Transculturalism and Teacher Capacity

Based on new research data, with a 135-teacher study over 8 countries, this book challenges the assumption that all teachers automatically have the expertise to teach cultural understanding and argues, instead, that there is the need for teachers to acquire transcultural expertise to teach cultural understanding effectively in the present age, rather than depending on current multicultural and intercultural approaches.

By outlining a new model to teach cultural understanding that is appropriate and relevant, this volume focuses on the expertise of teachers to address this gap in current teaching practice. Using the framework of education in Britain and its former empire, this book traces the role that teachers have played in teaching cultural understanding throughout history, and then uses the results of a recent international research project to outline recommendations for teacher education and professional learning that both develop and enhance the ability of teachers to address cultural understanding effectively in their work.

Transculturalism and Teacher Capacity: Professional Readiness in the Globalised Age is the perfect resource for any researcher, school leader and educational administrator, or those interested in education that prepares teachers to meet the demands of the profession in the current age.

Niranjan Casinader is Senior Lecturer in the Faculty of Education at Monash University, Australia.

Routledge Research in International and Comparative Education

This is a series that offers a global platform to engage scholars in continuous academic debate on key challenges and the latest thinking on issues in the fast-growing field of International and Comparative Education.

Titles in the series include:

Comparative Perspectives on Refugee Youth Education
Dreams and Realities in Educational Systems Worldwide
Edited by Alexander W. Wiseman, Lisa Damaschke-Deitrick, Ericka Galegher, and Maureen F. Park

50 Years of US Study Abroad Students
Japan as the Gateway to Asia and Beyond
Sarah R. Asada

Informal Learning and Literacy among Maasai Women
Education, Emancipation and Empowerment
Taeko Takayanagi

Parental Involvement Across European Education Systems
Critical Perspectives
Edited by Angelika Paseka and Delma Byrne

Transculturalism and Teacher Capacity
Professional Readiness in the Globalised Age
Niranjan Casinader

For more information about this series, please visit: https://www.routledge.com/Routledge-Research-in-International-and-Comparative-Education/book-series/RRICE

Transculturalism and Teacher Capacity

Professional Readiness in the Globalised Age

Niranjan Casinader

LONDON AND NEW YORK

First published 2020
by Routledge
2 Park Square, Milton Park, Abingdon, Oxon OX14 4RN

and by Routledge
52 Vanderbilt Avenue, New York, NY 10017

Routledge is an imprint of the Taylor & Francis Group, an informa business

© 2020 Niranjan Casinader

The right of Niranjan Casinader to be identified as author of this work has been asserted by them in accordance with sections 77 and 78 of the Copyright, Designs and Patents Act 1988.

All rights reserved. No part of this book may be reprinted or reproduced or utilised in any form or by any electronic, mechanical, or other means, now known or hereafter invented, including photocopying and recording, or in any information storage or retrieval system, without permission in writing from the publishers.

Trademark notice: Product or corporate names may be trademarks or registered trademarks, and are used only for identification and explanation without intent to infringe.

British Library Cataloguing-in-Publication Data
A catalogue record for this book is available from the British Library

Library of Congress Cataloging-in-Publication Data
A catalog record has been requested for this book

ISBN: 978-0-367-19378-2 (hbk)
ISBN: 978-0-429-20202-5 (ebk)

Typeset in Bembo
by Cenveo® Publisher Services

For Lee, who has always been with me, one way or another, throughout this academic journey

Contents

List of figures	ix
List of tables	x
Foreword	xi
Preface	xiii
Acknowledgements	xvii

1 Teaching for cultural difference: a temporal and spatial reflection   1

    1.1   Why the need to teach cultural understanding? *1*
    1.2   The nuances of globalisation *2*
    1.3   The cosmopolitanism of the past and the modern *5*
    1.4   The framework of consideration: defining the parameters of the discussion *10*
    1.5   Culture, faith and morality: teaching for the 'Other' *14*
    References   *25*

2 Cultural understanding and teaching expertise: a glimpse through British time and place   28

    2.1   Education as moral citizenship *28*
    2.2   The teacher and British educational morality: a temporal consideration *30*
    2.3   Pitfalls and conclusions: teachers as moral guides towards the 'Other' *48*
    References   *53*

3 Cultural education for the globalised age   55

    3.1   Culture and the global imperative: the garden of cultural education *55*
    3.2   Changing notions and contexts of cultural education *57*
    3.3   Transculturalism: a way forward for the 21st century *63*
    References   *67*

4 Cultural education in current policy and practice: a selective critique   70

4.1 The disjunctures of international comparisons 70
4.2 The substance of cultural education in policy 72
4.3 And whither the teacher? 83
References 84

5 Measuring transcultural capacity in teachers   88

5.1 The notion of professional readiness 88
5.2 Teacher standards and cultural expertise 90
5.3 Determining the cultural readiness of teachers 97
5.4 Project methodology 103
References 113

6 Transcultural capacity of teachers: a comparative analysis   117

6.1 Overview 117
6.2 Transculturality as a teacher attitude 118
6.3 The deeper characteristics of transcultural dispositions 121
6.4 Discussions and analysis 124
6.5 Conclusion 141
References 142

7 Building transcultural capacity in teachers: implications for teacher education and professional learning   143

7.1 Overview 143
7.2 Cultural displacement: the basis of developing expertise in cultural diversity as the norm 145
7.3 A personal epilogue: the cultural elephant – premonitions for the future 153
References 155

Index   158

Figures

3.1	Transpatiality	64
3.2	Three Paradigms of Cultural Education	66
5.1	Model of Cultural Dispositions of Thinking	108
6.1	Model of Cultural Dispositions of Thinking (Reprise)	118
6.2	CDT of Teachers across All Regions by Percentage of Participants	120
6.3	Attitudes of Teachers by Region: Global Mindedness and Change and Difference	122
6.4	Attitudes of Teachers by CDT: Global Mindedness	123
6.5	Attitudes of Teachers by CDT: Change and Difference	123
6.6	Number of Regions Visited by Cultural Disposition of Thinking (Percentage of Teachers in CDT)	132
6.7	Number of Regions Visited by Cultural Disposition of Thinking (Number of Teachers in CDT)	132
6.8	Travel Experience by Case Study: Number of Teachers	135
6.9	Travel Experience by Case Study: Percentage of Teachers	136
6.10	Living or Meeting Difference: Most Effective Means of Developing Cultural Understanding by Percentage of All Teacher Participants	137
6.11	Living or Meeting Difference: Most Effective Means of Developing Cultural Understanding by Number of Teachers and CDT	138
7.1	Teacher Participants: Years of Teaching Experience by CDT	145

Tables

1.1	Case Study Summary – Cultural Demographics	11
2.1	Principles of Intercultural Education	45
4.1	National Curriculum Summary: Selected Case Studies	72
5.1	The Australian Professional Standards for Teachers	92
5.2	Calculation of Cultural Dispositions of Thinking (% Coding)	111
5.3	Direction of Transculturality on Survey Responses (Example)	112
5.4	Scoring of Degree of Transculturality based on Change and Difference Statements (Example)	112
5.5	Calculation of Score on Attitudes to Change and Difference (example)	113
6.1	CDT of Teachers by Region – by Number of Teachers	120
6.2	CDT of Teachers by Region – by Percentage of Teachers	121
6.3	CDT of Teachers by School and Region	127

Foreword

Scholarly work on education in the last couple of decades has focused very much on how students acquire 21st-century skills. However, a child born today will likely live into the 22nd century, given more advanced medical technologies and the resultant higher life expectancy. In that sense, we should perhaps be examining what 22nd-century learning skills ought to be. Regardless, these learnings are associated with developing a child's capability to respond to and manage a wide range of issues that he or she will grow up with. They include critical thinking, creativity, communication skills, working collaboratively as well as personal and social skills. The argument is that children who have these skills will be able to engage in issues that are concerned with globalisation and global environmental change, or the downstream impact of these issues. Moreover, in addition to these 21st-century skills, children are also interacting more with students of other cultures, whether within local communities or through the Internet. How these cultural demographics will affect learning of these 21st-century skills is yet to be fully explored. Even more importantly, what kind of teacher is needed to help students gain this contemporary understanding about cultural diversity in our globalised society?

I was both delighted and humbled that Niranjan Casinader has asked me to write this foreword. While I am familiar with the developments in education and teacher education, the book proposes some exciting ideas about how to take education forward from the culturally diverse global society of today. This innovative book examines the expertise of teachers in relation to how they address the issues of cultural understanding, rather than just focusing on how they might teach students, arguing that teachers must possess transcultural expertise to achieve student learnings that are appropriate to the 21st century. Niranjan also provides a comparative discussion on how different countries and educational contexts have responded to the need to teach cultural understanding in their respective national curricula and on teacher expertise requirements. The variety of case studies used in the book also enriches the discussion with specific examples.

As a geography educator, I am also very happy that this book advances a willingness to contest ideas about contemporary globalisation and its supposed uniqueness in cultural, social, economic and political terms. This is supported by the introduction of a new, more nuanced mixed methods research approach in determining the cultural capacity of teachers. Subsequently, the use of research findings to develop and suggest new principles for teacher education and professional learning in the area of teacher capacity to teach cultural understanding provided me much food for thought in the way that I would design my own teacher education courses.

A key underlying aspect of the book is its salutary warning to teachers that attempts to be culturally inclusive need to take the complexity of the issue into account. Its discussion about the aims of cultural education and how these vary from place to place, and from context to context, highlights that it is not wise to assume that one approach to transcultural education will cover all circumstances. Instead, the book focuses on the broad principles that are required in such an approach, regardless of context.

As I read the book, I was encouraged by the many ideas that could help us educate our children and their children for the future. I hope you will enjoy reading the book as much as I did, and I am sure it is Niranjan's wish that the ideas in the book will inspire all educators working on these issues to improve their expertise so that the education we provide for children of the 21st and 22nd centuries will be both relevant and effective.

Dr Chew-Hung Chang
Chief Planning Officer, National Institute of Education
Associate Professor, Humanities and Social Studies Education Academic Group
National Institute of Education
Adjunct Professor, ECNU
President | Southeast Asian Geography Association

Preface

This book marks the third in an unofficial trilogy about the teaching of cultural understanding in the 21st century, all published by Routledge. The first book, *Culture, Transnational Education and Thinking: Case Studies in Global Schooling*, established the theoretical foundation of my work in this area. The second, *Transnationalism, Education and Empowerment: The Latent Legacies of Empire*, looked at the historical evolution of the notion of transnationalism and what I refer to as transculturalism, placed within a family history that I argued was an embodiment of these ideas in action; that is, they were not simply processes that have emerged as a result of globalisation in the late 20th century. The aim of this third book is to take those concerns to a classroom level by focusing on the assumed ability of teachers and other educators to teach about cultural understanding. It also seeks to prise apart some of the assumptions about teacher education and professional development in this increasingly significant part of teacher practice.

During my career as a teacher for over 30 years, working in Australian schools, but also with many ongoing and long-term connections with educators and education internationally, I became increasingly aware of the many differentials that existed in the environments within which I worked. One was the almost completely monocultural nature of the Australian teaching profession. By far the great majority of those whom I worked with, and the leadership teams for whom I worked for, were Anglo-European. In the teaching of Geography, my memory is that I only met one other teacher who did not come from that social sphere that has typified the European phase of Australian history. Alongside this background, my teaching became increasingly underpinned by concerns that would now be considered to be part of cultural education. My natural interest and instincts when undertaking my initial degree were in the area of development geography, largely because of my family's long-term work in the area worldwide. Within the school environment, this soon evolved to an interest in teaching about peoples and places in other parts of the world (always the core interest of geographers), but also to opening the minds and lives of the students whom I taught as to how and why peoples from other parts of the world might think and live in ways different to them.

Over the course of my career, and as I became more involved in leadership at various levels, the reality of the major issue became increasingly obvious; it was not so much the students who needed education about these matters, but the colleagues with whom I worked. The great majority of them were thoughtful teachers who were keen to do what was best for the students that they taught, but very few of them understood the context from which they were conducting their teaching; that is, their own cultural identity and their place in Australian society – what might be termed their own cultural geography. It was also striking that very few, if any, of my teaching colleagues outside the geographical education community saw any reason as to why they should become involved in teaching about cultural issues in the first place. They saw the responsibility of the various learning areas as being divided up by content and concepts, and cultural education (if it was relevant at all) was the concern of the Humanities teachers alone. Few saw any need for some coalescence in the approaches that the teaching staff of one institution should take in educating the children in their care in respect of some of the wider issues in life that cut across specific learning areas.

My focus on the role of teacher expertise rather than student learning in the area of cultural education was intensified when, whilst conducting my doctoral research alongside teaching full-time, it became clear to me that professional expertise in this area was a phenomenon that was of relatively less importance to educational researchers in this field. There was some work in this respect being conducted, but that was a general assumption that teachers who have been professionally educated would be able to take on and teach attitudes regarding cultural education with relatively little difficulty. My concern with this conundrum was further catalysed with the introduction of the Australian curriculum in 2010; I was deeply involved with its school implementation as a consequence of my role as a faculty leader. The gap between the reality of teacher expertise and the goals of the national curriculum became even more visible to me as some of my colleagues struggled to take on the mantle of being teachers of cultural understanding, even from within the general Humanities field. Consequently, it became one of the main drivers for my wish to shift my career into educational research after so many years working in schools.

I accept that some may find the themes and views expressed within this volume to be challenging and that a few may even find them controversial. The breadth of time and content addressed by some themes has inevitably led to the need for generalisations that seemingly ignore nuances that others might see as important, and I acknowledge the import of these necessary abbreviations of fact and history. However, I have attempted to situate my arguments not only with the literature that exists, but also within the wider context of philosophical and ethical discussion as to what education should be like in the 21st century. Whilst essentially founded in educational themes, the discussion has many interdisciplinary elements that feed off my ever-present and deep interest in a wide range of fields. That eclectic nature, I believe, is primarily a product of my being a geographer at heart, but it is also a function of my deep belief that cultural education, or teaching for cultural understanding, is a duty and obligation for all in society, and not just for educators.

Although I take full responsibility for the final way in which these ideas and propositions have been expressed and argued, they are the culmination of a number of years of discussions and debates, as well as collaborative research and authorship with a number of friends and colleagues, both in Australia and internationally. In particular, I wish to thank:

- John Loughran, former Executive Dean of the Faculty of Education at Monash University, and the Faculty as a whole, for providing research funds to enable this ongoing international research project, including sabbatical time to write the manuscript for this book.
- All the school principals and teachers who agreed to be part of this international project, one that will be ongoing as I continue to explore these concerns even further. Without them, no research to explore my theories and postulations would have been possible and I am very grateful for their cooperation. The ethical parameters of the project mean that I cannot name them or their schools, but their contribution has been foundational, regardless.
- My colleagues who assisted in finding schools and participants who were willing to be part of the research, both in Australia and overseas: Dr Phillip Wing Chan, Robyn Boswell, Associate Professor Shivali Tukdeo and Lalitha Nair.
- Joanne Gleeson, whose work as a research assistant on the project was exemplary, timely and insightful, always leading to lively, enjoyable and intuitive discussions.
- Associate Professor Clare Brooks from the Institute of Education, University College London, for facilitating a period as an academic visitor that included the enabling of school and library research in the United Kingdom.
- Academic friends and colleagues who have contributed to the evolution of my ideas and research through discussion, collaboration and other forms of practical help, especially Gillian Kidman, Jane Wilkinson, Jane Southcott, Howard Prosser, Fazal Rizvi, Catherine Manathunga and all the others who are too numerous to mention.
- Lucas Walsh, for his expertise and guidance as a co-researcher and author in the International Baccalaureate research project that initiated the wider research.
- Allie Clemans, as a co-author and enabler of prior research on the transcultural capacity of pre-service teachers.

In addition, I am particularly grateful to Associate Professor Chang Chew Hung from the National Institute of Education, Singapore, for his ongoing academic support and his kindness in agreeing to write the foreword to the book.

Special thanks are also due to my wide network of family and friends for their general support, particularly my youngest son, Simon, as well as my friend of 50 plus years and fellow educator, Peter van Cuylenburg, for his interest and willingness to discuss and philosophise about many of the ideas in this book, especially those relating to the realities and practicalities of teacher work and school life.

Finally, I am grateful for the work from the Australian team at Routledge for all of their support in the production of the book, including my editor, Vilija Stephen, her predecessor, Lucinda Knight, and editorial assistant, Marie Andrews.

Niranjan Casinader
June 2019
Melbourne, Australia

Acknowledgements

Parts of Chapters 3 and 4 are derived from ideas first published in the following journal articles:

Casinader, N. (2016). A lost conduit for intercultural education: School geography and the potential for transformation in the Australian curriculum. *Intercultural Education, 27*(3), 257–273. doi: 10.1080/14675986.2016.1150650.

Casinader, N. (2016). Transnationalism in the Australian curriculum: New horizons or destinations of the past? *Discourse: Studies in the Cultural Politics of Education, 37*(3), 327–340. doi: 10.1080/01596306.2015.1023701.

Chapter 1

Teaching for cultural difference

A temporal and spatial reflection

1.1 Why the need to teach cultural understanding?

The layers of complexity that designate the character of contemporary globalisation have been long established and discussed (for example, Crossley & Watson, 2003; Vertovec, 2009). Primarily, it is multifaceted (economic, social, cultural, amongst others), globally integrative, facilitated by developments in modern communications technologies, including the Internet, and embodied by the rapidity of change and the impact of that change on local, national, regional and global communities. Foremost amongst the latter is the increased demographic complexity of societies around the world, both in terms of cultural composition and movement of people, generating growing numbers of people whose lives are characterised by an increasingly complex web of global connectivities (Rizvi, 2009).

However, whilst all of these perceptions have credence, they have tended to be expressed in a quasi-mythical form, as if contemporary globalisation was somehow unique and never before seen in world affairs. In the context of certain characteristics, such a reverence has validity: modern communications technology, whether by land, sea, air or the ether, has enabled the global scale and pace of these changes like no era before it. For the first time in human history, an occurrence on one side of the world can have an almost immediate impact across all continents. In terms of cultural and demographic complexity, though, the picture is not as singular or unique as the deification of modern globalisation has implied. The intermixing of human cultures cannot be designated as being purely a modern phenomenon. The history of human beings on the planet, no matter where the study is focused geographically, is a history of demographic movement, of migration of peoples from one region to another, taking the culture(s) that they had developed in their place(s) of origin into a different context, creating impact in both visible and subliminal ways.

In that sense, there has always been cultural meetings and interactions as a result of migrations. What contemporary globalisation has created, however, is the facilitation of the speed, frequency and ease of that movement of people, ideas, artefacts and human responses, with the *entire* planet being the arena. It is this reconfiguration of local place that has had the most significant impact on the sociocultural nature of human societies and their interactions. Additionally, previous iterations of globalising forces of invasion and/or colonisation in world history have largely confined their impact to specific regions of the world, originally adjacent to the point of origin, but later expanded as transport technology and vision allowed; the sense of what was 'global' was defined by the existing knowledge of those directing the globalising. The empires of the past, whether Chinese, Assyrian, Moghul, Roman or European, were essentially contained in the geographical and temporal extent of their impact on global life; the transference of change was gradual and, to some degree, muted.

In contrast, the 21st century is characterised more than ever by the existence of a highly sophisticated butterfly effect; events and actions in one part of the world are more or less guaranteed to have a relatively instantaneous impact on other parts of the world, no matter how subliminal or deep. The eras or phases of past globalisations never had the potential to bring all parts of the geographical world into the one system so that they could be perceived as part of the same entity or framework for action. Their influence was both confined and constrained spatially, with the impact of new ideas or artefacts taking months, if not years, to reach the mass populations of previously unknown regions. It is certainly arguable that the European empires of the 19th century had and are still having a major impact on global affairs. However, the effects were not instantaneous, as they can be in the present age. Similarly, in the context of cultural understandings, it was not until the contemporary phase of globalisation that both the need and form of education in cultural understanding became highlighted as a truly 'global' necessity, rather than being limited to specific parts of the world in which significant cultural meetings and interactions were concentrated.

1.2 The nuances of globalisation

The tale of any history is, in reality, an amalgam of all the discernments and perspectives that are in play at the time, but historiography has generally been the concern of those who are left – or in charge – at the end of a global event. It is only in relatively recent times that, within the liberal world at least, a commitment to giving a voice to all sides of the historical prism has become accepted in the mainstream as being part of a democratic right.

The contention that the period of European colonisation between the 18th and 20th centuries is the only example of 'colonisation' that matters in the present day is an oversimplification, regardless of whether the argument is put from what can be broadly characterised as the opposing perspectives of neoliberalism or post-colonialism. For the former, the period was an exemplification of the 'rightness' of capitalism as cast in the Western mould, the reason why people in a growing number of States around the world now have a higher quality of material (if not spiritual) life, at least when measured by the indicators of an industrialised society. For post-colonial thinkers, such an argument is a product of those elements in present-day 'Western' societies that seek to promote and justify the historical superiority of the present created by their philosophy. In the post-colonial frame, the Age of European colonisation was the era of cultural and ethnic disruption (extending, in some cases, to genocide) that lessened or eradicated the rights of people to live as their own cultural evolution determined.

What tends to be diminished or ignored by both perspectives, however, is that the Age of European colonisation was only the most recent example of cultural-political powers extending their reach into geographical spaces far beyond their locational homes. There is also a tendency to see European colonisation as being a uniform beast, but as imperial studies show, there were stark differences between the British, Dutch, German, French, Spanish and Belgian approaches to and their application of colonial power. Further, it is generally acknowledged that colonisation within one empire often took varying forms on different places; for example, the British in the Caribbean, Africa and Asia (Darwin, 2008; Gould, 2008). Global history is replete with the building of empires that have extended the social, political, economic and cultural influence of specific powers that have originated from all parts of the world. The perception that the most significant act of colonisation is primarily confined to the act of white Europeans enforcing their will on peoples of colour over the last 250 years is not borne out by the reality of the past; human history is, in fact, the story of a whole series of colonisations, not all of which have emanated from the Euro-American axis. The rise and fall of older European-based colonial powers such as the Roman Empire (BC 27–476AD) has been equally matched or exceeded by other drives of dominance, including the growth of the Persian Empire between the 8th and 4th centuries BC, the impact of the Mongolian Empire across Eurasia created by Genghis Khan in the 12th and 13th centuries, the growth of the Chinese Empire in the 13th and 14th centuries, as well the establishment of powerful forces such as the 15th-century Inca Empire in what is now South America and the Aztec civilisation of Central America in the 14th and 16th centuries.

It would also be an overgeneralisation to maintain the line that the deep geographical integration of world trade that is frequently seen to characterise the contemporary phase of globalisation is a new phenomenon. The study of how civilisational symbols such as language, artefacts and foods have migrated across continents and oceans over time has shown that such consequences of the colonising process were occurring well before the emergence of the European empires such as those of Spain, Holland, Portugal and Britain. Collectively, these impacts are testament to the long-standing cultural impact of demographic movement throughout history. The extent of the influence throughout history of Arab traders from the present Middle

East, both pre and post the year zero in the Georgian calendar, can be seen in the diffusion of Arab peoples and the Islamic faith into large parts of what is now loosely described as the continent of Asia prior to the presence of European colonisers. Even within a continent such as Australia, substantial evidence exists that there was trade between the Indigenous peoples of the northern coast with the islands of Southeast Asia to the north, as well as trade between Indigenous nations across the extent of that continent.

Such contexts provide a partial explanation as to why some key nuances about differences and similarities between the different ages of globalisation appear to have been subsumed within the various overviews of contemporary globalisation. The exponential rate of change that is integral to modern globalisation aside, one of the constants has been that expansive globalisation – which is, and has been, the reality and effect of each historical wave of colonisation and its attendant demographic migrations – has been possible because of the technological advances developed by the globalising power(s) of the time, and specifically in relation to communications and warfare. In this context, technology is being used in its widest sense, and includes the development of new ways of conducting the movement and application of armed force. In each historical time period, it is possible to identify one or more key elements that were, in effect, as innovative and transformative as the development of the Internet in the late 20th century. Consequently, the system of fast-moving, well-trained cavalry that was the drivetrain of Genghis Khan's march across Eurasia can be equated to the organisation of the Roman legions and their skills of their engineers; the naval power and military weaponry of the European colonial powers of the 18th and 19th centuries were a similar advantage, as were the navigational and sailing skills of the Melanesian peoples who settled the Pacific.

In the moral contexts of the 21st century, at least in the Euro-American hemisphere, characterised by the evolution of the concept of natural inalienable human rights and dignity that is now enshrined in international law through the United Nations and its multilateral policymaking, such drives for political dominance through force are now frequently condemned as unequivocally unacceptable. By today's standards in democratic societies, this is a logical conclusion. But we cannot impose current moral standards on past events, especially if they have occurred in a multitude of historical times and sociocultural environments. To ignore the contexts in which they did occur is to discount the lessons that can be learned from them and to institute a form of obverse denial. Even in the modern world, not all people agree with the doctrine of natural human rights. In one sense, the continued existence and persistence of dictators, tyrants and violent extremists that straddle the current global political spectrum around is proof that human behaviour remains contrary and complex. To assume that uniformity of outlook is or should be the norm, regardless of whether the perspective be on either side of the political spectrum, is itself a form of political 'ostrichism' that denies any probability of a more realistic, complex reality. It is far more productive to accept that difference of outlook and opinion is not only the actuality, but also an expectation: acknowledge what has occurred, accept the consequences (acknowledging any positive with the negative), devise steps to redress the imbalances and take action to move forward.

1.3 The cosmopolitanism of the past and the modern

1.3.1 Older forms of cosmopolitanism

One of the most significant impacts of all historical migrations and colonisations has been the meeting of cultures that results from one group of people moving into the territory inhabited by another. On a purely logical level, the extent of this pattern of cultural meetings throughout human history adds weight to the case that the need for humans to develop cultural awareness and understanding about the 'Other' is not a new phenomenon. The meeting of and clashes between different cultures has been part of human interaction for millennia and, on that basis, it can be contended that the teaching and learning of some form of cultural awareness and understanding must have taken place in some form in the past, as necessary, even if the structures and modes of that education may not resemble those in the present.

It is, however, only in the last 20 years or so that any specific reference to cultural understanding as an essential part of educational provision has emerged on a large scale. The United Nations, through UNESCO, has been working in the broad field for over half a century, but it was only in the early years of the 21st century that a firm policy on the teaching of intercultural understanding was published (UNESCO, 2013). Similarly, it is only in the last decade or so that some countries have begun to recognise the reality of cultural demographic globalisation by mandating some form of cultural understanding as an inclusion in national curriculum frameworks; for example, Australia, New Zealand, South Korea and India.

The reasons for the timing of what can be historically viewed as a relatively sudden development in cultural education are diverse, but it cannot be ignored that these developments have occurred simultaneously with an increasing trend towards societal acceptance and recognition of human diversity in many societies around the world. Culture is merely one of the parameters of difference within human society and has to be placed into context with the progress made in certain regions in respect of human rights such as gender, sexuality and disability equality. Such change is neither universal nor consistent; to date, liberal changes of such nature have tended to be confined to sovereign States that follow a particular kind of Euro-American governmental democracy, such as the United Kingdom, Canada, the Republic of Ireland, the European Union, New Zealand and, to a lesser extent, the Democratic Republic of South Korea, Japan, the United States and Australia. In other parts of the world, there has been a distinct shift in the last decade to greater polarisation and extremism in respect of the consideration and awarding of such rights, an uncertainty that even extends to the political-social climate in countries usually considered to be bastions of democratic freedom, such as the United States.

The difficulty with this collective picture, however, is that it tends to skim over or even ignore some key patterns around this more visible focus on cultural understanding. Whilst it is true that historical contact has meant that there has long been a need for human beings to develop cultural understanding about the 'Other', the historical focus of that contact has been primarily economic. The chronology of contacts between different regions of the world, whether imposed by force or by mutual agreement, has been trade-based. Principally, they were economic-political ventures, driven by the desire of governing individuals or bodies to acquire resources to feed their own material growth. In many cases, where the basis of the contact was mutually negotiated, this meant that the contact between cultures often occurred on a simple vertical plane, with only *representatives* from different cultural environments coming into contact. For example, trade between China and Europe during the European Medieval period occurred because there was a continual exchange of goods by individual traders along the Silk Road. It was relatively rare for individuals from one end of the Silk Road to accompany goods all the way to the other.

Where colonisation of new regions did occur by force, the nature of contact was, in many ways, deeper and more involved. It is not within the short scope of this relatively brief overview to delve into all the complexities of historical imperialism, but several of the more permanent consequences of colonisations have been demographic and cultural. Many of the people involved in the colonisations stayed in their new surroundings and did not, as a rule, return *en masse* to their former home. For them, migration was permanent, with the result that much of the learnings about cultural interaction and interweaving on a mass scale occurred within the regions of contact over time. The consequence was an inevitable adaption on the part of both the culture(s) of both the invaded and the invader, often leading to a new hybrid culture or culture(s) that became established and recognised as the signifier of that region over time. One older example includes the collective impact of the colonisations of Ancient Britain, which saw the culture(s) of the Britons interwoven with those of the Angles and Saxons (from present-day Germany), the Danes (Scandinavia) and the Romans. The original indigenous cultures around the Mediterranean have been merged with a number of imperial waves over the centuries, including the Roman, Ottoman, Phoenician and Moor. In more modern times, the Anglo-Indians of India and the Burghers of Sri Lanka are further examples of long-term hybrid cultures that have stemmed from demographic movement.

So, if cultural meetings on a large scale have always been a feature of human history, what are the singular features about cultural interactions in the modern age that have led to a growing visible acknowledgement of a need for specific education in cultural understanding? There are two aspects of difference that seem to stand out: the demographic characteristics of modern cultural interaction; and the nature of modern cosmopolitanism.

1.3.2 Contemporary cosmopolitanism

In the age of contemporary globalisation, and particularly since the start of the millennium, the salient demographic shift is that the degree, extent and frequency of cultural meetings between individuals from different societies have become greatly enhanced. It is now the norm for individuals to travel frequently from one cultural context to another, whether this be for work or pleasure. Those contexts are not just limited to international movement, but can equally apply to movements on an intra-national level, or even within a particular city. The need to adjust to cultural interaction occurring on a daily basis is now more acute, especially as national populations have become more diverse as a consequence of these more varied patterns of demographic travel. As outlined in a number of publications over the last two decades, one of the constant themes in the impact of globalisation upon education in schools has been the emergence of strong cultural diversity in student cohorts; see, for example, Clay and George (2000), Tikly (2001), Casinader (2015), and Watkins (2015). Another of these key aspects of demographic change that has emerged from globalisation has been the increased fluidity of human movement, both temporary and permanent, as people develop the capability and desire to move out of places of origin into different parts of the world to live and work. Modern technology in transport and communications has intensified the proportion of those who move temporarily, but it has also expanded the horizons of young people globally and shown them the possibilities that might exist in other parts of the world beyond the confines of their local origins.

The second key difference is the modern nature of cosmopolitanism. In an important 2009 article in which he argued for education to adopt a more cosmopolitan approach – '… a mode of learning about, and engaging with, new social formations' (p. 254) – Fazal Rizvi (2009) highlighted that cosmopolitanism is not a new concept, contrary to some popular thinking. For example, he reminded us that some Ancient Greek philosophers such as the Stoics promoted a '… globally interrelated moral order' (p. 254); that, 'as an Enlightenment philosopher, Immanuel Kant was committed to a set of universal moral precepts. He viewed the world in terms of an integrated moral order, based on the promise of science as a language of universal laws that was applicable to the entire world, natural as well as social' (p. 255), and that both Britain and France constructed their colonial empires as a '… seamless entity, built around a core set of values and interests that were often viewed as 'cosmopolitan' (p. 256).

The key point about these different views, however, is that they are largely framed around visions of the 'world' that existed in the proponents' historical time and philosophical space. To the Ancient Greeks, knowledge of the planet was centred around Europe and its surrounds: hence the Mediterranean (Middle Earth) Sea. Kant, despite his apparent cosmopolitan pronouncements, only saw European culture as the mark of a civilised being, and his cosmopolitan frame of reference was therefore the world as he defined it (Kant, 1960). Britain and France both viewed their empires as being the places that acted as the central player to the rest of the world, with little overt knowledge or recognition of how or why other parts of the world were developing, unless it had an association on the operations of their own world. It should be remembered, too, that such insular and self-aggrandisement of a group's place in the world has been a universal and constant theme over culture, time and place. One of the main names that has been used by the Chinese for their own country – Zhong Guo – is associated with the 16th–19th centuries' belief that the country was the centre of the human world, the 'Middle Kingdom' being located between the 'barbarians' outside China and 'Heaven'. Many indigenous groups, such as some of the First Nations peoples of North America, identify themselves in their own language by references to themselves as 'The People'. In short, until the advent of contemporary globalisation, possessing a cosmopolitan outlook was defined by a people's knowledge of and perspective on the world as it was known to them, and characterised as identifying the unknown as comprising an enemy or cultural entity that was the opposite of themselves.

The singularity of contemporary globalisation is that, for the first time in world history, the impacts of human interactions and actions can now be observed and considered throughout the inhabited planet as a whole, more or less instantaneously. Consequently, for the first time, cosmopolitanism in the current age has come to incorporate the important characteristics of global citizenship, a commitment to maintaining a sustainable concern for the world as a whole that does not just focus on local or national regional interests. The quality, skill and propensity for cultural understanding has now become a human necessity, wherever one lives, rather than being more applicable to those whose daily interactions required it. Cultural interactions are embedded in the routines of daily life in multitudinous ways and are consequently an essential life skill, not an optional extra. It is that transition to globalised, daily cultural interactions, no matter how subtle or overt, that has made the inclusion of cultural understanding in modern educational provisions to be *sine qua non*.

Given the commercial and trade centrality to historical globalisation, it is not surprising that certain areas of society, such as business, have responded relatively rapidly to the changing circumstances, developing new ways of working and thinking that acknowledge that foundational shift in the demographics of global living. It was the work of economic/business thinkers such as Hofstede in the 1950s that were in the vanguard of post-war cultural education. There is now growing research evidence that, as the world of work changes in response to globalisation and other forces such as automation, the type of cultural education that young people receive must also change. Part of that shift is that there needs to be greater emphasis on developing skills in flexibility and global work, which includes an ability to exhibit cultural capacity (Foundation for Young Australians, 2017).

The degree to which educational systems in different countries have responded to this challenge is debatable. If we focus on the area of teacher expertise and the way in which pre-service educators are being trained and educated to work in this melting pot of cultural movement, there are signs that cultural diversity is being treated inconsistently and, at its worst, dismissed or ignored. For instance, Ohi et al. (2019) highlight that there is much research evidence that indicates '… many teachers and principals lack the knowledge, skills and confidence to engage with ICE [Intercultural Education] and ensure meaningful intercultural learning among students' (p. 4). The OECD 2013 TALIS Report on International Perspectives on Teaching and Learning indicated that less than 20% teachers had undertaken professional development about teaching in a multicultural or multilingual context during the past year, which mirrored the picture in the 2008 TALIS report (Ohi et al., 2019, p. 4). It is more concerning, however, only 13% of teachers saw a need for such professional learning in the first place (OECD, 2014, p. 4).

As will be discussed in later chapters, educational research studies to date that have focused on the teaching of cultural understanding on a global scale have tended to concentrate on the learning by students; investigation as to the professional readiness of teachers to deal with what is now a mandated aspect of mass education in many educational jurisdictions is far less visible. When teacher expertise is the focus, it is in the context of the *practicalities* of teaching in culturally diverse environments; in short, it is treated as a technical competence, and not necessarily as a professional capacity (see Chapters 3 and 4). One of the few exceptions to this was a 2015 Australian Research Council Linkage Report, the findings of which, whilst still focusing largely on student learning, included the statement that 'personal intercultural experiences, including travel, enhance teacher expertise' (Halse et al., 2015, p. 7). At a time when substantial educational research has reinforced the importance of teacher quality in the process of effective and meaningful student education, there seems to be a reliance on an assumption that teachers have the automatic capability and capacity to teach cultural understanding. It is this belief that this monograph seeks to confront and examine.

The remaining chapters of this monograph will focus more specifically on the state of teacher expertise in cultural education as it exists in the present day, with consideration of how this concern is connected with the way in

10 Teaching for cultural difference

which cultural education has been and is being approached in national education systems. In order to give that discussion a firmer context, the remainder of this particular chapter and Chapter 2 will discuss the basic philosophical rationale as to whether teachers should have responsibility for developing cultural understanding in students, using the framework of historical time and education within British cultural societal dimensions. In particular, it will seek to examine to what degree teaching about culture and communications between cultures has been seen as one of the core duties of the teacher through time and space. Conclusions drawn from this discussion will be used as the entry point into Chapters 3 and 4, which will look more closely at the role of teachers today – perceived and enacted – in the field of school-based cultural education. Is the contention of this monograph a new phenomenon, or merely a call for return to long-acknowledged basics?

1.4 The framework of consideration: defining the parameters of the discussion

1.4.1 Case studies

To undertake any global perspective that is constructed around cultural differentiation is itself fraught with pitfalls. As the literature has pointed out continually, the notion of culture is far from a fixed entity; there are always going to be multiple variations and interpretations of any one cultural identity, especially within those identities that are popularly perceived to be cohesive. To speak of a 'Western' culture, for instance, is to dismiss the multiple perspectives that are included within it. As illustrated by the recent splits in policy and direction within the members of the European Union, or those between the United States and its allies, there are substantial differences in a supposedly cohesive 'Western' outlook on life, including in matters relating to cultural difference. Similarly, there are a number of sovereign States that would define themselves as Islamic, but there is a world of difference between the mindset and attitudes of the monarchical State of Saudi Arabia, with its highly conservative form of Islam (Wahhabism), and the more democratically constructed societies of Indonesia and Malaysia. That complexity needs to be kept in mind constantly, especially when broader stereotypes and classifications are used, often out of convenience. Consequently, in recognition of these intricacies and to facilitate some comparative analysis, this monograph will limit its main discussions to the context of school teaching within countries or special status regions that have the common cultural heritage of being part of the British Empire, with some comparative reference to countries with different cultural bases where appropriate (see Table 1.1).

Three further points need to be highlighted as part of this justification. The first is that, without exception, all of these regions are now fundamentally multicultural, with sociocultural histories and populations that are inherently

Table 1.1 Case Study Summary – Cultural Demographics

Country	Cultural demographics	Source
Australia	• Australian-born (70.6%) • Overseas-born (29.4%) [Top Ten: England, China, India, New Zealand, Philippines, Vietnam, South Africa, Italy, Malaysia, Scotland] • 300 different cultural ancestries/300 + languages spoken at home • Top Ten: English, Australian, Irish, Scottish, Chinese, Italian, German, Indian, Greek, Dutch	Australian Bureau of Statistics, 2018 (3412.0 – Migration, Australia, 2017–2018)
Canada	• Canadian (32.3%), British origin (32.5%), French origin (13.6%), Aboriginal (6.2%) [First Nation, Métis, Inuit] • Multiple origins (41.1%) • 250+ ethnic ancestries (Chinese, East Indian, Filipino also in Top Ten)	Statistics Canada (2017) Ethnic and cultural origins of Canadians: Portrait of a rich heritage. Census 2016
Hong Kong Special Administrative Region	• Chinese: 96% • Non-Chinese: 4% (Filipino, Indonesian, European, Indian, Nepalese, Pakistani, Thai, Japanese, Other Asian)	Census and Statistics Department, Hong Kong Special Administrative Region
India	• Ethnic/cultural data not collected: latest census was 2011 • 4635 ethnic groups • Indo-Aryan (72%), Dravidian (25%) • Multi-faith (655): Hindu (80%), Islam (13%), Christian (2.3%), Sikh (1.9%), Buddhist (0.8%), Jain (0.4%) • Multilingual: Hindi and English are official languages • Hindi spoken by 44% population	CIA World Factbook Chandramouli (2015)
Malaysia	• Malay [Bumiputera] (61.9%) • Chinese (20.6%) • Indian (6.2%) • Others (0.9%)	Department of Statistics, Malaysia, 2018
New Zealand	• European (74%) [2013 Census] • Māori (14.9%) • Asian (11.8%) • Pacific Peoples (7.4%) • Middle Eastern/African/Latin American (1.2%)	Stats NZ Tatauranga Aotearoa, 2018
Singapore	• Chinese (74.3%) • Malay (13.4%) • Indian (9.0%) • Other (3.2%)	Singapore Department of Statistics, 2018
United Kingdom	• White (87.7%) • Black/African/Caribbean/Black British (3.0%) • Indian (2.7%) • Pakistani (1.6%) • Multiple Ethnic (1.2%) • Other Asian (1.1%) • Bangladeshi (0.6%) • Chinese (0.5%) • Other (1.6%)	Office for National Statistics, 2018

culturally diverse (see Table 1.1), with several also possessing strong and often dominant indigenous elements. As such, they are societies that, on the face of it, and regardless of the arguments about the culturally complex nature of contemporary globalisation, would appear to justify and mandate the specific inclusion of cultural understanding as part of their educational provision and in their demands of teachers. In most cases, the origins of their multicultural nature were in British colonialism, but their contexts have developed further through events after 1945 and modern globalisation. Nevertheless, it is too much of a simplification to ignore the reality that multiculturalism was an existing condition of some of these regions prior to European colonialism. In Australia and Canada, the range and number of indigenous peoples and cultures that were in place prior to British colonisation meant that these regions were already culturally diverse. It is only the Euro-American mindset that tends to group all non-industrialised societies into the one stereotype. The pre-European history of India was already replete with colonisations by different groups, including the Mughal Empires of the 16th and 17th centuries, a pattern that created a complex mosaic of Islamic and Hindu cultures throughout the subcontinent.

The second point, related to the first, is that, despite the limitations of such a sample, one consequence of this common element (British colonialism) in the histories of these case studies (Table 1.1) is that their educational systems have been influenced to varying degrees by British philosophies and practices, with English being often (but not necessarily the only) language of instruction. These countries, along with the Hong Kong Special Administrative Region, are the basis of a continually developing international research project on teacher attitudes and expertise in education that is the focus of Chapters 5 and 6, which comprise the practical exploration of the conceptual themes explored in this monograph. Consequently, collectively they provide a fertile foundation for meaningful, comparative interpretation of teacher attitudes and educational practices in the modern age.

The final point, which is itself a corollary of the second, is a counter to the logical criticism that to focus on educational systems that derive from colonial rule is to ignore the pre-colonial forms of education that existed previously, disempowering the cultural heritages of the colonised. In other words, the view is that such an perspective does not take into account that educational hegemony was maintained by the former colonial power through educational neocolonialism, in which 'Western' paradigms tend to shape and influence educational systems and thinking in the post-colonial era at the expense of local cultural traditions and thoughts (Sun & Roumell, 2017). However, within this particular case study set, the named places (aside from Hong Kong) have been independent for at least 50 years, with some past the century mark. As independent societies, they have had considerable experience in taking control of their own lives in a new context; the fact of colonisation cannot be eradicated, but it can be subsumed into a new national narrative that is owned by the people living in the post-colonial state. To dismiss this perspective as being morally weak is to deny self-agency to those who are now building their societies according to local wishes in the modern context, combining the new with the traditional: 'Institutions of formal education in post-colonial settings tell no simple story about how 'culture' is transmitted and yet they are key sites of the reproduction and refashioning of subjectivity, society and culture' (Simpson, 1999, p. 6). This is, of course, the ultimate meaning of self-determination. Education was one way in which the colonised chose to fight back against colonial rule by making decisions to deliberately use colonial policies for their own benefit (see also Casinader, 2017, Chapter 4):

> Education, in fact, has two attributes: reproduction and also production of unplanned, unexpected, and even undesirable effects in creating critical capabilities. Although the dominant class expects education to socialise the oppressed and marginalised into apathy, submissiveness and acceptance of the existing social order, it may create challenging and even revolutionary minds. (Assié-Lumumba, 2016, p. 19)

In a more specific example of how former colonies have integrated their pre-colonial and colonial pasts into a self-determined educational future, Metz (2015) highlights how '… contemporary discussions among sub-Saharan philosophers and thinkers about higher education have similarly focused substantially on the final ends of promoting development for the society as a whole, supporting local culture, and promoting moral personhood' (p. 1179), building upon the pre-colonial forms of education that were more '… centred on a disposition to relate communally with others' (p. 1179).

1.4.2 The concept of culture

Given the centrality of the meaning of culture to the themes in this monograph, it is important to highlight from the start that it will employ a definition of culture that is in line with a point of view that I have maintained and argued over recent years (for example, Casinader, 2014, 2016, 2017). Within this framework, the concept of culture emphasises the importance of an individual's *mindset* in determining the nature of their culture; that is, what they see as pertaining to their cultural identity. A 'cultural group' is therefore composed of people who have a similar mindset or outlook on life. This is in contrast to the long-standing ethnographic definition that sees culture and cultural identity as being constructed around the '… traditions, customs, beliefs, norms and perspectives …' (Jackson, 2010, p. 185) that a group of people have in common.

For writers such as Hall (1997), language is also a crucial part of the representational framework of the culture. However, I would strongly contend that language is not *necessarily* an *essential* aspect of a particular culture. Those who have the same cultural mindset may also relate to some, if not all, of these agreed ethnographic indicators, but they are not *ipso facto* vital to the determination of one's cultural identity. For instance, the scholarly and community work that is being conducted to revive and/or maintain the language of an indigenous or First Nations group whose language has been lost over time, in full or in part, is often perceived as being a sign of 'saving' a culture. For those who identify with that culture and feel the vibrancy of such a language connection, such a point of view holds truth. Alternatively, under the definition that culture is a mindset and not as a visible (or audible) set of objects and customs, I would contend strongly that a cultural group that has 'lost' its former language has no less authority to be considered a unique cultural group than those whose language still exists. In fact, the reality that the 'culture' has had to adapt and respond to that loss can be seen as a positive sign of cultural health, even if some elements of its form have changed. A living culture is one that has had to respond to change and become more organic, and is therefore more likely to survive through time. In some situations, such as those that exist with the demographic fluidity that is so characteristic of modern globalisation, the meeting of two or more cultures is more likely to result in new forms of cultural representation and identity, '... facets of culture and identity [that] are often self-consciously selected, syncretized and elaborated from more than one heritage' (Vertovec, 2009, p. 7). Frequently, the character and strength of our being is determined how we respond to the unexpected and unwanted, and not so much the elements over which we have some control. In consequence, the regions identified in Table 1.1 and the basis of the forthcoming discussion should be seen as being more separated by *cultural mindsets of life* than the more common, visible markers of cultural identity.

1.5 Culture, faith and morality: teaching for the 'Other'

1.5.1 Overview

In its simplest form, education for cultural understanding is essentially learning for a moral purpose. As part of that process, the teacher, try as they might to avoid it, must become an advocate for seeing the world in a certain way. Contentions and debates that surround such a specific imperative in the work of a teacher form an acute edge. The matter becomes one of ethics, as to whether a teacher has the right or the obligation to take on a particular philosophy. In countries like Australia, teachers have been frequently criticised by conservative elements in society for proselytising what are considered to be left-wing or socialist ideas; they have also been criticised by those on the other side of the spectrum for not taking advantage of their position to influence what are considered to be universal goods, such as the combating of prejudice, as well as for being unconsciously racist because of the assumptions – usually stereotypical – that they bring to their teaching when students from minority groups are in the class (Walton et al., 2014). At the same time, the importance of the part that they must play in countering cultural and racial prejudice in schools continues to be highlighted, such as with the current 'Othering' of South Sudanese students in Australian schools (Baak, 2019).

The complexities of addressing and navigating matters of moral contention (which are inevitably integrated into matters of cultural education) are such that it has been argued that the educational process has to be monitored and conducted through the medium of the teacher: '… this engagement with and criticism of the foreign and of one's own culture, the process of converting the native and familiar into the strange, can be regarded as an essential feature of adult or doctoral education. But it requires a teacher …' (McCarty & Hirata, 2010, p. 38). Teachers are not just conveyors of existing cultural attitudes and thoughts, but have the duty of enabling their students to take control of their own learning by deconstructing and reconfiguring it towards a new purpose. Instead of being reactive to instructions for change, they have a professional duty to be transformative in their actions as this is how meaningful education about social change takes place (Gutek, 2014). Hansen (2007) aligns himself with Dewey, highlighting that effective education in a democratic society must be itself metamorphic: 'Education involves reconstructing prior knowledge, understanding, and insight as the student takes in new questions, problems, perspectives, and realms of activity' (p. 25). Part of that learning is also subliminal, as students '… learn things from the teachers for which the teacher may be held responsible but which do not figure in the direct intentions of the teacher', and that includes when 'the teacher exemplifies moral virtues or vices' (Winch & Gingell, 2008, p. 211).

In short, whether they choose to be or not, teachers are moral educators, and it is therefore their professional obligation to be prepared to be so. How they undertake to fulfil this duty and obligation in a manner that creates a balance of views is more a matter of pedagogy, not core substance, but this then raises a further question: are there boundaries of morality on which teachers should hold a line in the classroom? In the current age, there are several areas on which there is now almost universal agreement on where such lines must be drawn (albeit largely in the world of more liberal governmental democracies): the boundaries in teacher–student relationships, bullying, personal abuse (including racial) and so on. Why, then, should cultural understanding be not included specifically in the list of teacher obligations? Inevitably, the difficulties lie in what is actually meant by cultural understanding, or who or what determines the boundaries of what is moral in terms of cultural understanding. A fuller exploration of what this attribute entails will be undertaken later in this chapter and then explored further at the beginning of Chapter 2, but for the purposes of tracing these broad historical transitions, the essential notion of 'cultural understanding' can be defined as an awareness of the existence of the 'Other' and how to relate to people who possess a different sense of cultural identity to your own.

1.5.2 Education, culture and faith

Throughout history, one of the dominant characteristics of any culture has been that they incorporate some form of spiritualism, whether that takes the form of belief in a faith that professes the following of one or multiple deities, or a belief in following a specific philosophy of life that tends to function without the attached detailed structures of an organised, hierarchical church. The mainstream faiths, such as Christianity, Islam, Judaism, Buddhism and Hinduism, are general examples of the former; Confucianism and Indigenous religions are examples of the latter, encouraged and facilitated by the focus of such belief systems on care and growth of the inner self rather than any reference to the external. Regardless, many see that '… [f]aith and culture always exist in a relationship of interdependence' (D'Orsa, 2013, p. 72).

If education is a reflection of a culture, and therefore a conduit for ensuring its maintenance or continuance in future generations, it is axiomatic that any public or government-controlled educational system is more likely to reflect the spiritual beliefs that underpin a particular culture, even in societies such as Australia, where the public education system is legally secular. Government or publicly funded schools tend to be non-denominational, although the degree to which they reflect the underpinning faith or faiths of society varies between countries. For instance, in Australia, there are tensions between the efforts of schools to respect all the faiths of their students, whilst not favouring one or the other, regardless of the denominational status of the school. Continual pressure from the more conservative elements in society argues that government schools, regardless of their secularity, and whilst acknowledging diversity of opinions on faith, should not be afraid to reflect and acknowledge the dominance of the Judeo-Christian faith in Australian society and history, even if the proportion of people who profess no religion has increased from 19% in 2006 to 30% in 2016 (Australian Bureau of Statistics, 2017).

In societies where there are multiple cultures, the educational system is more likely to reflect that same variation, often including independent or private schools established to educate children in the specifics of a particular faith within the broader context of wider societal concerns. Such is the case in Australia, Canada, the United Kingdom and New Zealand, as well in non-Euro-American societies, such as Malaysia. By and large, in such instances, and regardless of the individual national situations and debates in respect of how these schools are funded, it is the relevant faith organisations that take on the role of establishing and operating the schools to teach within the parameters of their cultural idiom. Inevitably, the values and outlooks embedded in the perspectives of different religions or cultural philosophies must have an influence on the ways that each faith or philosophy approaches the 'Other'. In turn, this becomes converted into an influence on the importance that faith-based schools place on cultural understanding as an educational obligation, the meaning of that cultural education entails and, consequently, the role of the teacher in the process.

However, what seems to be a relatively straightforward association is complicated by the apparent reluctance of human beings to focus on similarities in religions rather than differences. A key aspect of these culture-faith associations is that, contrary to the proclamations of some spiritual and religious leaders from across all these cultural philosophies, none of them can claim to promulgate one absolute version of that faith. Each has splintered into a number of sub-variants, which – often to the bewilderment of those who do not profess any faith – often seem to be separated by minimal points of difference. Through their very existence, these numerous variations highlight the fallacious assumption that cultures are straightforward constructions that are absolutes, with one only 'true' interpretation.

Consequently, although the Judeo-Christian branch can be divided into four general strands (Protestantism, Catholicism, Judaism and the Orthodox), it is often difficult to classify all of the variations as belonging to the same cultural family, especially when each of these four branches has multiple derivations; for example, the various Protestant churches (Methodist, Uniting, Anglican, Lutheran, Pentecostal and so on) and the multiple religious orders, charisms or branches of the Catholic church. Whether the differences between these variations are major or minor depends, of course, on one's perspective. Adherents to a particular faith invariably see even small points of difference as being crucial points of separation. Similarly, the notion of Islam as a united religion, a trope frequently pursued in the Euro-American media, ignores the fact that there are three main factions of Muslim belief, all with adherents whose belief orthodoxy covers the full spectrum from doctrinaire to liberal: the Sunni (85% of Muslims), the Shiites and the Sufis. Buddhism itself has three major branches (Theravada, Mahayana and Vajrayana). Each of the main variations and their 'subcultures' are consistently dogmatic as to the rightness of their own beliefs. This is no better demonstrated by the example of Roman Catholicism, where Catholic schools are often required to use approved texts in their religious teachings and services that consistently refer to Catholics as 'Christians' in outlining their religious and educational expectations. There is no overt suggestion that other Christian churches even exist, with the clear message being that there is only 'the one' (Catholic) path for Christians to follow. Similar statements of belief superiority can be found in various interpretations of Islam, Judaism and Protestantism. Other variations can be less dogmatic, such as in most Uniting and some Anglican schools in Australia, which often choose to teach their faith in the context of comparative religious courses that give the student a wider perspective on their own beliefs.

This splintering of moral outlooks can be seen as a reflection of the reaction of each particular outlook to the existence of the 'Other' and the notion of what cultural understanding might, or might not, mean. It is an unpalatable reality of history that most of the extreme examples of human conflict have often arisen from a total intolerance and unacceptance of the 'Other', including those expressed in religious terms, even if the disagreement is between two branches of the same faith. More often than not, that religious superiority has been infused with, and sometimes masqueraded by, a strong degree of political power, using the religion as a moral justification of action. In doing so, the notion of religion as being core to culture, used in a deeply ethnographic sense, has been the definer of what might be called the historical regional cultures of global societies.

Thus, as illustrated in Table 1.1, Christianity has been long associated with Euro-American societies, despite its origins in the heart of Central Asia or the Middle East (Dawson, 1998; D'Orsa, 2013). Confucianism, through what is referred to as a Confucian Heritage Culture (CHC) – 'one that is heavily influenced by the teachings of Confucius … a society's values, beliefs, rituals and ceremonies …' (p. 3) – is now not only embedded in China and Hong Kong, but can also be found in other regions where emigrants from China now form a key part of the local population; for example, Taiwan, Singapore, Malaysia, Korea and Japan. Other examples of regional religious associations include the Middle East and large parts of Southeast Asia with Islam; Buddhism in large sub regions of Central and Southeast Asia; and the spaces where indigenous systems of faith are most strongly held, including Papua New Guinea, large parts of central South America and Australasia.

Consequently, education, however it is constructed in any region, reflects the opinions that are held by the inhabitants of a culture about 'Other' societies and/or communities that may have been built on differing religious principles, no matter how minimal the differences might be. The teaching of cultural understanding in each of those societies therefore favours and is favoured by an interpretation that defines believers from other faiths as the 'Other' and unacceptable. The reality of these attitudes was, of course, made even more complex by the splintering of the major religious outlooks into subgroups whose mutual antagonism was, in some ways, more condemning of the 'Others' in completely different faiths. The paramilitary attitudes of the Roman Catholic and Protestant followers in cases such as the 'Irish Troubles' in Northern Ireland and the Republic of Eire of the 20th century, the divisions of Sunni and Shia Muslims in the Middle East and Southeast Asia, along with other conservative Islamic variations such as Wahhabism in Saudi Arabia, have all contributed to such a demonisation of the 'Other' in some form; it is far from being a purely post-colonial construct.

By choosing to confine the national case studies to be utilised in this monograph to those that have a direct connection to the period of British colonialism, it is inevitable that the role of religion in the evolution of the teacher's role will comprise a significant part of that discussion. On face value, it appears that, in this context, the focus will be on the Judeo-Christian faith that has long been identified and argued as being the foundation of Euro-American or 'Western' civilisation, of which Britain has been a core part. What tends to be often omitted in considerations of a British imperial history, however, is that British colonialism, although highly promoting of Christianity, was often accepting of existing faiths and traditions. It was not unusual, for instance, for the peoples of India to retain their Hindu or Muslim faiths whilst also adopting Christianity. In colonial British Ceylon (Sri Lanka), Buddhism, Hinduism and Islam continued to exist side-by-side with Christianity, despite clear encouragement for the promotion of Christianity by the Colonial Office and the local administration.

For the United Kingdom itself, one of the legacies of colonialism has been a 21st-century population that is highly culturally and faith diverse (see Table 1.1). In large part, this willingness to defend religious freedom was allied to the tradition of liberalism that was developing within British conceptions of democracy, the same tradition that led eventually to the abolition of slavery and that is argued by the conservatives in Australian politics today. Consequently, despite the clear expectation that education was the main means by which the superiority of British societal imaginary could be inculcated throughout the Empire as well as Great Britain itself, it also provided a pathway through \which a British conception of cultural education could be disseminated, one that did contain an underlying sense of some form of cultural understanding, albeit one constructed with British sensibilities to the fore.

1.5.3 Faith and cultural understandings: a comparative interpretation

The academic study of religions tends to divide the different faiths into three broad groups: World Religions, encompassing the handful of religions that are found globally, such as Christianity, Islam and Buddhism; New Religious Movements; and indigenous Religions (Harvey, 2000). For the purposes of this monograph, however, the first two are being considered as being combined into one. The nomenclature around the description of indigenous religions, now sometimes referred to as First Nation religions, is a contentious field. As Harvey (2000) has pointed out, previous use of terms such as 'traditional' has been criticised for its implication that such faiths are somehow backward when compared with those classified as World Religions, that they are '… simple [or] mere fossils from the earliest evolution of humanity' (Harvey, 2000, p. 7). Such views are, of course, both arrogant and ignorant, and demean the fact that all religions, including the indigenous, are 'traditional' in the sense that they ascribe to the substance of the past, honouring '… what previous generations did as [being] formative and of abiding significance' (Harvey, 2000, p. 9).

In line with the tendency of each religion or philosophy to demonise 'Other' spiritual ontologies to varying degrees, there are broad differences between even related faiths or cultural philosophies that suggest the various ways in how the tenets of moral education – and therefore attitudes to the 'Other' – were and are expressed. The different interpretations that the various world's faiths or religions might place on their principles of what can be called 'moral citizenship' can be both described and explained, by two factors that, on the surface, are more about form than substance. In reality, however, they are far more fundamental.

The first of these is the way in which different faiths have consolidated their core beliefs and practices and then communicated them to future generations. For example, the religions of Judeo-Christianity, Islam, Buddhism, Confucianism and Hinduism are all philosophies that are primarily constructed around written word texts that purport to be the words of the founder(s). In contrast, indigenous belief systems globally tend to be more centred on oral traditions; the recording and dissemination of faith principles are through speech rather than a form of writing in the Euro-American sense, supported by the symbolism and significance or various forms of artwork and artefacts. It could be argued that the lines of moral citizenship in traditional/indigenous beliefs are more likely to be subjectively influenced as transmission from generation to generation has no 'objective' reference. Such a perspective, however, reflects a 'Western' cultural bias that puts more premium on the written word than more personal and community forms of contact. It also does not acknowledge a fundamental flaw in the logic of faiths that are defined by reference to written texts, which can also be criticised for lack of objectivity. As summarised by Marcos (2010):

> Texts, even if they exist, are not at the core of [indigenous] belief structure. If we try to systematize the religions that are transmitted through oral traditions with the methods used for systematizing religions rooted in textual traditions, we will distort and misinterpret them. Historical and textual methods presuppose a fixed narrative as a basis for analysis. Oral traditions are fluid, flexible, and malleable ... a tradition that is in continuous change. (p. viii)

As historical and theological documents, the religious texts of the different faiths in the case study set, as they have survived, are all secondary sources that have been transcribed – and sometimes translated – from previous iterations. Their meanings have been derived through a sequence of interpretations, decided upon following intensive study and debate from scholars within the faith, as well as outside. In such circumstances, it is hardly unexpected that there are so many splinter groups of the original faith, each reliant on a different interpretation of the texts. Invariably, the meaning of these historic texts, including the guides of understanding they offer in respect of the 'Other', depends upon the underlying tone and intention adopted by the interpreters(s). They are heavily dependent on human subjectivity and personal interpretations, especially if these interpreters have tended to be members of the clergy of the faith or philosophy. The lines of moral citizenship obtained from the variety of religious texts are therefore more likely to be aligned with the contemporary societal ethos pertaining to the actual times, society and languages of the respective interpreters, rather than the texts themselves.

The second factor of differentiation is arguably one that is a more fundamental determinant of why different faiths might see moral citizenship differently and, through this, the view of the 'Other' that might be taught in education that is framed within a religion. Essentially, whereas some faiths or philosophy place more emphasis on the individual, others are more collective or community minded in their approach to life. Researchers such as Wang and Torrisi-Steele (2015) and Dahl (2010) argue that 'Western' or Euro-American cultures, most of which are associated with and were established by various interpretations of Christianity, are connected by their general emphasis on the importance of individualism and self-reliance, the importance of independent learning and the productive use of self-reflection in making judgements: '... The independent spirit that is part of Western society lends itself very well to problem solving and creative innovation' (Dahl, 2010, p. 19). Dahl (2010) goes even further than this, however, and is even more forthright on what she sees as the cognitive superiority of Western societies: '... the freedom found in Western education provides the critical and analytical ability ... [that] has given the West its technological edge' (p. 18).

In contrast, philosophies such Confucianism, along with indigenous religions, emphasise the importance of the collective or communal perspective on the world, which leads to a moral educational focus on the significance of considering the totality of a situation; that is, a recognition of the value placed on the holism of interdisciplinary thinking (Di, 2017). There is an emphasis on communitarianism, '... the view that responsibilities to the family and community have priority over the rights of the individual' (Minnis, 1999, p. 177). Self-reflection and the ability to be self-critical are still important, but instead of a self-directed priority, this individual action is undertaken as part of a drive towards a collective goal. The final emphasis is on a greater respect for and the significance placed upon the progress of the individual as a member of a *community*, whether that be of the immediate family or a wider web of family relationships. It is also a philosophy that is not so influenced by any rigidity in geographical location, extending into

> China and other parts of East Asia, such as South Korea, Japan, Vietnam, Singapore, and Taiwan. These societies, despite having their own unique identities, share common Confucian cultural values: society

emphases of harmony and filial piety, respect for the elderly, moderation, collectivism, operates via hierarchical social structures, and values family-centeredness. (Sun & Roumell, 2017, p. 178)

The importance placed on the retention of Confucian principles is no better illustrated by the example of Hong Kong. Before British colonisation, the movement of mainland Chinese into Hong Kong had led to the creation of Chinese schools based on Confucian traditions. Under the British, education was '… a curriculum that originated from a traditional English grammar school model influenced by local trying these traditions' (Eng, 2012, p. 5). Education remained a province for the societal elite until the 1970s, when the British introduced a system of 9 years of compulsory, free education for all. The impact of that policy on what is seen as the holism of Confucianism has been of concern to the governance of post-1997 Hong Kong; Confucian conceptions of moral virtue and citizenship were seen to have diminished under the decades of British colonial rule prior to the hand back to China in the 1990s, with the government '… concerned that civic education was not focusing on moral judgements and social justice, just specific knowledge' (Chan & Chong, 2012, p. 51). The irony here is that it appears that the examination-centred, high-pressure educational environments typical of academically competitive Chinese societies such as Hong Kong and Singapore is not readily compatible with the type of self-reflection required for the skills needed for such goals in Hong Kong, that is the development of the ability to make moral judgements in light of the principles of social justice; '… creativity, self-esteem, critical thinking skills or independent learning' (Chan & Chong, 2012, p. 51).

For researchers such as Ozoliņš (2017), however, such differentiations are not helpful, arguing relationships with other human beings was central to both 'Eastern' and 'Western' societies, with both seeking a peaceful and cohesive society:

> Human beings need education in order for them to develop their ability to relate to others and to cultivate the virtues needed to be good and humane persons. These virtues and attributes are crucial elements in the development of a just, harmonious and humane civil society. (p. 374)

In the same vein, Kato (2016) also says that the similarities between Eastern and Western outlooks on life are more salient than is usually acknowledged. Both Eastern and Western perspectives possess common humanistic elements in the importance placed on the '… philological study of ancient texts, imitation of ancient literature, and a profound love of letters …' (Kato, 2016, p. 23). In a similar vein, de Botton (2012) points out that Christian, Western philosophers such as Matthew Arnold and John Stuart Mill were of the view that the purpose of education was to create cultured, knowledgeable human beings who would leave the world in a better place (p. 102), which does imply a form of concern for the wider community beyond the individual. Such thoughts have a distinct synchronicity with the Confucian outlook, in which '… educating people and helping them to cultivate virtues becomes important to enhance a more human and harmonious relationship in society' (Cheng-Tek Tai, 2011, p. 25). These similarities would suggest that both Christianity and Confucianism have an innate concern for the 'Other' that would be reflected in any education or teaching based upon their respective principles. The priority placed on that aspect, however, and the way in which that concern is exemplified and enacted, suggests that Confucianism may see it as more of a natural or self-evident priority. Scholastically, this translated into a first-principle belief that all people are entitled to an education, even if the type of education varied with the social standing of the individual (Cheng, 2016).

It appears, then, that Christianity's concern for the 'Other' comes with provisos. In the classic European perspective, Kant (1960) saw Christian education as being specifically to aimed to develop moral training within the cultured individual, and that meant those who had the capability of using reason (p. 4). It was from the educated individual with an interest in the common good that societal improvement would emerge:

> All culture begins with the individual, one man gradually influencing others. It is only through the efforts of people of broader views, who take an interest in the universal good, and who are capable of entertaining the idea of a better condition of things in the future, that the gradual progress of human nature toward its goal is possible. (Kant, 1960, p. 17)

To Kant, education of the uneducated by the 'educated' was the mark of a civilised society, suggesting a prejudicial, class and racially based edge to his attitudes in this context. Non-Europeans were equated to uncivilised, 'savage nations': 'The uncultivated man[sic] is crude, the undisciplined is unruly' (Kant, 1960, p. 7). In alignment with Kant, de Botton (2012) contended that Christianity does ultimately focus human action on the self, and not the community at large, because it sees people as being dependent upon the Christian faith for their self-esteem. The religion promotes people's feelings that they are in need of a Christian faith because it emphasises the fallibility and weakness of human beings:

> it has no patience with theories that dwell on our independence or our maturity. It instead believes us to be at heart desperate, fragile, vulnerable, sinful creatures, a good deal less wise than we are knowledgeable, always on the verge of anxiety, tortured by our relationships, terrified of death–and most of all in need of God …
>
> (de Botton, 2012, p. 112)

Further, the ability to think about matters beyond our own selves has become '… of secondary importance to a more practical ability to bring consoling and nurturing ideas to bear on our disturbed and irresolute selves' (de Botton, 2012, p. 112). The end result is that Christianity in practice has effectively forgotten the ultimate meaning of its own Good Samaritan parable by redefining the notion of who is a 'neighbour' and what it means to be 'neighbourly'; it is not just those who are physically close to us: 'the neighbourhood that is constructed by our relations with distant people is something that has pervasive relevance to the understanding of justice in general, particularly so in the contemporary world' (Sen, 2009, p. 172).

What writers such as Ozoliņš fail to take into account, therefore, is that Euro-American societies tend to see societal harmony as being based on the welfare of the individual and what they perceive as the truth of reality, as opposed to the more holistic notions of philosophies such as Confucianism, in which consideration of the whole – and therefore the possibility of the 'Other' – is more heightened. As Regnier (1995) mused in thoughts about North American societies, the

> … dominant North American culture [has] both a deep distrust of holistic styles of understanding, [seeing them] as separating people from any grounded experiences they might have through a veil of verbal abstraction … many First Nations have traditions which valorize holistic learning and champion the development of human sensibilities. (p. 384)

In the end, however, these differences in perceptions of moral citizenship between cultural philosophies are more or less negated by the underlying premise of all faiths and religions. Whilst there may be general tolerance of other faiths' existence, the very existence of the different religions highlights that each one (along with each variant of their mainstream) has the inherent belief that its own cultural-moral perspective on people and the world is the only truth. Within that singular declaration of superiority is contained the belief of each that it is their faith or philosophy has the 'correct' construction of moral character. Contrary to the general view of British society in the age of colonisation, and the significance that post-colonial thought places on the British imaginary being transferred to the colonies through education and the media of the time, it was not only Christianity that taught principles of behaviour as part of a community. All of its major philosophical competitors – Islam, Hinduism, Buddhism, Confucianism and the collective body of what can be referred to as indigenous or First Nation belief systems – had and have very clear images of what it means to be a moral citizen in their own contexts. In the Islamic tradition, for example morality is defined by teachings that '… provide a system that inculcates a spiritual personality that functions practically in this world' (Mogra, 2010, p. 159), a balance between the '… the duality of materialism and spirituality …' (pp. 201–202).

As will be discussed in Chapter 2, it was not until the emergence of a notion of cultural understanding that incorporated the acceptance and embracing of difference as an inalienable human condition and right, one that was not reliant on the imprimatur of a theological superiority to accept the existence of the 'Other', that teachers were freed theoretically to teach a form of cultural understanding that was more attuned to the fully globalised society of the contemporary age.

References

Assié-Lumumba, N. D. T. (2016). Evolving African attitudes to European education: Resistance, pervert effects of the single system paradox, and the Ubuntu framework for renewal. *International Review of Education, 62*(1), 11–27. doi: 10.1007/s11159-016-9547-8.

Baak, M. (2019). Racism and Othering for South Sudanese heritage students in Australian schools: Is inclusion possible? *International Journal of Inclusive Education, 23*(2), 125–141. doi: 10.1080/13603116.2018.1426052.

Casinader, N. (2014). *Culture, Transnational Education and Thinking: Case Studies in Global Schooling*. Milton Park, Abingdon: Routledge.

Casinader, N. (2015). Culture and thinking in comparative education: The globalism of an empirical mutual identity. In J. Zajda (Ed.), *Second International Handbook on Globalisation, Education and Policy Research* (pp. 337–352). Dordrecht, the Netherlands: Springer.

Casinader, N. (2016). A lost conduit for intercultural education: School geography and the potential for transformation in the Australian curriculum. *Intercultural Education, 27*(3), 257–273. doi: 10.1080/14675986.2016.1150650.

Casinader, N. (2017). *Transnationalism, Education and Empowerment: The Latent Legacies of Empire*. Milton Park, Abingdon: Routledge.

Chan, R. W. M., & Chong, A. M. L. (2012). The applicability of peer learning and peer assessment in Hong Kong: A cultural perspective. In B. C. Eng (Ed.), *A Chinese Perspective on Teaching and Learning* (pp. 43–60). New York, NY: Routledge.

Cheng, C.-yi. (2016). Modern versus tradition: Are there two different approaches to reading of the Confucian classics? *Educational Philosophy and Theory, 48*(1), 106–118. doi: 10.1080/00131857.2015.1084219.

Cheng-Tek Tai, M. (2011). An Asian perspective of western or eastern principles in a globalised bioethics. *Asian Bioethics Review, 3*(1), 23–30.

Clay, J., & George, R. (2000). Intercultural education: A code of practice for the twenty-first century. *European Journal of Teacher Education, 23*(2), 203–211. doi: 10.1080/713667276.

Crossley, M., & Watson, K. (2003). *Comparative and International Research in Education: Globalisation, Context and Difference*. London, England: RoutledgeFalmer.

D'Orsa, T. (2013). Catholic curriculum: Re-framing the conversation. *International Studies in Catholic Education, 5*(1), 68–82. doi: 10.1080/19422539.2012.754589.

Dahl, M. (2010). *Failure to Thrive in Constructivism: A Cross-Cultural Malady*. Rotterdam, the Netherlands: Sense.

Darwin, J. (2008). Britain's empires. In S. Stockwell (Ed.), *The British Empire: Themes and Perspectives* (pp. 1–20). Oxford, England: Blackwell Publishing.

Dawson, C. (1998). *Christianity and European Culture: Selections from the Work of Christopher Dawson* (G. J. Rusello Ed.). Washington, DC: Catholic University of America Press.

de Botton, A. (2012). *Religion for Atheists*. London, England: Hamish Hamilton.

Di, X. (2017). Educational philosophy – east, west, and beyond: A reading and discussion of Xueji (學記). *Educational Philosophy and Theory*, *49*(5), 442–451. doi: 10.1080/00131857.2016.1233092.

Eng, B. C. (2012). Introduction: Why a Chinese perspective to teaching and learning. In B. C. Eng (Ed.), *A Chinese Perspective on Teaching and Learning* (pp. 1–13). New York, NY: Routledge.

Foundation for Young Australians. (2017). *The New Work Order*. Retrieved from https://www.fya.org.au/report/new-work-order/.

Gould, E. H. (2008). Britain's empires. In S. Stockwell (Ed.), *Foundations of Empire, 1763-83* (pp. 21–38). Oxford, England: Blackwell Publishing.

Gutek, G. L. (2014). *Philosophical, Ideological and Theoretical Perspectives on Education* (2nd ed.). New Jersey, NJ: Pearson Education.

Hall, S. (1997). The work of representation. In S. Hall (Ed.), *Representation: Cultural Representations and Signifying Practices* (pp. 15–74). London, England: Sage Publications/The Open University.

Halse, C., Mansouri, F., Moss, J., Paradies, Y., O'Mara, J., Arber, R., ... Wright, L. (2015). *Doing Diversity: Intercultural Understanding in Primary and Secondary Schools*. Melbourne: Deakin University. Retrieved from https://en.unesco.org/interculturaldialogue/resources/161.

Hansen, D. T. (2007). John Dewey on education and the quality of life. In D. T. Hansen (Ed.), *Ethical Reasons of Education: Philosophy and Practice* (pp. 21–34). New York, NY: Teachers College Press.

Harvey, G. (2000). *Indigenous Religions: A Companion*. London: Cassell.

Jackson, R. L. (Ed.). (2010). *Encyclopedia of Identity* (Vol. 1). Thousand Oaks, CA: Sage Publications.

Kant, I. (1960). *Education* (A. Churton, Trans.). Ann Arbor, MI: University of Michigan Press.

Kato, M. (2016). Humanistic traditions, east and west: Convergence and divergence. *Educational Philosophy and Theory*, *48*(1), 23–35. doi: 10.1080/00131857.2015.1084216.

Marcos, S. (2010). *Women and Indigenous Religions*. Santa Barbara, CA: Praeger.

McCarty, L. P., & Hirata, Y. (2010). East meets west in Japanese doctoral education: Form, dependence, and the strange. *Ethics and Education*, *5*(1), 27–41. doi: 10.1080/17449641003590605.

Metz, T. (2015). How the west was one: The western as individualist, the African as communitarian. *Educational Philosophy and Theory*, *47*(11), 1175–1184. doi: 10.1080/00131857.2014.991502.

Minnis, J. R. (1999). Is reflective practice compatible with Malay-Islamic values? Some thoughts on teacher education in Brunei Darussalam. *Australian Journal of Education*, *43*(2), 172–185. doi: 10.1177/000494419904300206.

Mogra, I. (2010). Spirituality in the life and career of Muslim teachers. *International Journal of Children's Spirituality*, *15*(2), 159–173. doi: 10.1080/1364436X.2010.497651.

OECD. (2014). *TALIS 2013 Results: An International Perspective on Teaching and Learning*. Paris, France: France OECD.

Ohi, S., O'Mara, J., Arber, R., Hartung, C., Shaw, G., & Halse, C. (2019). Interrogating the promise of a whole-school approach to intercultural education: An Australian investigation. *European Educational Research Journal*, *18*(2), 234–247. doi: 10.1177/1474904118796908.

Ozoliņš, J. T. (2017). Creating the civil society east and west: Relationality, responsibility and the education of the humane person. *Educational Philosophy and Theory*, *49*(4), 362–378. doi: 10.1080/00131857.2015.1048666.

Regnier, R. (1995). Bridging western and first nations thought: Balanced education in Whitehead's philosophy of organism and the sacred circle. *Interchange, 26*(4), 383–415. doi: 10.1007/bf01434743.

Rizvi, F. (2009). Towards cosmopolitan learning. *Discourse: Studies in the Cultural Politics of Education, 30*(3), 253–268. doi: 10.1080/01596300903036863.

Sen, A. (2009). *The Idea of Justice.* Cambridge, MA: The Belknap Press/Harvard University Press.

Simpson, A. (1999). The labours of learning: Education in the postcolony. *Social Analysis: The International Journal of Social and Cultural Practice, 43*(1), 4–13.

Sun Qi, & Roumell, E. A. L. (2017). Interrupting the mindset of educational neocolonialism: Critical deliberations from east and west international adult educators. *Asia Pacific Education Review, 18*(2), 177–187. doi: 10.1007/s12564-017-9482-9.

Tikly, L. (2001). Globalisation and education in the postcolonial world: Towards a conceptual framework. *Comparative Education, 37*(2), 151–171.

UNESCO. (2013). *Intercultural Competences: Conceptual and Operational Framework.* Paris, France: UNESCO.

Vertovec, S. (2009). *Transnationalism.* Milton Park, Abingdon: Routledge.

Walton, J., Priest, N., Kowal, E., White, F., Brickwood, K., Fox, B., & Paradies, Y. (2014). Talking culture? Egalitarianism, color-blindness and racism in Australian elementary schools. *Teaching and Teacher Education, 39*, 112–122. doi: https://doi.org/10.1016/j.tate.2014.01.003.

Wang, V. X., & Torrisi-Steele, G. (2015). Confucian and western teaching and learning. *International Journal of Adult Vocational Education and Technology (IJAVET), 6*(1), 52–64. doi: 10.4018/ijavet.2015010104.

Watkins, M. (2015). Culture, hybridity and globalisation. In T. Ferfolja, C. Jones-Diaz, & J. Ullman (Eds.), *Understanding Sociological Theory for Educational Practices* (pp. 146–162). Port Melbourne, Australia: Cambridge University Press.

Winch, C., & Gingell, J. (2008). *Philosophy of Education: The Key Concepts* (2nd ed.). Milton Park, Abingdon: Routledge.

Chapter 2

Cultural understanding and teaching expertise

A glimpse through British time and place

2.1 Education as moral citizenship

In terms of its etymology, the role of the teacher in the British idiom, regardless of the specific cultural or societal context, time or place, has always focused very much on the relationship between educator and student. Consequently, in its modern frame, the interpersonal skills of teachers are seen to be an essential attribute, an '... awareness of self and of others, emotional stability and control, and the capacity to form satisfying interpersonal relationships' (Aspin, 1973, p. 199). Philosophically, it is a matter of what is being learned and understood by the student through the intermediary of the teacher; the student is receiving the benefits of the knowledge, understanding and skills of the other. The basic act of education is taking the knowledge and understanding of one person from one level to another through the actions of the more learned individual.

However, the learning relationship should not be one of indoctrination or mere transmission. The word 'education' derives from the Latin 'educere', or 'to lead out', which has clear connotations that teaching should be seen more as a mentoring process; it is not an act of domination, but a process of guiding someone into a higher level of knowledge and understanding. Such a concept of education is very much in line with contemporary notions of the role of a teacher, but nevertheless, the question remains as to the nature of the context of that guidance and what it comprises. Theoretically and philosophically, there is no barrier to the use of direct instruction in the mentoring or guidance of a person; pedagogical and counselling variety that is appropriate to the circumstances and the individual are the keys to effective learning in any context. In that sense, there should be no hurdle that would prevent a teacher from encouraging a student to develop a particular perspective or point of view, assuming that it would enhance their ability to best utilise the socio-economic environment in which they live; that is, to ensure that they have the capacity to be active and worthwhile members of their contemporary society.

These parameters of relevance and utility are aligned with the long-established view that education is the fundamental means by which a way of life and its accompanying mindset (that is culture) is nurtured, inculcated and transmitted to future generations: 'Education in all its forms is the primary instrument of enculturation. [It] defines the whole human being as a member of a given society with its worldview, ethos and social representation' (Assié-Lumumba, 2016, p. 14). Some of the knowledge, values and skills to be imparted are vocationally oriented, designed to help the learner find an occupation or place in the society in which they live and are expected to play a part. However, there is another pattern that is repeated strongly through and across societies and time; that one of the key facets of a teacher's role is to imbue a moral sense of citizenship that enables the student to relate and connect to the society in which they live. They are therefore '… concerned with the intellectual development of a whole person, at least, and … also concerned with [their] moral, civic, aesthetic and career development' (King, 1970, p. 29). This 'making of a citizen' has been a focus of education since the times of Plato in Ancient Greece. Contemporary notions of democratic citizenship education today – that education should prepare people for life in a democratic society – reach back not only to Dewey, but also to Rousseau (White, 1996). From this perspective, it is the role of education to create a mental perspective in the individual that highlights the essential elements of what it means to play a part in a particular society, emphasising what is agreed by people in that society to be important to them as a collective group.

In reality, though, the views that are expressed in such conception of citizenship at any particular time in history are more likely to be of those in societal power, and not necessarily the population at large. Moreover, the elements that are seen to comprise moral citizenship vary between societies, and so it is therefore inevitable that what is meant by a moral sense of citizenship, and the scope of that obligation, has varied between cultures, time and place. Included in the framing of a society's notion of moral citizenship are the views and perspectives that reflect attitudes towards people who are either unknown or different; the 'Other'.

This inescapable variety of possible perspectives in cultural outlooks makes it inappropriate to attempt the improbable within the scope of this monograph. Consequently, as presaged in the last chapter, this introduction to the historical notion of teachers being responsible for the teaching of cultural understanding will focus on a sample of countries that have, at some stage in the last 300 years, found themselves under the aegis of the former British Empire. In that, it continues the motifs of the author's last two books (Casinader, 2014, 2017) in which my own life experiences within British imperial education have acted as a launching pad for exploration of wider educational themes.

2.2 The teacher and British educational morality: a temporal consideration

2.2.1 Overview

Historically, within the broad British context, I contend that there have been three main historical phases in the work of a teacher in respect of their responsibilities as an educator of cultural understanding. None of these periods are mutually exclusive, with examples of each being clearly discernible in different places globally at any time in history, especially since the Age of Industrialisation in Europe. Each can be characterised differently in several ways: the likelihood and the degree to which people might be exposed to the 'Other'; the basis on which that cultural difference is identified; and the way(s) in which people of a specific culture respond to the discovery of that cultural difference.

The first phase can be applied to all societies that were (or are) typified by a strongly hierarchical social and political structure, encompassing forms of organisation that have a feudal-like social configuration based on levels of mutual obligation. Such societies are exemplified by those in Europe during its medieval period, or similarly, in China up to the fall of in the line of its imperial dynasties in 1949. In this form, society is headed by some form of monarchical or hereditary leader and is dominated by an agrarian economy. The focus of community is/was on the local environments in which people actually lived, typically rural communities or neighbourhoods in relatively small urban areas.

The second phase originates with the transformation of society that was initiated by the process of modernisation, epitomised by the Age of Industrialisation in 18th-century Europe and onwards. As in the first iteration, the focus of community in this phase is not just on the local social communities in which people lived, but also on the process of rural-urban migration that inevitably accompanies any degree of societal industrialisation. The result is a mounting focus on rapidly growing urban communities, both in terms of geographical extent and numbers. As people become less tied to small, local rural communities, their attachment to the country or the nation-state in which they live – and which is now replacing the security of their former village community – becomes more heightened.

The third period, which is still in process, is highlighted by the age of contemporary globalisation since the 1990, but has its origins dating back to 1945 and the emergence of internationalism. During this period, and especially since the 1990s, there has been a rapid reconceptualisation of world society as a global entity, as much as it is composed of local and/or national communities. As a result of this enlarged scale in the perception of community, a vastly expanded paradigm of citizenship has developed and the parameters of what is encompassed by moral citizenship have adjusted accordingly. Individuals are now seen to have responsibility to world society and people outside their local places of origin or residence in a manner that goes way beyond the expectations in previous generations, taking on a cosmopolitan frame that is inherently characterised by a global sense of citizenship and obligation. In the first two periods of transformation, the 'Other' was primarily represented by differences in the people living in the next village or the adjacent country, principally because travel beyond the community of residence and/or work was not a viable or desired option for the majority. The physical distance between oneself and the 'Other' was distinctly less than it might be now, even if that zone of separation was equally difficult to cross psychologically. In the third transformation, however, the 'Other' is not just local or national, but also as likely to be international and/or global. The intensity of cultural difference in any meeting may be heightened to the point of extreme disengagement in its worst instances because the degree of cultural difference is now more visible and tangible. It is this greater likelihood of meeting and being part of cultural difference that makes the necessity of teaching of cultural understanding far more of a specific educational imperative than has been in the past. The moral sense of citizenship, which this monograph argues has been at the heart of the teaching role throughout the centuries, albeit often hidden and in different forms, has now become a salient necessity in the globalised age.

2.2.2 Phase 1: the religious as educator

In broad terms, it can be argued that the primary educators of a child are, and have always been, his/her parents and other adults who are part of his/her wider community and environment. This is one educational expectation that has transcended time, place and culture, even though the perception of what is 'family' has become increasingly diverse. The notion and reality that the entirety of a local community – or, at least, a child's extended family – is responsible for the upbringing of a child remains core to the cultures of many in the modern age, especially those whose master cultures are collective or community-focused in their outlook. For instance, the tribally defined African communities throughout that continent, the extensive web of Chinese diaspora throughout Southeast Asia and the rest of the world and the deep kinship connections within Australia's Indigenous (Aboriginal and Torres Strait Islander) clans, regardless of whether they live in rural or urban contexts, are all current examples of how that wider sense of community responsibility and education is still very much part of the modern situation. In these 'traditional' connections, the place of the community elders, in conjunction with other spiritual and philosophical leaders, is central to the education and upbringing of a child, especially when boys and girls reach the age at which they are ritually welcomed into adulthood and their education is recontextualised/ritualised accordingly. Wisdom and educational responsibility are seen as the privileges of the experienced adult, highlighting the depth to which those kinship links in life and education are still relevant.

In the early years of Anglo-Saxon Britain, which extended from the 5th to the 11th centuries, these same sets of localised educational priorities and responsibilities were still in play, and remain so, albeit with a different emphasis. Whilst the role of parents was still an important component in educating a child about the practicalities and vocational needs of a life, depending upon one's gender and status in a highly stratified society, the institution of the early Christian (that is, Roman Catholic) church played a major role in both establishing and defining the need for a more specific form of education. Formal education was reserved for young males high on the social scale, a system that served to meet the dual requirements of managing and governing a country where religion and governance (at this stage, through the monarchy) were deeply intertwined. In this phase, learning and schooling was based on the traditions of the Roman Empire, focused on the learning of Latin (the official language of the Church and the Bible), grammar and Psalms, a practicality as much as anything else, since the native British language had never been written down (Orme, 2006, p. 17). Since the clergy were the only ones who had a knowledge of Latin, which was taught as a foreign language, the teachers in this early phase of British history were the bishops, the senior clergy, abbesses, monks and nuns, with many specialising in teaching the young, even if they had no formal training in the art. Teachers were not seen as professionals in themselves; instead, teaching was perceived as part of the duty of being a member of the clergy. Education was for the chosen few and not for the masses. Cathedrals and monasteries were the

> ... centres of literacy, since their members worshipped with books and studied religious texts, and each needed to recruit boys and men to sustain their activities in the future. The schooling of these recruits had to be organised internally because no other schools existed locally. (Orme, 2006, p. 18)

Given the relatively low numbers of clergy, lay student numbers were essentially limited to the children of royalty and senior mobility (Orme, 2006). Teaching, though, was a part-time activity, with '... clergy[doing] their teaching alongside the duties of saying daily worship, just as Anglo-Saxon clergy had done, even where the school was open to outsiders' (Orme, 2006, p. 163).

By the time of the European Middle Ages, the essence of education had shifted somewhat in response to the growing importance of trade, both economically and as a social class. It was now essentially concerned with the arts and skills of conducting business (that is, trade) and the documentation of governance. There were essentially three main groups of children who were educated: the clerks, stewards and bailiffs, who were servants of the monarch and nobility; the apprentices in trades or crafts where writing, recordkeeping and financial accounting were essential; and the aristocracy. Even though the numbers of students had increased, the numbers of clergy were still relatively low; nevertheless, the role of the teacher – or the schoolmaster, for teachers were overwhelmingly male – was still one embedded in the life of the clergy.

The move towards teachers being seen publicly as stand-alone professionals was taking place, however, as the demands of clergy life and for education increased. By 1200, there was an emerging class of specialised teachers, very largely male, but not exclusively:

> There may have been mainly women instructors in towns, ministering to girls, small boys, or both. Very likely they concentrated on the lower end of the curriculum: the ABC, the reading of Latin prayers and primers, and perhaps the reading of works in French or English. (Orme, 2006, p. 167)

The sense of moral citizenship taught by educators in this phase, therefore, can be largely characterised as one of obedience to your designated place in society and meeting the obligations of that position within the class system. Cultural understanding was not so much directed at learning about the unknown, for the great majority of people in Britain, unless they were merchants, traders and explorers, remained largely within their local communities. Instead, it was largely an insulated, self-directed affair, focused on learning about one's own cultural identity as reflected in your position in society. This class-occupation dualism still exists in some modern sovereign states, such as with the caste system in India (especially rural India), where, despite the system being officially made illegal, status in society is often still closely attached to one's occupation, even though it is less prevalent than before.

Children – or, to be more precise, male children, for feudal structures tend to reflect strong patriarchy – inevitably followed the paths of their parents in terms of profession or occupation, and more than likely, in terms of the location of their residence. The introduction of the Anglo-European tradition of creating and using surnames to differentiate between people with the same first (Christian) name only serves to reinforce the way in which one's individuality was determined by the occupation a male might hold or to whom they were related. The now common Anglo-European names such as Smith, Wilson, Johnson, Taylor, Weaver and so on were the outcome of that fundamental need. The teaching of morality was essentially replicated or condensed into the teachings of the church and the expectations of the Christian faith. The centrality of Christianity to society as a whole and the educational system, such as it existed, was paramount.

2.2.3 Phase 2: the rise of the layperson as teacher

The last centuries of Medieval Britain saw the beginnings of the transition in the role of teacher from being associated with the clergy to a more specialised profession composed of lay people. From the 13th to the 18th centuries, Britain, along with other European centres such as the Netherlands and the Italian city-states, developed an economy focused mainly around trade as well as agriculture. This period of growth culminated in the agricultural revolution of the 18th century, which enabled greatly increased volumes of farm production with less labour at a time of steady population growth. Trade became increasingly the primary source of wealth generation, offering a range of new jobs and employment. The waves of plague that had struck Europe during the Middle Ages had helped to break down the feudal system of obligation by creating a shortage of labour supply for work on the land. The situation was exacerbated by the higher quality of living offered by industrial work in the towns, producing materials for the new agricultural revolution. The impact of that process, which proceeded to increase agricultural productivity with less labour, along with the Industrial Revolution that followed, made urban areas a more attractive centre of human life and activity. People had to move from the rural areas to the growing urban communities in order to find work. In consequence, as the complexity of British society increased, the role of the teacher also began to shift. The number of clergy could not keep up with increasing demand for educated citizens who could work in the burgeoning trade sector, with all its necessary financial accounting, recordkeeping and agreement making. By the 13th century, a small yet distinct class of teachers as a separate profession was beginning to emerge (Orme, 2006).

By the time of the Age of Industrialisation, the increasing specialisation of the workforce and the demand for labour had created an influx of rural-urban migrants, creating large areas of slum housing and social disadvantage in the rapidly growing towns and cities. An industrialised workforce, however, required a more educated labour force, a task that was clearly way beyond the resources of the church and clergy. Teaching increasingly became a specialised profession, but the nature of teaching also had to respond to the challenges of having to educate numbers of children in sizes and extent never before seen. The result was a government-administered system of mass education that was, for the first time, regulated to some degree by government. In doing so, the profession of teacher as a separate entity within organised society was introduced; the 19th century can be seen as the era when, within the British imperial context, teaching came to be considered and acknowledged as an occupation in itself, and it was only at this time that systematic teacher education began, as the shortage of competent teachers was seen as a barrier to the introduction of mass education (Dent, 1977).

As a consequence of this socio-economic transformation, the type of moral citizenship expected as an outcome of education itself became far more complex and nuanced. From being a conveyor of basic knowledge and skills, reinforcing the past, the teacher, I would argue, began to become more of a proactive moral and cultural educator, promoting the new personal and attitudinal qualities that were seen to be important drivers and supporters in the new industrialised society. The modern form of human society was driven and controlled, not so much by personal obligation and community expectation, but by personal drive for economic – and therefore social – improvement.

However, throughout this transitionary – albeit long – period, the moralities of good citizenship taught by both religious and lay teachers still remained centred on the precepts of obligation and duty as determined by Christian principles. The initial signs of teacher training could be seen in the work of groups such as the Society for Promoting Christian Knowledge in 1699, which had the specific goal of ensuring teachers avoided vice and debauchery (Dent, 1977, p. 1). Other groups saw teachers as needing to mirror Christian missionary qualities, namely, an '… harmonious combination of religious fervour, scholarly ardour for study, a high respect for professional expertise, and personal humility' (Dent, 1977, p. 13). This combination of strength in academic learning and faith was a notable feature of writings on teacher qualities and obligations in the 17th, 18th and 19th centuries; see, for example Brinsley (1627), Snell (1649), Coote (1673) and Scott (1866). In 1777, George Chapman summarised a teacher as requiring expertise in the classics, able to communicate knowledge, being conscious of the needs of their students and being a role model in religious and other aspects: 'Pious and ingenuous in his mind, prudent and humane in his temper, regular and polished in his manners, temperate and plain in his[sic] way of life …' (Chapman, 1773, p. 105).

By the mid-19th century, this combination of spiritual and educational obligations was still very much in place. Jellinger Symons, in a treatise on establishing a school (Symons, 1852), argued that teachers needed to be of high religious, moral and intellectual character, as 'if our education is to be education at all, it must moralize and Christianize. It must educate the heart as well as the head and hand' (p. 2). John Scott, who was Principal of the Wesleyan Training Institution, set out a number of teacher expectations and qualities (Scott, 1866), including focused academic study ('to improve the mind itself, with all its powers, should be your enlightened aim', p. 65), to see religious belief as the 'highest of human attainments' (p. 11), to possess sympathy and feeling for children, to not see financial reward as the main motivator and, most importantly, 'to bring the children well forward in secular learning, to form their manners, and to produce upon their minds proper moral and religious impression' (p. 11).

Theoretically and realistically, only the State has the resources to implement such a system of mass education, or education for a large number of people across the country at the same time. However, governmental acceptance of this new responsibility was not a process that occurred naturally or in haste. Consequently, at a time when the direct hold of the church(es) on educational processes was being diluted, and despite the progressive developments towards the democratisation of society throughout much of the 19th century – such as the Reform Act of 1832, which democratised the demand for education by giving the right to vote to over a million adults – it was the churches who, along with philanthropic organisations and individuals, continued to 'pioneer' the provision of basic education to the masses through the establishment of schools, not only in Britain, but also throughout the British Empire (James, 1998; Seth, 2007; Casinader, 2017).

As is often the case in governmental policy, contradictions abounded. As early as 1802, it was evident that politicians understood the need for large-scale education of the population in order to meet the needs of the industrialising society and economy:

> In the debates preceding the Education Act of 1870, it was vigorously argued that teaching was a social service, and an essential one, too. Teaching ensued moral standards, provided better-equipped recruits for industry and the armed forces, and enabled democracy to function more efficiently. (Gould, 1973, p. 55)

Nevertheless, they were not keen to accept the financial responsibility for such a transformation. Prime Minster Peel's Factory Act (1833) mandated that employers had to ensure that young apprentices received instruction in reading, arithmetic and writing within their first 4 years, but it was not until 1870 that Britain's Education Act enabled the implementation of a system of large-scale education across the country, education that was free, compulsory and – most significantly – nondenominational. The nexus between religion as the primary education provider and the general population had finally been broken, at least in theory.

The impact of these significant shifts on the work of teachers in respect of teaching cultural understanding in the form of the morality of citizenship was, in many ways, pedagogically driven. Limited financial and human resources meant that teaching had to be conducted as efficiently as possible; large class sizes and direct instruction were the primary convention of the day. But in terms of might be referred to the development of individual character, it is arguable that the most substantial change was the decline in the role of an individual's local community and family in developing moral outlooks. Although urban communities retained some of the interactions that were, and are, typical of rural communities, the concept of a village as a collective educator of young people disappeared to a large degree. Instead, given the number of hours that children began to spend within them, the school began to replace the local social community as the primary zone of personal development, at least for those who attended school. Just as is the case today, parental knowledge of future places of work became mired in the past, as technology and economic change created employment that could not be anticipated, especially if the parents had received little or no education beyond maybe some vocational on-the-job training. The schoolmaster – for, aside from governesses for the daughters of wealthier families, the profession was still dominated by men – was now becoming the major adult influence on the ideological and philosophical development of the child.

By the end of the 19th century, I would argue, the Age of Enlightenment throughout Europe and the gradual democratisation of British society, which had commenced around the late 17th century, had created a paradigm of moral citizenship that incorporated specific notions as to the role of the teacher, one that was increasingly independent of (but not exclusive of) the original religious imperative. The influence of European philosophers such as John Locke and Immanuel Kant can be seen in the gradual establishment of the principle that education of children needed to be a rational, developmental and individual process. In so doing, they also help to create a specific role and *profession* for the teacher, one that had responsibility for developing the character of the child in order to prepare them to meet what was perceived as the norms of the times. For instance, Locke (Locke & Gay, 1964) and Kant (1960) were both firm on the importance of learning discipline and developing positive work habits:

> Education includes the nurture of the child and, as it grows its *culture*. The latter is firstly negative, consisting of discipline; that is, merely the correcting of faults secondly, culture is *positive*, consisting of instruction and guidance (and thus forming part of education). *Guidance* means directing the pupil and putting into practice what it has been taught. (p. 2)

As Gay commented, it took over half a century for the work of John Locke and others '… to defuse the notion that children are human, with their own rights, their own rhythm of development, and their own pedagogical needs' (Locke & Gay, 1964, p. 3). This is not to say that writers such as Locke were proponents of mass quality education. Locke himself was writing about the education of the sons of gentlemen (the patriarchy of contemporary society was not in his scope of contestation), but he, along with philosophers such as Kant (1960), did set in place some very clear expectations of the expertise that a teacher needed to bring to bear on the educational process. The development of morality in the child was seen as the primary objective of education, for

> virtue is the first … of those endowments that belong to one man or gentleman, as absolutely requisite to make and valued and beloved by others, acceptable or tolerable to himself. Without that, I think, he will be happy neither in this, nor the other world. (Kant, 1960, p. 99)

In Locke's view, this virtuous quality incorporated qualities such as a kindly and measured religious belief (extremism in religious fervour was not encouraged), respect for the truth, wisdom and good breathing; learning of knowledge came second to the acquisition of such moral qualities. Similar attributes were enunciated by Kant, for whom education was about culture, for culture was a knowledge of morality; none of his four goals of education, which included the teaching of faith, being good-humoured and displaying an even temperament (Kant, 1960, p. 111), referred to learning of knowledge at all. Culture was not an ethnographic concept, nor a psychological perspective. In the classic European outlook, it referred to those activities that cultivated the mind to the point that a person was able to think and act with flexibility and understanding, qualities that came with an appreciation of literature and the arts.

The work of the teacher also had to be supportive of the responsibilities of teaching that needed to be fulfilled: '... so the tutor's example must lead the child into those actions he would have them do' (Locke & Gay, 1964, p. 78). Interestingly, in an ironic twist that, in many ways, is a reflection of 21st-century educational thought, Locke also placed great emphasis on the ability of the teacher to encourage inquiry in children by nurturing a desire for new knowledge:

> Curiosity in children ... is but an appetite after knowledge, and therefore ought to be encouraged in them, not only as a good sign but as the great instrument nature has provided, to remove the that ignorance they were born with, and which without this busy inquisitiveness will make them dull and useless creatures. (Locke & Gay, 1964, p. 88)

In order to achieve this, Locke indirectly highlighted the need for the teacher to know their student; without it, they could not engage them in learning:

> The great skill of the teacher is to get and keep the attention of his scholar: whilst he has that, he is sure to advance as fast as the learner's abilities will carry him; and without all his bustle and bother will be to little or no purpose. (Locke & Gay, 1964, p. 126)

Kant (1960) was even more specific, arguing that the duty of the teacher was to develop culture in a student, as

> it is culture which brings out ability. Ability is the possession of the faculty which is capable of being adapted to various for ends. Ability, therefore, does not determine any ends, but leaves that to circumstances as they arise afterwards. (p. 19)

What is interesting, however, is that the 19th century also contained indications that expectations were slowly changing. The obligations of a teacher were slowly moving beyond the religious imperative, expanding to include engendering young people with a disposition to think about ideas, rather than just receiving them. For instance, there were pronouncements from school leaders that teaching professionals were now expected to do more than just communicate a Christian, British view of the world:

> Education, by opening new sources of pure pleasure, is an incentive to mental activity. (Newlands, 1824, p. 7)
>
> The end of education is the improvement of the powers and faculties of the mind, not the infusion of knowledge, however important. (Milligan, 1889, p. 10)

To some extent, the increasing democratisation of education throughout the Ages of Enlightenment and Industrialisation did translate into a form of cultural understanding related to its modern context; that is, consideration about other people, if not in a wider sense. Compared with more 21st-century-like sensibilities, philosophers such as Locke and Kant were distinctively elitist in their conceptions of education and the role of the teacher. As mentioned earlier, Locke was more concerned with the education of the sons of nobility. Any consideration that he gave towards the education of the working class was very much in the mould of the moral value of building a strong work ethic and the condemnation of idleness (see Locke & Gay, 1964). Likewise, Kant was very strident in his condemnation of those who were not part of his ideal world. All non-Europeans were seen as being 'savage' (Kant, 1960, p. 4). Only enlightened people (which, in Kant's construction, were only those who subscribed to a Christian God) have the ability to develop reasoning, which meant that Kant was effectively equating the start of civilisation with the art of writing. Thus, when Kant (1960) refers to the importance of moral training in education as it 'imparts to man a value with regard to the whole human race' (p. 31), the impression is one of paternalism, not of equality. Ironically, for both Locke and Kant, the base of this morality was the Christian faith that was so central to both their lives. Those who were non-Christian were considered to incapable of developing reason and, therefore, regard for others: 'The divine law must at the same time be recognised as Nature's law, for it is not arbitrary. Hence religion belongs to all morality ... Morality, then, must come first and theology follow; and that is religion' (Kant, 1960, p. 112).

In broad terms, therefore, this phase in the evolution of the British teacher, as a cultivator of moral character and cultural understanding, would last until after the World War II. At that point, the global world order changed in ways that had not been possible after the Great War of 1914–1918, although it was that earlier period of conflict that set the scene for the changes after 1945. If the Great War was the 'apogee of nationalism' in global politics,

World War II was the 'apogee of internationalism' (Sluga, 2013, pp. 79–80). The profession of the teacher as a stand-alone expert, and who was not necessarily part of the clergy, was still an illusion in reality. The dominance that Christianity had maintained in both directly and indirectly guiding and justifying the evolution of British society through the Age of Colonialism and into the first half of the 20th century persisted.

For British governments, the perceived supremacy of Christianity as a faith – especially in its Protestant variations – was a public tool to be used for support in their drive to acquire resources to feed the industrialisation and colonisation process. Since imperial funding was a continual issue (the act of acquiring and defending colonies was an expensive undertaking), British authorities were more inclined to support church and private organisations that wanted to take on the key colonial role of cementing British notions of citizenship, moral and otherwise, through educational ventures in all parts of the Empire. Whether supported or not by central government or colonial authorities, the establishment of any large-scale education system in imperial colonies was often initiated or undertaken by various churches or missionary societies, at little or no cost to the metropolitan government. The heads of many of these schools, along with many of their teaching staff, were invariably from the clergy or, at the very least, people with strong church connections. It is a pattern that is maintained until the present day, even though the number of secular schools has increased dramatically in the intervening period. In colonial India and Ceylon (Sri Lanka), early education was at first instituted by missionary societies, overseen by the colonial administrators (Ceylon) or the East India Company (India), and not the Colonial Office (see Seth, 2007; Casinader, 2017). A similar approach in Britain itself persisted until the Education Act of 1870, which established the role of elected government in providing education for all. Thus, it was in the Age of Industrialisation that church-based or church-established schools became the precursor of mass public education systems, each of them providing the ideal medium for the religious characterisation of individual student.

In another sense, it can be also argued that the advent of industrialisation decreased people's need for reliance on religion as a rationale of life. The societal shift enabled individuals to free themselves from the religious parameters of medieval times in exchange for upward social mobility through the 'sale' and application of their own skills and labour. However, in so doing, the religious influence on the role of the teacher became far more enmeshed that it had been when the clergy had been the main source of teaching. Even as the years of mass education progressed from the late 19th century, the provision of education was increasingly a dual-sector affair, separated between institutions of power; that is, the government and the numerous schools and systems set up by the various denominations of the Christian church. The degree to which government and religion developed and governed education throughout the growing British Empire of the 19th and 20th centuries was as diverse is the Empire itself, as exemplified by the contrast between India and Ceylon (Sri Lanka), about which I have written elsewhere (Casinader, 2017). For instance, the dominance of Scottish clergy and religiously minded educators who established, staffed and led the many non-government schools throughout the colony of Ceylon (Sri Lanka) was typical of the colonial connection.

Even taking into account the myriad variations with which teachers have approached the teaching of the 'Other', the role of the teacher as an educator in cultural understanding throughout this phase was essentially one of creating educated children (still almost overwhelmingly male) who had developed the eternal paradox of the democratically minded Christianised education: an individual who has the power to reason based on knowledge, combined with the tension of seeing value and worth in all human beings, and yet having the firm conviction that the only way in which that value and worth could be recognised by adopting the Christian cultural perspective. To be 'cultured' was to be a member of and a subscriber to the European perspective on the world. What varied, of course, as is the case today, were the views on which that Christian perspective were interpreted in terms of skin colour and culture as a way of life. The bifurcation of teachers between those who saw skin colour as a negative symbol and measure of ability, and those who did not, led to a great diversity in how teachers responded to the imperative of teaching morality as an essential aspect of British Imperial citizenship.

Pedagogically, however, the status of teacher as the main fount of knowledge and understanding remained a constant. Education was largely a one-way process, with the transference of understanding from the teacher to the student. In this way, the perceived benefits and benevolence of the British character and approach to life were transmitted to students throughout Britain and its Empire, and it was this that comprised the moral education that underpinned the British educational approach. This meant that the teacher had become a professional responsible for the generation and maintenance of national identity, the means by which the norms and priorities of British society would be passed on to future generations, and that included attitudes towards cultural difference. By the end of the 19th century, the significance of teacher influence on the creation of a child's attitudes to life was beginning to be recognised; it was just about not the transference of knowledge. As a Glasgow headmaster outlined in a speech to an educational institute in 1889,

> Education [is] ... the harmonious development of all the powers of a child's physical, intellectual, and spiritual nature, and the teacher as agent, in many cases, the main agent, in accomplishing this development. (Milligan, 1889, p. 1)

During this phase, by and large, people remained physically and emotionally tied to their place of origin, and teachers were not an exception to this rule. Those who went to colonial territories far away from 'home' to teach in the British idiom did so in the full expectation that they would return to Britain at some point in their lives, even if it was just before the time of their death. No matter how long the time spent overseas, migration was essentially a temporary affair. Those from colonised territories who had acquired British citizenship as a result took advantage of their new opportunities by travelling to Britain to take on further education, but most had the intention of returning 'home' at some stage. Deeper knowledge and understanding of how people beyond British 'civilisation' thought, lived and died became the privilege of those British educators who travelled to work in the outer reaches of the Empire, but also of the colonised who were able to develop a new knowledge and understanding of how their enhanced and expanded 'local' world operated.

In hindsight, it can be argued that the status of the teacher as the dominant leader in the process of education was, in large part, a direct consequence of the transport and communication technologies that were available to them at the time. One point that often appears to be forgotten in current educational debates is the reason why pedagogy has been able to develop and evolve in the last 50 years or so to a more student-centred approach. Technologies now exist that enable students to access knowledge in the form of information and ideas by themselves, without the aid of a teacher. The growing wealth of the expanding middle class means that the public have increasing economic and educational capacity to take on and use that technology as it is developed. In 19th-century imperial Britain, though, the capacity to purchase books – which were effectively the World Wide Web of the day – was limited to the upper classes. In terms of mass education, the cost of producing books, and even writing implements such as pen and paper, were high enough to put them out of the reach of most students and families. The practice of direct instruction, accompanied by large classes, the use of personal slates (writing boards) and the most basic of blackboards, was a function of the socio-economic and technological state of society at the time. It was not until the technological revolution of the post World War II era that the costs of producing and accessing information became progressively low enough to make access to ideas and content available to all, without necessarily going through the teacher at the front of the class. In such a context, the development of any cultural understanding within students was very much in the hands and minds of the teachers in front of them, and in the environment of imperial Britain, that meant that students would only be able to consider the views of the 'Other' as they evolved through the learning and teaching of the school educators themselves.

2.2.4 Phase 3: the teacher as global professional

The evolution of global society after World War II had four major interrelated impacts and influences on the role of the teacher as the conduit for education in cultural understanding. The first was technological, the culmination of the post-1945 revolution, assisted by the rapid improvements afforded by the scientific advances made through such events as the first Moon landing in 1969. Air travel gradually came into being as an increasingly affordable form of civilian transport, and by the 1980s and beyond, the cost of that travel became low enough to be within the reach of the ordinary citizen, whether living in Britain or in another part of the now rapidly diminishing empire. It was not long before the technological revolution resulted in the creation of the global computer network that came to be the Internet or the World Wide Web.

As has been addressed elsewhere (Gopinath, 2008; Vertovec, 2009; Pieterse, 2015), the dramatic evolution of what can effectively be termed a speedy, affordable global public transport system has had the effect of reducing the impact of distance on daily domestic and work lives; a lessening of the geographical friction of distance. People still migrate from one part of the world to another, but maintain their connections with their place of origin far more easily and in much more comprehensive ways. In doing so, they develop the multiple connectivities (Rizvi, 2009) that are now the core characteristics of a large proportion of the world's population. The communications revolution in media has resulted in a shift from people around the world watching a Moon landing on of a fuzzy black-and-white TV (a feat that itself was undertaken with the computer power of a 21st-century electronic calculator) to a situation where the vast majority have potential instant access to events being held in all parts of the world at all times of day and night, only dependent upon their ability to access depth of coverage, whether financial or otherwise. Consequently, it is now far more commonplace for people to meet others from different backgrounds, cultures and variations of cultures on a daily basis, both physically and virtually. That exposure to difference, a theme which will be explored in more depth in the beginning of Chapter 3, has meant that there is a greater likelihood of people from one particular culture having to meet, live and work with others from another culture; in short, the need for cultural understanding of the other has become a necessity of life, and is no longer an optional extra.

The second impact was socio-political and centred around the formation of the United Nations. Although initiated by the 1945 Great Powers for the purposes of stabilising the international order as a deterrent against global conflict, the organisation has become both a symbol and practical substantiation of cultural diversity. As a global body, built in part on the notion of national equality, particularly in the General Assembly, it has become a voice for types of cultural expression from all parts of the world, growing in membership as decolonisation created a new paradoxical imaginary of independent and yet interdependent sovereign States. As has been researched and written about from multiple perspectives, including the fields of comparative and international education, the decolonisation process, which followed the trauma of World War II and the establishment of the United Nations as an international meeting place of cultures on a theoretically equal basis, has also generated a greater propensity and likelihood of people from different backgrounds to meet and work together, both out of choice and necessity. Prior to 1939, world affairs were dominated by the Western or Euro-American States, with societies and educational systems built fundamentally on the profession of a Christian outlook and the values of the moral outlook embedded within it. The social, political and philosophical complexity of world society that followed 1945 created threads of uncertainty at all levels of life, regardless of status, class and outlook, especially as the then-British colonies began to utilise the impetus created by the World War II to generate transitions to independence:

> What set mid-twentieth-century internationalism apart however was the extent to which, for a relatively brief moment and among a considerable swathe of mainstream and marginalized public opinion, the discarded utopian precepts of the earlier period suddenly took on the semblance of political realism. (Sluga, 2103, pp. 79–80)

Through agencies such as UNESCO, with its emphasis on education and cultural growth that prioritised local attitudes and ways of life in a balance with what were perceived to be the necessities for global cooperation and stability, the United Nations has consistently promoted notions of cultural acceptance and diversity as a basis for policymaking. The emergence of contemporary globalisation in the 1990s, facilitated, promoted and actualised by the technological revolution referred to previously, necessitated and assisted an increase in the attention paid to the development of global policy in the area of education, cultural understanding and global citizenship.

The third impact has been the emergence of a concept of moral citizenship that is not dependent on the relationship between education and faith, one that owes its origins to the other dramatic shift in global thinking about cultural relationships that has occurred since the end of the World War II. The emergence of a new sense of universal human rights, instantiated in the principles and agreements of the main multilateral organisation in global politics, the United Nations, has provided global society and national governments with the nearest the world has seen to a universal understanding of what is meant by cultural understanding and acceptance of the 'Other'. Amongst others, legal historians such as Samuel Moyn (2010) have argued that developments such as these were not possible prior to World War II, for it was only after that conflict that the notion of universal human rights – including those relating to cultural self-determination – came into existence; any rights relating to humans that existed prior to that time were prescribed by belonging to a sovereign State; that is, national citizenship. The whole notion of a universal set of international human rights was the basis for the concept of a global form of citizenship.

The work of global agencies such as UNESCO has created avenues for collaboration and interaction between sovereign States towards improving the quality of life across the world in its most basic aspects, including education. In doing so, a global context has been created in which it is now possible to have a global policy document that outlines what is meant by cultural understanding, together with recommendations as to how it should be taught (UNESCO, 2006). More significantly, in the context of this monograph, the documents that have emerged from the UN deliberations over time highlight, more than ever, the importance of and the obligation for school educators to teach about cultural understanding, regardless of whether such priorities are seen as politically advantageous and expressed as a government directive through national curriculum. The Universal Declaration of Human Rights (United Nations, 1948) itself highlights the umbilical cord between education and the gaining of cultural understanding:

> Education shall be directed to the full development of human personality and to the strengthening of respect for human rights and fundamental freedoms. It shall promote understanding, tolerance and friendship among all nations, racial and religious groups, and shall further the activities of the United Nations for the maintenance of peace (United Nations, 1948, Art. 26.2).

In terms of how education should enable this progression, the UNESCO Guidelines on Intercultural Education outlines three principles (Table 2.1), all of which emphasise that the teacher must take responsibility for developing these notions within students. The development of appropriate learning

Table 2.1 Principles of Intercultural Education

Principle I	Intercultural Education respects the cultural identity of the learner through the provision of culturally appropriate and responsive quality education for all.
Principle II	Intercultural Education provides every learner with the cultural knowledge, attitudes and skills necessary to achieve active and full participation in society.
Principle III	Intercultural Education provides all learners with cultural knowledge, attitudes and skills that enable them to contribute to respect, understanding and solidarity among individuals, ethnic, social, cultural and religious groups and nations.

Source: UNESCO (2006).

materials, pedagogy, assessment and teacher training are all emphasised as being fundamental to the achievement of these goals.

However, just because such declarations have been made and even agreed to by member of United Nations, does not mean that they have become implemented at the national level. Education is not alone in being treated in such a selective manner as far as UN policy recommendations are concerned. Even though sovereign States and national governments might be required to work towards these policies as a matter of international law, especially if they are signatories to them, it is too often the case is that nation-states will only implement UN agreements if their governments of the day perceive that kind of action as being politically advantageous.

The fourth factor, and arguably the most important educationally at the level of teacher practice, has been the gradual democratisation of education at a philosophical level throughout the 20th century in the Euro-American sphere. This shift has been driven largely by the impact of educational thinkers such as John Dewey,[1] who is often seen as a seminal influence on education as it is conceptualised in the modern – and, at least, 'Western' – world. Conceptually, the notion of democratic education acts as the thread that transforms the combination of the other three impacts into an educational imperative; that all teachers are educators in cultural understanding and must therefore be ready, prepared and educated to meet it. Consequently, the process of transforming the role of a teacher into a proactive agent of change was already in train before the transformations induced by the post-1945 era, especially in respect of teaching a form of socio-cultural consciousness that included an awareness of differences in ethnicities and cultures (Willis, 2012).

For some, it is the association with Christianity that has driven the link between the socially just nature of democratic education and Western cultures:

> This persistent attachment to Greek ideas inculcated rational enquiry into the culture and defined the nature of authority and governance. Christianity's lessons in ethical behavior and social justice added to this in a way that made England and the rest of Western Europe unique.

---

[1] The importance of democratic conceptions of education in relation to teacher capacity in cultural understanding is slightly ironic given some of the background of one of its most keenly revered originators. As Fallace (2012) has suggested, Dewey did not become a cultural pluralist until the mid-1920s and it was only then that he began 'emphasizing the necessity of cultural diversity and interaction for a healthy deliberative democracy' (p. 14). Even then, he remained true to the elements of the paradigm of ethno-superiority typical of his times, seeing 'the social world as a series of developmental linear steps leading from the primitive to the civilized' (p. 16). He saw the necessity of designing curriculum so that it reflected the social and cultural history of the race and child and promoted the value of interaction between different, yet equivalent, cultural approaches to life. Western forms of civilisation were still the pinnacle of human achievement and Dewey considered those who were not civilised to be inferior.

Where in other places people turned to authoritarian regimes for security, Western Europe's political power shifted to people and democracy. (Dahl, 2010, p. 26)

The democratic perspective on education that has become connected with aspects of contemporary Western outlooks is, however, not as new as some of its proponents might wish to believe. At its heart, democratic education is a humanist approach and, in that sense, has a lineage that dates back to the early days of Western philosophy in Ancient Greece. It is based on the principle of social justice that gives opportunity for self-growth and development to all:

> A genuinely liberal education dispenses with cutthroat, crass competition; or softens the competitive edge so no one bleeds. It teaches the respect for the laws of social justice; replaces the law of the jungle with the laws of democratic governance: creates win-win situations in which every man, woman and child enjoys the human rights-including the right educational equality and excellence. (Suri Prakash & Esteva, 1998, p. 12)

In turn, this then enabled the existence of a

> society with enriched, expanding interaction between all its members. In such a society, people will find it important to ensure that resources are distributed so that all have the fullest possible opportunities to engage in the forms of process of communication, interaction, and meaning-making. (Hansen, 2007, p. 8)

Such conceptions have a connection with the thoughts of earlier humanists such as Erasmus in the 16th century, who thought it important to break away from the contemporary focus on teaching logic and grammar to include a sense of civic-mindedness. The analogy of the teacher as a gardener, cultivating and nurturing the growth of young minds was part of this tradition (Bushnell, 1996), with the principle of acceptance of others at the base of the educational approach:

> ... the belief that people are largely responsible for what happens on this earth; committed to tolerance, attention to the differences among people and the need to treat them with equal respect: shapes by a cheerful acceptance of ambivalence and contradiction; and informed by an almost painful historical consciousness, which sees the past as estranged yet able to illuminate present concerns. (p. 17)

What really separates the notion of democratic education from earlier paradigms, however, is the specific and enhanced role that it gives to teachers in influencing the growth of the students in their care whilst adjusting their professional practice to meet the needs of individual students. They are not demigods, but part of a community that is collectively working towards a goal that is centred on the well-being of the student, and through them, the future of society:

> ... teachers, as individuals and as a teaching community, [help] the very different students in their care to find a place and a voice in the democratic polity. Because students come with different values, skills, and self-perceptions, those seeking to educate democrats need to be sensitive to that inheritance. (White, 1996, p. 6)

2.3 Pitfalls and conclusions: teachers as moral guides towards the 'Other'

Whether this maelstrom of pre-millennium ideas had a more significant impact on global society than the changes after World War I is debatable and is better addressed in a more specific discussion elsewhere. However, the impact of these progressive events on British education and the role of the teacher can now be understood more comprehensively in hindsight. Arguably, it was the emergence of the atomic bomb and how society viewed the prospect of such a future that made the biggest difference. Education between the world wars essentially had to adjust to a world in which dramatic generational and social change was largely confined to Europe and, to a lesser extent, the Middle East. That is not to say that there were not consequential long-term implications in countries and areas outside those regional blocs – the casualty rate amongst Australian troops in 1914–1918, for instance, was one of the highest of any country that had armed forces involved in the Great War – but it was within those two particular areas of the world – even taking into account the transformations that were emerging in China – that the greatest shifts in social and political class and structure took place at the time. The psychological trauma of the Great War, which changed the concept of military conflict from being one of adventure to that of grim reality, set the scene for what was to occur two decades later.

After 1945, educational systems and the teachers who staffed schools found themselves teaching students who were now living in an era of change and challenge in which the entire world was implicated. It was an environment in which the reality of global annihilation was a distinct possibility; rapid societal change was not only inevitable, but endemic. The former relative predictability of childhood and youth was increasingly disappearing, and the tensions of future employment and lifestyle were polarised – the reality of the disappearance of old industries and lines of work versus the possibilities and greater material wealth of new work areas and practices.

For teachers, the long-term import of these shifts has been much deeper than just the inevitable changes in educational curriculum, systems and pedagogies.

Cultural understanding and teaching expertise 49

In fact, I would posit that one of the most significant and yet, less known and understood, impacts has been a shift in the psychological complexity of what it means to be a member of human society. From a world in which citizenship, and the moral implications of that citizenship, was largely determined by national and even local presumptions and attitudes, the notion of what is meant by such a concept has become more diverse, complex and far more difficult to navigate in an educational sense. As the contemporary features of globalisation have encouraged the modern sense of cosmopolitanism referred to earlier, it has become more evident that the notion of what is meant by a 'good' moral citizen is not a universal concept. As a result, the teaching of cultural understanding, or living with the 'Other', has itself become a more demanding, multifaceted and composite professional capacity or attribute.

As part of this enforced shift in thinking, the hold that Euro-American or 'Western' ideals have had on the notion of moral citizenship has declined markedly. The contrast between the principles of rights and obligations is one exemplar of this:

> [In the past] Southeast Asia, emphasis was placed on one's duties and responsibilities within the family and larger community, the concept of rights being imported from the west. Today, Southeast Asian states stress a balance between rights and duties, although some analysts argue that the balance remains skewed towards duties. (Minnis, 1999, p. 177)

Another example of this difference, as outlined by several writers, is the difference between 'Western' democratic conceptions of education and Confucian/Chinese positions on learning, even though both might have elements of a humanistic perspective. The difference, however, is on how either of these ideological perspectives interprets the concept of humanism. For example, Bai (2011) has argued that Western influences in language have distorted the essence of Chinese attitudes to life, and therefore, to education:

> [the] traditional way of Chinese life ... is closely associated with a traditional language. The interruption of this life by the Western way of life and the introduction of foreign linguistic framework and terminology have ruined this traditional way of life and traditional language. (p. 616)

Notions of social justice are not necessarily universal. Bai (2011) reasons that, under the Confucian perspective, equality of education still needs to be more nuanced and take into account that differences are real and cannot be subsumed under a typical Western inclusive approach that is meant to cater for all:

> social justice ... cannot be achieved by an equal education because we cannot wish away students' differences, and it can only be realistically

achieved by educating the best and the brightest to care for the disadvantaged and by inventing social and political mechanisms to ensure this care. (p. 620)

Instead, '... Confucians tried to teach everyone, but [offers] different levels of education to different people' (Bai, 2011, p. 621). Cheng-Tek Tai (2011) also highlights that compassion is far more deeply ingrained into the Confucian mindsets because it does not flow from the logic of reason, which is often used as the basis of justification in a Euro-American context:

Compassion is more of a virtue than a principle to Confucianism... something internal that motivates a person to act spontaneously to adhere to the recognised norms... A virtuous person does what he does not because he is forced by law or by someone else. (p. 25)

Decolonisation and political independence from the British Empire meant that teaching systems and schools in the newly independent states were increasingly staffed and led by local educators rather than British expatriates, although old patterns were, and are, often resistant to change. Within the ever-decreasing British Empire, the curriculum and pedagogies employed were still often British in origin or official derivations of them, a pattern that persists today, even in highly modernised countries such as Singapore, where the final school examinations that are chosen to assess students are supplied and monitored by British universities. Since education is one of the key conduits through which multilateral global organisations such as the United Nations have worked in order to improve the quality of life of the people, it is not surprising that much of the bilateral and multilateral aid provided to newly independent countries after 1945 has been in various forms of educational provision, including the training of teachers, curriculum development and pedagogical learning. Universities throughout the Euro-American world, and increasingly so in newly established global powers such as India, depend financially to a large extent on the provision of consultancy and education (both on-campus and virtual) to educational systems in countries that were formerly part of the colonial world.

In the educational systems of many former British colonial territories, such as India, Singapore, Malaysia and Hong Kong, English still remains the primary language of instruction, even if placed alongside local languages in parity. It would be wrong to attribute the apparent continuity of colonial practices is purely down to force of habit and colonial influence, however; many of these decisions have been made deliberately by the current governments of the countries involved as part of an educational strategy to enable their students to have access to the global employment market. In that sense, it is more accurate to label such decisions as being the outcome of contemporary globalisation as a whole, in which English, along with languages such as

Spanish and Mandarin, both of which are spoken by around 400 million of the world population, are seen to be economic, social and politically advantageous assets. Nevertheless, there are still countries, such as Sri Lanka, which made the decision after independence to remove English is the primary language of instruction; schools that did not follow that policy became ineligible for government support. In that country, the decision has been effectively tainted by the extreme Sinhalese nationalism of its post-independent governments, which, for political reasons, did not give the other long-standing local languages of Tamil and, to a lesser extent, Arabic, equal status as a national language. In that context, it is not surprising that many of its high-level schools, most of which were established originally under British imperial rule by the colonial administration or missionary/church-based groups, have chosen to maintain English as their primary language of instruction, forgoing the right to government funding in the process (Casinader, 2017).

At a more fundamental level, teachers operating within this new post-1945 Euro-American context have been no longer able to teach to a form of moral character or citizenship that has stayed essentially static in character for several centuries. The local environments in which individual teachers conduct their work are now far more complex social organisms; it cannot be assumed that students in the one classroom live in the one local community or come from a similar environment, which would give some stability and unity to the way in which teachers approach the teaching of their students. Instead, the students in a class are likely to represent a diversity of backgrounds, cultural, social, economic and otherwise; Christianity is not guaranteed to be the dominant faith, and many will have no faith at all, even in schools that are religiously based. There will be a greater range of disabilities represented amongst the students in the one class for the teacher to teach. Of course, these are not characteristics that are specific to the Euro-American environments within the British colonial heritage, such as Britain itself, Australia or Canada. The same complexities, with all their local nuances and individual challenges, can be found in regions such as Malaysia, Singapore, New Zealand and Hong Kong, but, as discussed earlier, different constructions of moral citizenship mean that these variances are being approached in quite different ways. In short, whereas the teachers of previous generations prior to 1939 could be generally sure that they would be teaching a reasonably uniform cohort, the reverse is now true. Difference is now the norm, a situation that has demanded teachers develop flexibility and adaptability in all that they do. Part of that suppleness is an ability to not only teach children from different cultural backgrounds from a theoretical point of view, but to be engaged with them as a point of *normality*, not as a point of difference. The ability to teach understanding about the 'Other' in a way that is external to the self and one's home society, whatever that might be, has now become one of the key determinants, if not the most significant, challenge to a teacher's effectiveness.

The basic duality in the role of the teacher – developing the moral character and preparing for the vocational – is one aspect of the teaching role that is not changed in its intent over time. It remains today, but its form has been altered dramatically. The extent of its old usages can be seen in those whose individual lives are still very much encased with their community, such as the outlooks of those who identify as belonging to the indigenous or first nations peoples within a region. In contrast, within modernised societies, the role of the community has been adopted, or some might prefer, usurped by the school, whether provided by the government or independent agencies. If the purpose of teaching cultural understanding is to develop a more accepting attitude towards the positions and ways of living of others, that it can be said that the longstanding connection between religion and education has tended to muddle the message as far the teacher and their role is concerned. The theoretical differences between them, which could have been collated into a more universal pattern of understanding, have been exacerbated and extrapolated by the extremist elements across all faiths, creating philosophies that mirror a highly splintered view of moral citizenship. Students are taught according to the fears of the 'Other', as interpreted by some of the leaders of their faith, past and present. Consideration of cultural difference tends to be confined to accepting variations with one's own broad cultural outlook, but even that is not a firm pattern, as the extreme examples of Shia-Sunni Muslim and Protestant-Roman Catholic confrontation illustrate.

All cultures, to some degree, have some inherent fear of the 'Other'; it is the purpose of education to elevate and enervate people to live with and beyond the confines of their own cultural identity. Human beings have the capacity to reason and justify any stance that they may wish to take, so the prime purpose of cultural education must be therefore the ability to think beyond one's self and see the wider picture of global humanity. As utopian as this may sound, the greater complexity of human society at this stage of history requires active intervention to reduce the possibility of conflict. It is not a case of removing difference of opinion, but of ensuring that enough awareness and understanding of the 'Other' exists so that there is some basis for compromise and future coexistence. Extremism, or retreating into bunkers on either side, far from being an assertion of personal freedom, is a withdrawal into the unthinking corruptions of past when it was generally uncommon to have a frequent connection with the 'Other', unlike today.

At a fundamental level, education needs to provide students with learning that will enable them to participate in a world that has many interpretations of democratic action. For that to occur, students need to 'develop dispositions and competences like tolerance, the ability to negotiate and to make informed decisions' (Winch & Gingell, 2008, p. 55), as well as a deep understanding of the history and culture of the society(ies) in and with which they live. Schools, teachers and students cannot see themselves as being separate from the world in which they are situated, for the process of living life is itself an education

(Wang & Zhang, 2007). In this context, the role of the teacher is to free students from the constraints of an insular, localised knowledge that does not enable them to see the world and 'Others' in a wider perspective (Bushnell, 1996, p. 5).

References

Aspin, D. (1973). On the 'Educated' person and the problem of values. In D. E. Lomax (Ed.), *The Education of Teachers in Britain* (pp. 193–217). Chichester, England: Wiley.

Assié-Lumumba, N. D. T. (2016). Evolving African attitudes to European education: Resistance, pervert effects of the single system paradox, and the Ubuntu framework for renewal. *International Review of Education, 62*(1), 11–27. doi: 10.1007/s11159-016-9547-8.

Bai, T. (2011). Against democratic education. *Journal of Curriculum Studies, 43*(5), 615–622. doi: 10.1080/00220272.2011.617835.

Brinsley, J. (1627). *Ludus literarius: or, the grammar schoole shewing how to proceede from the first entrance into learning, to the highest perfection required in the grammar schooles, with ease, certainty and delight both to masters and schollers onely according to our common grammar, and ordinary classicall authours: begun to be sought out at the desire of some worthy fauorers of learning, by searching the experiments of sundry most profitable schoolemasters and other learned, and confirmed by tryall: intended for the helping of the younger sort of teachers, and of all schollers.* London, England: Felix Kyngston for William Leake.

Bushnell, R. W. (1996). *A Culture of Learning: Early Modern Humanism in Theory and Practice.* Ithaca, NY: Cornell University Press.

Casinader, N. (2014). *Culture, Transnational Education and Thinking: Case Studies in Global Schooling.* Milton Park, Abingdon: Routledge.

Casinader, N. (2017). *Transnationalism, Education and Empowerment: The Latent Legacies of Empire.* Milton Park, Abingdon: Routledge.

Chapman, G. (1773). A treatise on education with a sketch of the author's method. In A. M. George Chapman (Ed.). *Master of the Grammar-School of Dumfries.* Edinburgh: T. Cadell.

Cheng-Tek Tai, M. (2011). An Asian perspective of western or eastern principles in a globalised bioethics. *Asian Bioethics Review, 3*(1), 23–30.

Coote, E. (1673). *The English School-Master ... Now for the 32 Time Imprinted, etc.* London, England: A. Maxwell for the Company of Stationers.

Dahl, M. (2010). *Failure to Thrive in Constructivism: A Cross-Cultural Malady.* Rotterdam, the Netherlands: Sense.

Dent, H. C. (1977). *The Training of Teachers in England and Wales 1800-1975.* Sevenoaks, England: Hodder and Stoughton.

Fallace, T. (2012). Race, culture, and pluralism: The evolution of Dewey's vision for a democratic curriculum. *Journal of Curriculum Studies, 44*(1), 13–35. doi: 10.1080/00220272.2011.641588.

Gay, P. (1964). Introduction. In P. Gay (Ed.), *John Locke on Education* (pp. 1–17). New York, NY: Bureau of Publications, Teachers College, Columbia University.

Gopinath, C. (2008). *Globalization: A Multidimensional System.* Thousand Oaks, CA: Sage Publications, Inc.

Gould, S. R. (1973). The teaching profession. In D. E. Lomax (Ed.), *The Education of Teachers in Britain* (pp. 53–68). Chichester, England: Wiley.

Hansen, D. T. (Ed.) (2007). *Ethical Reasons of Education: Philosophy and Practice.* New York, NY: Teachers College Press.

James, L. (1998). *The Rise and Fall of the British Empire*. London, England: Abacus.
Kant, I. (1960). *Education* (A. Churton, Trans.). Ann Arbor, MI: University of Michigan Press.
King, E. J. (1970). *The Education of Teachers: A Comparative Analysis*. London, England: Holt, Rinehart, and Winston.
Locke, J., & Gay, P. (1964). *John Locke on Education*. New York, NY: Bureau of Publications, Teachers College, Columbia University.
Milligan, J. (1889). *Is Teaching a Profession? Inaugural Address Delivered to Glasgow Branch of Educational Institute of Scotland*. Glasgow, Scotland: Bryce & Son.
Minnis, J. R. (1999). Is reflective practice compatible with Malay-Islamic values? Some thoughts on teacher education in Brunei Darussalam. *Australian Journal of Education, 43*(2), 172–185. doi: 10.1177/000494419904300206.
Moyn, S. (2010). *The Last Utopia: Human Rights in History*. Cambridge, MA: Belknap/Harvard.
Newlands, W. (1824). *A Philosophical Essay on Education*. In. London, England: Printed by J. Haddon, Tabernacle Wells.
Orme, N. (2006). *Medieval Schools: From Roman Britain to Renaissance England*. London, England: Yale University Press.
Pieterse, J. N. (2015). *Globalization and Culture: Global Mélange* (3rd ed.). Lanham, MD: Rowman & Littlefield.
Rizvi, F. (2009). Towards cosmopolitan learning. *Discourse: Studies in the Cultural Politics of Education, 30*(3), 253–268. doi: 10.1080/01596300903036863.
Scott, J. (1866). Well trained teachers essential to good schools. *An Address to the Students in the Wesleyan Training Institution*. London, England: Westminster Training College, Westminster.
Seth, S. (2007). *Subject Lessons: The Western Education of Colonial India*. Durham and London, England: Duke University Press.
Sluga, G. (2013). *Internationalism in the Age of Nationalism* (1st ed.). Philadelphia, PA: University of Pennsylvania Press.
Snell, G. (1649). *The Right Teaching of Useful Knowledg [sic], to Fit Scholars for Som [sic] Honest Profession, etc*. London, England: William du-Gard.
Suri Prakash, M., & Esteva, G. (1998). *Escaping Education: Living as Learning within Grassroots Cultures*. New York, NY: Peter Lang.
Symons, J. (1852). *School Economy: A Practical Book on the Modes of Establishing and Teaching Schools*. London, England: John W. Parker and Son.
UNESCO. (2006). *UNESCO Guidelines on Intercultural Education*. Paris, France: UNESCO.
United Nations. (1948). *United Nations Declaration of Human Rights*. New York, NY: United Nations Retrieved from http://www.un.org/en/universal-declaration-human-rights/.
Vertovec, S. (2009). *Transnationalism*. Milton Park, Abingdon: Routledge.
Wang W., & Zhang K. (2007). Tao Xingzhi and the emergence of public education in China. In D. T. Hansen (Ed.), *Ethical Reasons of Education: Philosophy and Practice* (pp. 95–107). New York, NY: Teachers College Press.
White, P. (1996). *Civic Virtues and Public Schooling: Educating Citizens for a Democratic Society*. New York, NY: Teachers College Press, Columbia University.
Willis, R. (2012). *The Development of Primary, Secondary, and Teacher Education in England: A History of the College of Teachers*. Lampeter, Ceredigion: The Edwin Mellen Press.
Winch, C., & Gingell, J. (2008). *Philosophy of Education: The Key Concepts* (2nd ed.). Milton Park, Abingdon: Routledge.

Chapter 3

Cultural education for the globalised age

3.1 Culture and the global imperative: the garden of cultural education

As outlined in the previous chapter, the third and most contemporary phase of teachers as historical cultural educators can be said to have begun with the drive for a global sense of co-operation that emerged out of the political, social and economic detritus of the World War II. The formation of the United Nations was the focal point of a wide-ranging multinational strategy to develop a means of reducing, and even eradicating, the possibility of future global and/or civilisational conflict. The variety of agencies that have been developed under the aegis of the United Nations are themselves indicators that the global leadership of the time was aware that the journey towards such a goal was multifaceted, and would entail international co-operation to address a variety of necessities, ranging from the basic needs of human life (food, water, shelter and so on) to the need for integrated systems of world behaviour across all aspects of economic, social and political life. It was hoped that such systems would help to lessen the attraction of self-interested nationalistic drives for progress. Regardless of whether that ideal has been realised which is a matter for a different forum, the main strategy fostered by the United Nations has been to encourage international agreements that furthered global activity that was beneficial to the majority, rather than to the advantage of just a few.

The formation of UNESCO as one of the first major UN agencies was also a recognition of three key preconditions towards the achievement of the goal of international harmony: that the reduction of conflict was equally dependent on the interdependence of all aspects of society, beyond the economic and political; that a drive towards an improved quality of life for all – that is, the removal of global inequalities, at least economically – would help to reduce international tensions; and that not only was education a central conduit for lessening the gap, but that a full knowledge and understanding of cultures around the world was also essential if global co-operation was to be achieved. Additionally, it has been argued that this global acknowledgement of the existence of cultural differences, combined with the educational imperative of learning about them, was an outcome of what has been generally acknowledged as being collective Western guilt about the cultural depredations that were umbilically identified with the causes and realities of the World War II (Skillington, 2013). The evidence of the Holocaust and Nazi treatment of anyone outside their perceived notions of Aryan superiority was very much in physical and psychological view in the years after 1945.

The apparent sociocultural generosity in the construction of the United Nations was tempered nevertheless, to a degree, by the reality of the economic and political context in which it was conceived and the way in which it has operated. Despite its partial trappings of national equity, such as the fact that all member states have one vote in the General Assembly, regardless of size or economic power, the existence and membership of the Security Council and the power of veto afforded to specific sovereign States still ensure that global policies, initiatives and progress across the economic, social and political fields are ultimately still determined by the direction of a limited number of nations. Allowing for the rebirth of China as a site of paradox, a free market economy directed by a one-party state, all of these States are adherents to what can be loosely classified as a collection of singular models of Western-style, industrialised development. Variations to that approach have not been generally encouraged as genuine, contrasting alternatives in national strategy. The initial existence of the former Union of Soviet Socialist Republics (USSR, now Russia) as a founding member of the Security Council was very much more a function of global power struggles than ideological synchronicity. Similarly, the more recent inclusion of China in the same grouping only followed the country's adoption (outwardly at least) of a freer market economic approach and its emergence as a major global power. The process of decolonisation after 1945 has seen most newly independent states aiming for national socio-economic success in the same mould as the industrialised West, even if the eco-political strategies they have adopted might have varied from those used by the industrialised West in its rise to economic prominence.

If the post-1945 era was the catalyst for the generation of a specific interest in education about national cultures, it can be argued that it was not until the 1960s that the field began to be a focus of interest for educational researchers. By that time, the process of decolonisation was by and large complete. One of the most visible consequences of the dismantling of empire – politically, at least, if not economically and socially – was the assertion of national identity by the newly independent nations which were, almost exclusively, situated outside the foundational geography of the Euro-American Western alliance; that is, Central and South America, Africa and Asia. Instead of being buried within the imperial identities of colonial powers, countries such as India, Brazil, Kenya, Indonesia and Malaysia were able to promulgate the value and essentiality of their national existences, a process in which the identification and consolidation of a recognisable cultural identity was central.

In addition to the collective realisation about the cultural base of Nazism that was referred to earlier, this promotion of national identities and cultures was a direct consequence of the decolonisation process and a reaction to the historical diminution of local cultures that had occurred in many colonial contexts. Knowledge of different national cultures therefore became a political necessity and learning about different cultures an educational priority, especially in Euro-American contexts that were determined to avoid the consequences of the culturally founded prejudices of the past.

3.2 Changing notions and contexts of cultural education

3.2.1 Multiculturalism: the initial context

The post-1945 focus on addressing cultural ignorance as part of the wider goal of minimising international conflict (if not achieving the more utopian goal of eradication) had significant indirect and direct consequences for education. This is not the place to delve more deeply into the ways in which international and comparative education has evolved since that time (see, for example Crossley & Jarvis, 2000; Casinader, 2014), but the shift in world sentiment – at least in those societies and countries that had been part of the Allied bloc – did have the effect of making the teaching and learning about cultures in different parts of the world an educational priority. The changing international political landscape, with a range of regions gaining independence from the previous colonial order progressively during the 1950s and early 1960s, was also a driver for a rise in interest about the cultural context of the newly independent sovereign states, a process that was both encouraged and facilitated by the work of the United Nations and its various agencies.

The initial focus on facilitating knowledge about different cultures eventually developed to become multicultural education. Fundamentally, multicultural education is an ethnic pluralist approach (Leeman & Ledoux, 2005) that emphasises knowledge about individual cultures within a society. As a concept, however, it did not emerge as a comprehensive framework until the late 1960s and early 1970s. Its origins and use were linked very closely to the Euro-American sphere (Portera, 2008), especially in societies such as the United States, Canada and Australia, where the recognition of different cultures was beginning to be translated into government policy. Although there is some debate as to the exact origin of the term, there is general agreement that the concept of multiculturalism was first utilised in the report of the Canadian Royal Commission of Bilingualism and Biculturalism, which was published between 1967 and 1970. It was first incorporated into Canadian government policy in 1970, to be followed by Australia in 1973, when the newly elected Whitlam government instituted the first Australian Minister for Multicultural Affairs (Jackson, 2010).

There were two factors that encouraged the adoption of the concept of multiculturalism by numerous countries throughout the Euro-American sphere. First, there was an increasing awareness of the rights of the cultures of indigenous minority groups, as well as the obligation to protect those rights; and second, the increasing recognition of one of the outcomes of post-1945 migration patterns, which saw many Western countries becoming more culturally diverse as a consequence of global population movements, commencing with European refugees displaced from their home territories by the impacts of war on continental Europe. The adoption of multiculturalism was perceived to be a means of '… allowing [immigrants] to keep and maintain the distinct ethnic and linguistic identities regardless of their status of residency and citizenship' (Jackson, 2010, p. 480). As an educational tool, though, '… multicultural/pluricultural education aims to promote knowledge and tolerance of people with different cultural backgrounds who form part of the same socio-political unit …' (Cots & Llurda, 2010, p. 51). As a consequence, multiculturalism came to be defined very much in terms of ethnic difference, which, in many countries, was also seen as a reflection of differences in skin colour. One of the more salient examples of this was in the United States, where the concept still holds great prominence (Portera, 2008), but has been expanded beyond that of ethnic or cultural difference to include other issues of social justice beyond ethnicity, such as gender, sexuality and class (Sleeter & Grant, 2009).

It was not long, however, before the use of multiculturalism as a term and concept was being criticised on a number of fronts, including politicians across the ideological divide, a controversy that persists to this day in some parts of the world. One of the major criticisms centred, and still does, on the many regional variations in the meaning of the term; there is relatively little consistency internationally, which means that any development and sharing of ideas in the educational sphere across different socio-economic contexts is often of limited value. As Spiteri (2017) has highlighted, 'Each country has its own particular historical context through which its multicultural outlooks(s) and curricula have been developed' (p. 23). In the aforementioned US context, the term is, for all intents and purposes, an umbrella term for '… a wide variety of groups all marked by difference, from the disabled to indigenous populations, from sexual orientations to speakers of languages other than English' (Aman, 2014). In the western part of continental Europe, multiculturalism is far more focused on the notion of acceptance and hospitability towards migrants from different cultures. Similarly, but with more of a reverse connotation, the term has been more used in Australia as referring to the existence of different ethnic/cultural groups within the one society as a result of immigration (Connell, 2007). Despite the fact that, aside from oft-quoted examples such as the Democratic People's Republic of Korea, very few countries are monocultural and use multiculturalism to engender national unity (Kymlicka, 2003), the conservative side of Australian politics has frequently expressed views that reflect the 'fragmentation objection' (Shorten, 2010, p. 57) to multiculturalism. In other words, it creates division and envy between different groups and does not encourage social cohesion; assimilation and integration are seen as being far more effective and justifiable (Editorial, 2017).

The difficulty with all these variations in definition and scope is that they not only create confusion and misunderstandings, but also create their own stereotypes that are difficult to dislodge: 'Different in meaning, united in consequences: part of the critique that the concept generates is that each of these variations fosters its own simplifications, generalizations or collective amnesias' (Aman, 2014, p. 26). Byram and Guilherme (2010) have commented that the tensions about terminology arise because of the difference between those who study and research cultures and those who educate about cultural engagement. Indeed, the separation between the different regional conceptions was no better exemplified by the publication of a six-volume book series that was grandly (and misleadingly) titled '*History of Multicultural Education*' (Grant & Chapman, 2008), and which had an almost exclusively North American focus.

In the same vein of oversimplification, another issue with the use of multiculturalism is that it promotes an essentialisation of culture (Gundara, 2008; Gundara & Portera, 2008; Kahn, 2008). By identifying specific groups as part of a broad classification, any benefits in addressing gaps in cultural knowledge are gained at the expense of proliferations in generalised stereotypes. There is little or no recognition that any one culture incorporates a range of manifestations and should not be seen as inviolably homogeneous and constant; they are organic entities that are continually adapting in response to new ideas that meet with them (Aman, 2014, p. 8); 'the history of all cultures is the history of cultural borrowing' (Said, 1993, p. 217). Furthermore, the oversimplification of reality that results from the use of multiculturalism is also condemned because of its origins that were embedded in decolonisation. In postcolonialist eyes, it is argued that the promotion of multiculturalism was, and is, being used as a substitute for the continued promulgation of 'Western' cultures as the norm to which all peoples should aspire:

> ... the multicultural classroom, however celebratory or respectful of cultural diversity, can only be a deliberately Western site; transmitting only the culture/s of the West. In that limited capacity, while very useful for 'western' 'cultural workers' taking their first steps in hosting and hospitality toward the Otherness of the Other, it cannot do anything in terms of initiation into the cultures of the pluriverse. The pluriverse of cultural diversity cannot be nourished or regenerated through the project of education. For education is of modern western origin. Multicultural education is an oxymoron. (Suri Prakash & Esteva, 1998, p. 16)

3.2.2 The move towards interculturality

The difficulties with the concept of multiculturalism led to the emergence of interculturality as a new basis for cultural education in the 1980s. As highlighted by Aman (2014), it was primarily a European enterprise initially:

> To commemorate the 25th anniversary of the International Association for Intercultural Education (IAIE) in 2008, Jagdish Gundara and Agostino Portera edited a special issue of the journal *Intercultural Education*, in which interculturality was cast as the most important educational initiative for addressing problems of inequality – racism, xenophobia, socio-economic marginalization – throughout the world. (Aman, 2014, p. 2)

The shift was also encouraged by the emergence of theoretical consolidations of a global society (Coulby, 2006). As a concept, interculturalism was seen as being more representative of the human interactions between different cultures that were required in order to develop the capacity of people to become aware of and understand the power relationships of privilege within and between cultures; '... realities are constructed and shaped by social, political, cultural, economic, and ethno-racial values' (Hassim, 2013, p. 5). Educationally, this could be achieved if students could learn '... to recognize, tolerate and, at best, understand cultures other than that of the state into which people are born' (Coulby, 2006, p. 246).

Given its global context, the notion of intercultural understanding and education has become the basis of all global and international initiatives in cultural education, reflected as it is in the policies and programs of the United Nations. Surprisingly, perhaps (although it is also a reflection of the multitudinous confusions in the concept of cultural education), it took the United Nations until the millennium to publish its intercultural education initiative (UNESCO, 2006). Within its policy, intercultural education is necessary as it '... provides all learners with cultural knowledge, attitudes and skills that enable them to contribute to respect, understanding and solidarity among individuals, ethnic, social, cultural and religious groups and nations' (UNESCO, 2006, p. 37). More specifically, intercultural understanding is more than just the capacity to know and understand how and why people of a particular culture live their lives; it is also the ability to look for, and understand, the importance of developing individual agency in order to redress imbalances in existence, that is '[t]o depoliticize intercultural education is to cut it off from many of the possibilities of political action and redress' (Coulby, 2006, p. 249). Compared with multiculturalism, intercultural education is characteristically more proactive and effective as a changer of personal attitudes as it '... encompasses both cognitive and affective domains ...' (Perry & Southwell, 2011, p. 254). It utilises the knowledge obtained about other cultures (that is multicultural knowledge) to create changes in perspectives such as empathy and respect. It is a process that necessitates changes in the four dimensions of knowledge, attitudes, skills and behaviours (Perry & Southwell, 2011, p. 255). As a result, interculturalism has a '... educational and political dimension ...' (Portera, 2008, p. 484) that cannot be seen in multicultural education; the inner concept of social justice is at the core of its meaning. It is an equal opportunities approach, in which the knowledge gained about different cultures is actively used to combat disadvantage for the culturally marginalised (Leeman & Ledoux, 2005).

3.2.3 The problems of asynchronicity: multiculturalism, interculturalism and the 21st century

The development of the conceptual framework of interculturality was a response to the growing demographic and cultural complexity of societies as an outcome of the increasingly complex migration patterns of modern globalisation. However, the intellectual and practical debate as to the efficacy of terms such as multiculturalism and interculturalism has continued to be evident in both academic discourse and the actions of governmental authorities in different parts of the world. The persistence of multiculturalism as a primary concept in government and intellectual discourse within the United States, albeit in a much more complex configuration, along with the simultaneous use of interculturalism, is but one example of this ambiguity. As with multiculturalism, the conceptual history of interculturalism has been also distorted by a continued confusion as to what intercultural education means, the multiple interpretations of which Dervin (2014) refers to as the 'polysemics' of the intercultural; the debate has been distorted by the '... fluidity and complexity of the concept' (Guo, 2010, p. 25).

The discussion has been also muddied by the persistent slippage and unsureness as to the meaning and value of multiculturalism when compared to interculturalism; the salient identifiers have been mixed. On the one hand, there is the strong philosophical argument made by writers such as Coulby (2006), who, along with others such as Hassim (2013), put forward the view that the two are individually distinct, and should not be used interchangeably. In Europe, conceptual support for the use of interculturalism remains strong, primarily because of its perceived emphasis on the building of bridges between cultures and the importance of communication. In Australia, educational policy at the national (Australian Curriculum Assessment and Reporting Authority [ACARA], 2019) and state levels is not always consistent. In its school curriculum framework (Victorian Curriculum and Assessment Authority, 2019b), the State of Victoria separates and interweaves the two concepts by framing the importance of developing intercultural understanding so that social cohesion is maintained in a multicultural society (Victorian Curriculum and Assessment Authority, 2019a). However, the use of multiculturalism as a term prevails in other areas of the same government's administration, illustrating how multicultural and intercultural are used seemingly interchangeably, with little wider understanding of the differences in meaning. For instance, despite its educational focus on developing intercultural capability in students (Victorian Curriculum and Assessment Authority, 2019a), June 2019, the State Government of Victoria also has a Victorian Multicultural Commission, the role of which is to '… promote multiculturalism in Victoria and provide a voice for people from culturally and linguistically diverse communities … [as well as] promotes the benefits of multiculturalism and supports the maintenance of cultural heritage' (State of Victoria, Department of Premier and Cabinet, 2019). The idea of community voice and communication between community elements is very much an intercultural concept, not a multicultural one. A similar emphasis on intercultural themes of communication across cultures in a multicultural context can be seen in the state of New South Wales (NSW). Its Multicultural NSW entity

> … promotes community harmony and social cohesion in one of the most culturally diverse states in the world. We come from more than 262 countries, speak 275 languages and dialect, and follow 144 different religious beliefs …', and aims to '… Engage with all sections of society and break down barriers to participation'. (State of New South Wales [Multicultural NSW], 2019)

Both are perfect examples of the tension that comes from '… promoting desirable forms of multiculturalism within state institutions and promoting desired forms of interculturalism within individual citizens' (Kymlicka, 2003, p. 14).

Elsewhere, the continuing 'multicultural-intercultural' debate has meant that there remains a significant interweaving in the use of the two terms. Intercultural approaches have been criticised for being merely variants of a liberal interpretation of multiculturalism, one whose only significant addition is that it incorporates the concept of multinational citizenship (Meer & Modood, 2012). Other researchers have been firm in their argument that the two are distinct; multiculturalism is concerned with the facts of an ethnic or cultural group's existence, whereas interculturalism is communication between different groups. Another variation is that multicultural education helps students to see or 'diagnose' the cultural power imbalance and interculturalism provides a solution (Leeman, 2003). Such reflections, however, tend to diminish the fact that intercultural education also differs in its highlighting of global citizenship, through which the place of the nation-state is de-emphasised. In contrast, multinational citizenship, or multicultural education, operates on the premise that it is the sovereign State that will remain the main arena for citizenship and societal development.

3.3 Transculturalism: a way forward for the 21st century

3.3.1 Criteria for a new construction in cultural education

The continued debate and confusion as to the nature of interculturalism and what it specifically involves, along with the almost parallel persistence in the use of multiculturalism as a base for government policy, demands a resolution. Moreover, what is required is a strategy that takes the debate into an entirely new context, one that is appropriate for the education of young people in the years that comprise *their* future, and not the years of their parents' *past*. That new approach needs to accomplish two further goals:

a   First, it needs to build upon the notions of multiculturalism and interculturalism in a logical manner that advances the idea of cultural education.
b   Second, it needs to separate itself from the multi-stranded confusion surrounding the two existing concepts through a completely separate etymology. Part of the confusion surrounding both multiculturalism and interculturalism is the way that both have been duplicated in 'visible form' instead of being transformed in response to different conceptualisations. A complete break from the past and a rebirth of terminology will reinvigorate the discourse into a future perspective, rather than staying trapped in a continuous glance back to the past.

The most significant flaw with the concepts of multiculturalism and interculturalism is that they were both conceived well before the beginnings of the contemporary globalisation. Consequently, the current globalised context is completely at odds with the world in which the concepts of multiculturalism and interculturalism were developed and evolved. In the world of the 1970s and 1980s, the ability to move around the planet as part of daily life and routine was heavily constrained by both socio-political and economic structures, as well as by social constraints such as class and financial resources. The meeting of people from different cultures was, by a large, not a common experience, confined mainly to the following of media pathways that were embedded in print and film, and far from instantaneous. The reality of the first half of the 21st century is quite the reverse. One of the consequences of this more complex diffusion of global population has been an increasingly culturally diverse population in regions that have previously been characterised as being largely culturally homogenous. The meeting of cultures is now the norm, neither the exception nor an occasional occurrence. Consequently, both multiculturalism and interculturalism were constructed on the perception that cultural difference was a combination of being relatively unexpected and constituting a difficulty or barrier that had to be overcome.

3.3.2 The conditions for a transcultural approach

The wider context for a new approach to cultural education has also been influenced by one other key factor: alternative perspectives and changes in the conception of culture. The long-term pattern of global demographic changes resulting from enhanced migration flows has had an impact on considerations of both the concept of culture and the nature of individual cultures. As outlined in the work of researchers such as Rizvi (2011b) and Vertovec (2009), as well as my own (Casinader, 2014), these ideas have morphed and developed in response to globalisation. One of the products of this process, it has been argued, has been the development of a globalised culture or 'global imaginary' (Rizvi, 2011a) that reflects the emergence of other phenomena, such as what I have referred to as a 'trans-spatial sensibility' (Casinader, 2017). The essence of this new perspective of cultural identity (see Figure 3.1) is that, for an increasing proportion of the world's population, place is no longer the *automatic* determinant of their cultural identity,

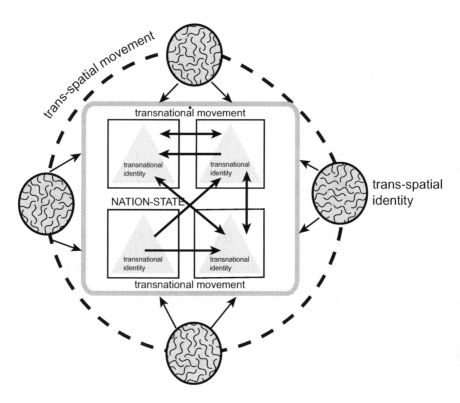

Figure 3.1 Transpatiality.

Source: Casinader (2017) (reprinted by permission).

actions and behaviour. Migration is no longer the incontrovertible action that it once was when transport and general communications technology could not capture the immediacy of the modern world. The present relative affordability of air travel means that migrants can return to places of origin far more often, drawn, as they are, by the desire to maintain personal relationships. The ever-evolving suite of personal communications technologies has also diminished the 'tyranny of distance' by enabling regular, cheap contact between people in different places. In the same vein, place of residence has become far more a possibility of choice, as these same technologies enable people to live in one part of the world and work in one or multiple places elsewhere, whilst simultaneously maintaining the multiple personal networks that provide stability to life and identity.

As a result of these myriad complexities, the nature of culture and cultural identity has become far more fluid, taking on more of a mind-centred construction that is quite often independent of all aspects of the ethnographic contexts within which culture has been previously and traditionally defined, for example values, customs, beliefs, artefacts (including clothing and foods) and language (Casinader, 2014). Cultural identity is a matter of internal personal belonging and integrity, not *necessarily* identified or classified by 'visible' parameters such skin colour, religion, art or language. For some, such factors may be crucial in defining their own culture or identity; for others, they will be less important or even non-existent. Migration across all of its dimensions has now created a global society in which cultural diversity is the norm, not the exception, and within which the concept of possessing a cultural identity borne out of multiple heritages is part of mainstream societal fabric, and not an aberration, exception or outlier:

> ... identity is something both discovered and created. It is not a natural characteristic, a property owned solely by the individual. It is a way of feeling, thinking and behaving achieved and developed through encounters with others in a social context... identity belongs properly to the sphere of action of a culture. (Büyükdüvenci, 1996, p. 25)

In this completely new global context and a time of rapid change, approaches to cultural education that are founded on concepts that are more than half a century old are even more of an anachronism. Both multiculturalism and interculturalism were developed conceptually prior to the age of contemporary globalisation; that, is prior to 1990, either before or just coincident with the start of the internet revolution (see Figure 3.2). Even a focus on an evolved sense of interculturalism, such as now taking place within Europe (Faas, Hajisoteriou, & Angelides, 2014; Catarci, 2015; Fuentes, 2016), fails to fully acknowledge the more substantial shifts that globalisation presents for cultural education. There is now a need to encourage the development of a *transcultural* educational approach.

66 Cultural education for the globalised age

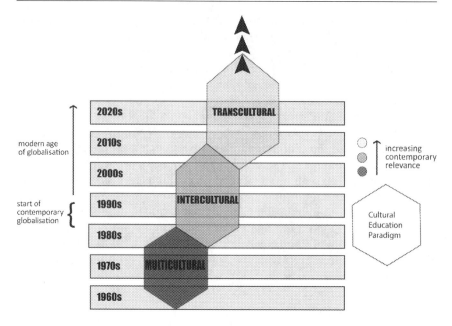

Figure 3.2 Three Paradigms of Cultural Education.

As illustrated in Figure 3.2, it is important to emphasise that, as a paradigm of cultural education, transculturalism is not a total rejection of either multiculturalism or interculturalism; instead, it should be viewed as a sequential progression from both. The concept of transcultural education is a third developmental stage that is an advance from multicultural education (which was dominant in the 1960s–1980s, see Figure 3.2) and intercultural education (dominant from the 1980s to the present day in the 2000s). As the initial paradigm, multiculturalism involves gaining a deeper informational knowledge about different cultures and cultural identities. The second stage or paradigm then explores the ways in which people might communicate across cultural boundaries and the power relationships between cultures that may be in play (interculturalism).

However, as reflected in the paradigm characterisation of Figure 3.2, multiculturalism and interculturalism are now increasingly irrelevant as the main conceptual underpinning for cultural education, even if they retain importance as initial foundations for any program. The current and future global societal context, which is dramatically different from that which existed in the last half of the 20th century, requires a new paradigm of cultural education that is more attuned to the characteristics of human societies in the 21st century. Transculturalism comprises an attitudinal shift that not only acknowledges and accepts the existence and value of different cultures and cultural identities within a society, but also sees the existence of those cultural differences as part of the *norm* and *reality* of society. These differences do not represent an exceptional 'problem' that needs to be addressed, for cultural diversity is now the common or existing societal characteristic. It needs to be perceived as a *positive* connotation, rather than being nominated or feared as a negative area of concern. Consequently, what is now known as intercultural education needs to be modified and transformed into a new transcultural approach, as part of which, the study of cultural difference needs to be seen, approached and taught as part of the standard societal norm, and not as a phenomenological problem that needs to be treated in isolation.

A transcultural approach to education in cultural understanding, therefore, first builds on the knowledge about different cultures that has been gained through multicultural education, before integrating the intercultural focus on the ability to communicate between cultures, as well as the awareness of the power difference that can be at the heart of cultural interactions. The key difference between interculturalism and transculturalism is the capacity of transculturalism to look beyond cultural variations as embodying matters of concern, to the point where those with transcultural understanding have the capability to work within and between very different cultural contexts. In the process, the notion of global citizenship that is part of both interculturalism and transculturalism is intensified. Instead of fear and uncertainty, cultural differences are considered and acted upon more as natural variations of the complex organic existence of humankind. The capacity to respond to variations in expectations and behaviour is an intrinsic element within the state of transculturalism itself.

Furthermore, another of the key aspects of transculturalism is that it is more a future-oriented approach to cultural education than either multiculturalism or interculturalism. The emphasis is on engagement of the mind, a reflection of a re-conception of culture as being far more than just being an anthropological set of attributes. Instead, it is constructed around a mindset, an adaptable perspective on life and a context that stresses the importance of transcultural understanding for global citizenship. In short, in a transcultural approach to education, cultural diversity is considered to be part of the natural pattern of human existence rather than a deviation from a supposed Euro-American norm. Without such an enhanced open approach to cultural education, we run the risk of trapping teachers and their students in the constraints of the past, '… becoming the puppets of monolithic home cultures …' (Büyükdüvenci, 1996, p. 26), inhibiting their ability to construct their own cultural identity in a form that is more appropriate and relevant to the world of their future in the last half of the 21st century.

References

Aman, R. (2014). *Impossible Interculturality? Education and the Colonial Difference in a Multicultural World*. (Linköping Studies in Behavioural Science No. 182). Linköping, Sweden: Linköping University.

Australian Curriculum Assessment and Reporting Authority (ACARA). (2019). *The Australian Curriculum*. Sydney, Australia: Author.

Büyükdüvenci, S. (1996). Philosophical conceptions of identity and culture. *Studies in Philosophy and Education, 15*(1), 25–26. doi: 10.1007/BF00367509.

Byram, M., & Guilherme, M. (2010). Intercultural education and intercultural communication: Tracing the relationship. In Y. Tsai & S. Houghton (Eds.), *Becoming Intercultural: Inside and Outside the Classroom* (pp. 2–22). Newcastle upon Tyne, England: Cambridge Scholars Publishing.

Casinader, N. (2014). *Culture, Transnational Education and Thinking: Case Studies in Global Schooling*. Milton Park, Abingdon: Routledge.

Casinader, N. (2017). *Transnationalism, Education and Empowerment: The Latent Legacies of Empire*. Milton Park, Abingdon: Routledge.

Catarci, M. (2015). *Intercultural Education in the European Context: Theories, Experiences, Challenges*. Farnham, Surrey, Burlington, VT: Ashgate.

Connell, R. (2007). *Southern Theory: The Global Dynamics of Knowledge in Social Science*. Crows Nest, Australia: Allen and Unwin.

Cots, J. M., & Llurda, E. (2010). Constructing and deconstructing interculturality. In Y. Tsai & S. Houghton (Eds.), *Becoming Intercultural: Inside and Outside the Classroom* (pp. 48–65). Newcastle upon Tyne, England: Cambridge Scholars Publishing.

Coulby, D. (2006). Intercultural education: Theory and practice. *Intercultural Education, 17*(3), 245–257. doi: 10.1080/14675980600840274.

Crossley, M., & Jarvis, P. (2000). Introduction: Continuity, challenge and change in comparative and international education. *Comparative Education, 36*(3), 261–265.

Dervin, F. (2014). Towards post-intercultural teacher education: Analysing 'extreme' intercultural dialogue to reconstruct interculturality. *European Journal of Teacher Education, 38*(1), 71–86. doi: 10.1080/02619768.2014.902441.

Editorial. (2017, March 21st). Turnbull evokes Howard on multiculturalism. *The Sydney Morning Herald*. Retrieved from https://www.smh.com.au/national/turnbull-evokes-howard-on-multiculturalism-20170320-gv1ofu.html.

Faas, D., Hajisoteriou, C., & Angelides, P. (2014). Intercultural education in Europe: Policies, practices and trends. *British Educational Research Journal, 40*(2), 300–318. doi: 10.1002/berj.3080.

Fuentes, J. L. (2016). Cultural diversity on the council of Europe documents: The role of education and the intercultural dialogue. *Policy Futures in Education, 14*(3), 377–391. doi: 10.1177/1478210316630467.

Grant, C. A., & Chapman, T. K. (Eds.). (2008). *History of Multicultural Education*. New York, NY: Routledge.

Gundara, J. (2008). Civilisational knowledge, interculturalism and citizenship education. *Intercultural Education, 19*(6), 469–479. doi: 10.1080/14675980802568269.

Gundara, J. S., & Portera, A. (2008). Theoretical reflections on intercultural education. *Intercultural Education, 19*(6), 463–468. doi: 10.1080/14675980802568244.

Guo, Y. (2010). The concept and development of intercultural competence. In Y. Tsai & S. Houghton (Eds.), *Becoming Intercultural: Inside and Outside the Classroom* (pp. 23–47). Newcastle upon Tyne, England: Cambridge Scholars Publishing.

Hassim, E. (2013). An 'intercultural understanding' view of the Asia priority: Implications for the Australian curriculum. In K. Redman (Ed.), *Occasional Paper 131*. Jolimont, Australia: Centre for Strategic Education.

Jackson, R. L. (Ed.) (2010). *Encyclopedia of Identity* (Vol. 1). Thousand Oaks, CA: Sage Publications.

Kahn, M. (2008). Multicultural education in the United States: Reflections. *Intercultural Education, 19*(6), 527–536. doi: 10.1080/14675980802568327.

Kymlicka, W. (2003). Multicultural states and intercultural citizens. *Theory and Research in Education, 1*(2), 147–170.

Leeman, Y. (2003). School leadership for intercultural education. *Intercultural Education, 14*(1), 31–45.

Leeman, Y., & Ledoux, G. (2005). Teachers on intercultural education. *Teachers and Teaching, 11*(6), 575–589. doi: 10.1080/13450600500293258.

Meer, N., & Modood, T. (2012). The multicultural states we're in. In A. Triandafyllidou, T. Modood, & N. Meer (Eds.), *European Multiculturalism: Cultural, Religious and Ethnic Challenges* (pp. 61–87). Edinburgh, Scotland: Edinburgh University Press.

Perry, L. B., & Southwell, L. (2011). Developing intercultural understanding and skills: Models and approaches. *Intercultural Education, 22*(6), 453–466. doi: 10.1080/14675986.2011.644948.

Portera, A. (2008). Intercultural education in Europe: Epistemological and semantic aspects. *Intercultural Education, 19*(6), 481–491. doi: 10.1080/14675980802568277.

Rizvi, F. (2011a). Beyond the social imaginary of 'clash of civilizations'? *Educational Philosophy and Theory, 43*(3), 225–235. doi: 10.1111/j.1469-5812.2009.00593.x.

Rizvi, F. (2011b). Experiences of cultural diversity in the context of an emergent transnationalism. *European Educational Research Journal, 10*(2), 180–188. doi: http://dx.doi.org.ezproxy.lib.monash.edu.au/10.2304/eerj.2011.10.2.180.

Said, E. W. (1993). *Culture and Imperialism* (1st Vintage books ed.). New York, NY: Vintage Books.

Shorten, A. (2010). Cultural diversity and civic education: Two versions of the fragmentation objection. *Educational Philosophy and Theory, 42*(1), 57–72. doi: 10.1111/j.1469-5812.2008.00504.x.

Skillington, T. (2013). UN genocide commemoration, transnational scenes of mourning and the global project of learning from atrocity. *The British Journal of Sociology, 64*(3), 501–525. doi: 10.1111/1468-4446.12029.

Sleeter, C. E., & Grant, C. A. (2009). *Making Choices for Multicultural Education: Five Approaches to Race, Class and Gender*. Hoboken, NJ: John Wiley and Son.

Spiteri, D. (2017). *Multiculturalism, Higher Education and Intercultural Communication: Developing Strengths-Based Narratives for Teaching and Learning*. London, England: Palgrave MacMillan.

State of New South Wales (Multicultural NSW). (2019). About Multicultural NSW. Retrieved from https://multicultural.nsw.gov.au/about_us/about_mnsw/.

State of Victoria, Department of Premier and Cabinet. (2019). DPC portfolios, entities and agencies. Retrieved from https://www.vic.gov.au/dpc-portfolio-entities-and-agencies#victorian-multicultural-commission.

Suri Prakash, M., & Esteva, G. (1998). *Escaping Education: Living as Learning within Grassroots Cultures*. New York, NY: Peter Lang.

UNESCO. (2006). *UNESCO Guidelines on Intercultural Education*. Paris, France: Author.

Vertovec, S. (2009). *Transnationalism*. Milton Park, Abingdon: Routledge.

Victorian Curriculum and Assessment Authority. (2019a). Intercultural Capability: Rationale and Aims. Retrieved from http://victoriancurriculum.vcaa.vic.edu.au/intercultural-capability/introduction/rationale-and-aims.

Victorian Curriculum and Assessment Authority. (2019b). Victorian Curriculum: F–10. Retrieved from https://victoriancurriculum.vcaa.vic.edu.au.

Chapter 4

Cultural education in current policy and practice

A selective critique

4.1 The disjunctures of international comparisons

The transition of worldwide societies into a reimagined global context over the last 40 years has had consequences for educational provision within regions. Educational systems, schools and educators have had to adapt their curriculum and pedagogical frameworks to cater for the changing learning needs of their student populations, the characteristics of which have undergone a relatively rapid transformation as part of society's foundational demographic shift; in Coulby's words, '... the need to recognize, tolerate and, at best, understand cultures other than that of the state into which people are born has never been more vital' (Coulby, 2006, p. 246). However, the debate as to how these different levels of educational systems should address such new cultural dimensions in their programs of teaching and learning has been ongoing, especially in terms of policy and curriculum structure.

By necessity, the outlines in the conceptual evolution of cultural education discussed in the last chapter were broad in scope. In the same vein, any discussion of how those conceptual frameworks have been translated into school-based policy and practice must be equally generalised. It is not within the parameters of this particular monograph to provide a detailed international description and analysis of the multitudinous ways in which cultural education has been implemented in different parts of the world; that, in itself, is a major piece of research that deserves its own volume, but it is important in terms of the context of this book to highlight certain features of how cultural education has been and is being manifested in schools. I acknowledge the limitations and selectivity of the themes presented in this chapter, but it is my intention that they serve as a catalyst for a continuation and widening of the discourse.

In line with the chronology put forward in the previous chapters in respect of teacher expectations and cultural education, the focus and goal of cultural education in schools across the Euro-American sphere prior to 1945 was essentially one of assimilation and integration into the 'Western' mainstream. The research that is the focus of this particular monograph has its basis in the evolution of education within the British Empire, for reasons outlined earlier in this monograph and in line with the approach adopted in the two earlier books that serve as unofficial precursors to this particular publication (Casinader, 2014, 2017). As has been discussed in a variety of forums (for example Seth, 2007), education within the British colonial context had the same overall purpose as the educational system(s) being developed and implemented within Britain itself; namely, the validation and continuation of British values and way of life. The same can be said of educational systems, both indigenous and modern, within North America, Europe, Africa and Asia. However, as was argued in Chapters 2 and 3, it was not until after World War II that cultural education aimed at increasing people's general acceptance of other ways of life became more specific.

Beyond such generalisations, however, any attempt to summarise international comparisons in this educational field must acknowledge and be cognisant of the complex, myriad nuances that exist in societies globally. In this research context, one of the most apt examples of the dangers of generalisations was the extensive six-volume 'History of Multicultural Education' published in the early 2000s. Its title was, and remains, slightly misleading, inferring that it was an internationally focused venture. The reality, whether by accident or design, was that it was a history of multicultural education within the United States alone, as exemplified by a summary of the focus of the initial volume, which dealt with conceptual frameworks and curricular issues:

> The articles in this volume illustrate the initial and continued debates over the concepts, definitions, meanings, and practices that constitute multicultural education. The authors articulate how to represent the **history and citizens of the United States** [author emphasis], best what types of content should be covered in public schools, and the type of learning environments that best serve the needs of all students. (Grant & Chapman, 2008, p. xiv)

The US-centric focus was also reinforced by the list of journals from which the articles within the collection were drawn, nearly all of which were exclusively of US origin, with only a minority having a fully international perspective.

Consequently, as discussed in earlier chapters, the potential for inappropriate global generalisations is one of the major reasons for this particular monograph to focus on one particular sociocultural context, specifically, societies that have been influenced strongly by the imperial period of British colonisation. Additionally, it is acknowledged that the range of countries represented in this sample is not representative of all the major facets of human society, whether classified geographically, ontologically or ethnically. However, aside from Africa and the Caribbean, they do represent a broad spectrum of British colonial histories: the metropolitan core (the United Kingdom); the settler colonies (Australia, Canada and New Zealand); the 'Jewel in the Crown' and the heart of the former empire (India); and three examples of former colonies with distinctly different origins and structures (Malaysia, Singapore and Hong Kong). Essentially, they are sovereign States– or, as in the case of Hong Kong, a Special Administrative Region – with jurisdictions that have a strong historical association with Euro-American societal ideas as expressed through the British perspective, including those in education. The expectation exists, therefore, that should be some degree of commonality in how the notion of cultural understanding is presented in their national curriculum frameworks, as well as an expectation that there should be some identifiable difference(s) as a consequence of the variety of the individual contexts across the set of case studies.

4.2 The substance of cultural education in policy

4.2.1 Overview

In many ways, the advent of the millennium can, in retrospect, be seen as the initiation point for a distinctive shift in the direction of national curriculum frameworks. As illustrated in Table 4.1, one of the common features of all the countries in this particular study is that the early years of the 21st century have seen a radical reconstruction of school education, particularly in terms of curriculum and purpose. The ways in which the teaching of cultural education has been structured and emphasised within those curriculum frameworks, though, are strikingly varied. As a general rule, with the exception of New Zealand, it is the former colonies from outside the Anglo-European settler societies that have placed a much greater emphasis on the notion of a national curriculum and, as shall be discussed shortly, a far more specific

Table 4.1 National Curriculum Summary: Selected Case Studies

Country	Curriculum	Date of national curriculum introduction (current/updates)
Australia	Australian Curriculum	2010 (2016)
Canada	No national curriculum: provincial educational frameworks	
Hong Kong	Hong Kong School Curriculum	2001 (2014 and 2017)
India	National Curriculum Framework	1975 (2005)
Malaysia	National Curriculum	1956 (2013)
New Zealand	New Zealand Curriculum	1992 (2007)
Singapore	Singapore Curriculum	1997 (regular rotational updates until present)
United Kingdom (England)	national curriculum for England	2013 (2014)

priority on the teaching of cultural awareness and understanding as a compulsory part of school education.

It is arguable that cultural diversity has been one of the major factors in determining the chronology surrounding the introduction of national curriculum frameworks in the countries comprising this particular study. As illustrated in Table 4.1, the fact that there was no national curriculum in the former colonial power (and even then, confined to England, not the United Kingdom) until 1988 and in one of its major white settler colonies (Australia) until 2010 is in stark contrast to the relative rapidity with which other newly independent countries formulated national curriculum frameworks after political independence, as well as the frequency with which those regions have reviewed and updated those original statements. Such proactive policy was a reflection of the belief that, given that education had been one of the major areas of British colonial influence, it was appropriate to use it as a transformative vehicle for cementing and cohering the national identity of the newly decolonised region.

4.2.2 Contradictions and expectations: the Anglo-European legacy

In Australia, the problems generated by a Constitution that is based on the defence of state rights were the major hindrance in generating a political and social environment conducive to a unified educational approach (for more detail, see Kennedy, Marland, Sturman, & Forlin, 1996; Harris-Hart, 2010; Casinader, 2016). Its federal system of government means that no national action in education can be devised or implemented without the agreement of all the states, which have primary responsibility for the administration and delivery of school education. For similar reasons, there is still no national curriculum that cuts across the provinces of Canada. The first attempt at a national curriculum in New Zealand was in 1944, and it was not until the early 1990s that a second version was created. For most of the countries in this group, though, the period since 2010 has been a time of great change, a trend that can be viewed as being a direct consequence of the multifaceted impact of contemporary globalisation on the aims of school-based education and its need to prepare young people for the world to come. In a global society that it is continually undergoing and responding to change, that future is becoming even more difficult to predict.

The same variation in approach can be seen in the differing significance placed by the case studies in this research project on the importance of addressing the aforementioned demographic cultural complexities that are now a salient characteristic of 21st-century societies. The differences between the case studies with a dominant Anglo-European heritage and those from Central/Southeast Asia are marked. Canada and the United Kingdom are the only case studies without some form of a national curriculum. In the United Kingdom, where education is controlled by its various regions, such as England and Scotland, the English curriculum is a de facto national curriculum on the basis of geographic and demographic coverage. In Canada, like Australia, its Federal system of government places responsibility for education at the provincial (state) level, and the differences between the thirteen provinces are quite marked. On the one hand, there are jurisdictions such as British Columbia, which is in the process (2019) of transitioning to a new curriculum that '… provide[s] students with an education that is still rigorous, but also flexible and innovative, one from which they gain the knowledge, skills, and abilities they need to succeed in today's modern world' (Government of British Columbia, 2019a). One of the underpinnings of the new curriculum is a set of core competencies, which includes that of Positive Personal and Cultural Identity (Government of British Columbia, 2019b). It is a document that stands out in comparison with other Canadian provinces and similar countries such as Australia and the United Kingdom because it explicitly connects respect for one's cultural identity with respect for others, and that such an understanding is essential to a 'healthy sense of oneself' within a pluralistic society; an understanding of 'relationships and cultural context' is foundational (Government of British Columbia, 2019b, p. 2).

Few of the other Canadian provinces have such clear statements of cultural understanding that underpin their curriculum frameworks. Alberta and Ontario have specific references to the education and perspectives of the First Nations, Métis and Inuit peoples (Government of Alberta, 2019; Government of Ontario, 2019) and New Brunswick makes reference to the importance of Native Studies, along with the development of provincial and Canadian identities (Government of New Brunswick, 2019). The other major provincial commitment to cultural education is evident in Québec, which has its dual language context of French and English placed foremost. A similar emphasis on the construction of an assured sense of personal identity and a worldview in students is highlighted, with a clear statement on the importance of ensuring that culture is embedded in learning to the point that all school boards are required to have a cultural policy committee:

> No matter what subject you teach, the activities and resources suggested here have been designed to support and inspire you in carrying out stimulating projects – projects that focus on culture as a source of knowledge and learning.
>
> Culture knows no boundaries; it can therefore be integrated into all school subjects, making learning more enjoyable and enriching for all students. Moreover, culture is not confined to the arts alone but extends into other areas of learning such as languages, professional and personal development, social sciences, mathematics, and science and technology.

Additionally, it has been shown that culture can create a strong sense of belonging in the school and contribute to student retention and the construction of students' identities.

There are so many good reasons to integrate culture into schools! (Gouvernement du Québec, 2019b)

Perhaps the most interesting component in the Québec case is the compulsory study of cultural geography, making the province one of the few examples where the primary learnings about cultural difference and diversity have been ascribed to a particular subject discipline. Of particular note is the context of critical and reflective learning in which that education is positioned; the aim is clearly to develop a positive and empathetic approach to a pluralistic society:

By studying the world's cultural areas, students come to understand the relationships that societies maintain with the space they transform into territories organized in a particular way. In addition, by considering the relationships that societies within these cultural areas maintain with each other, students develop their capacity for critical thinking. Examining other cultures as well as their own culture gives the students a better understanding of the world in which they have an opportunity to become involved as citizens. The Cultural Geography program aims to:

– help students understand the diversity and complexity of the cultures in the world
– help students develop a geographic perspective that fosters their understanding of other cultures. (Gouvernement du Québec, 2019a, p. 2)

Unfortunately, the situation in the other two predominantly Anglo-European democracies is inconsistent and disappointing. In the United Kingdom (England), there is hardly any explicit reference to the notion of cultural understanding within the current national curriculum at all (Government of the United Kingdom, 2019), which appears to be at odds with the fact that the country recognises the modern complexity of British society by asking respondents to most specifically nominate their ethnic/cultural heritage in the census. Although 81% of the population in 2011 defined themselves as being "white British" (Office of National Statistics, 2019), the population of the United Kingdom also comprises significant minorities from South Asia (India/Bangladesh) and the Caribbean. There is, however, a very clear reference to cultural/ethnic harmony in that part of the curriculum that relates to secondary school citizenship education, in which students are expected to have learned, by the end of Key Stage 4 (equivalent of 16 years of age), about the '… diverse national, regional, religious and ethnic identities in the United Kingdom and the need for mutual respect and understanding'

(Government of United Kingdom, 2014, p. 3). Furthermore, there is a far more explicit expectation set out in another document from the Ministry of Education to schools in England that are maintained by the government. The document sets up the belief that each school should '… promote pupils' spiritual, moral, social and cultural (SMSC) development …' (Government of United Kingdom, 2013, p. 3) as part of the teaching of fundamental British values, which include the belief that students should '… be encouraged to regard people of all faiths, races and cultures with respect and tolerance' (Government of United Kingdom, 2013, p. 4). A concerning aspect about this statement that it is presented as non-statutory advice to a specific set of schools; in other words, it is not set out as a mandatory expectation that is applicable to all school education in England, let alone the United Kingdom.

The contrast in this respect between United Kingdom and the other former settler colonies of Australia and New Zealand is very marked. From its beginnings, the first national Australian curriculum, which was progressively introduced from 2010, has had an expectation that, regardless of learning area, teachers were expected to infuse 'intercultural understanding' into teaching and learning, where appropriate. The attribute is specified as one of the seven General Capabilities that all students meant to acquire and develop throughout their primary and secondary education (Australian Curriculum Assessment and Reporting Authority [ACARA], 2019). The existence of this capability was a direct consequence of the educational policy document that was the foundation of all that has happened in Australian school education over the last decade or more. In 2008, the annual meeting of Commonwealth and State Government Education ministers agreed on the 'Melbourne Declaration on Educational Goals for Young Australians', which outlined an agreed national direction for the future of Australian education. One part of that statement, which also set the creation of a national curriculum in train, was an explicit statement that Australian students were to be educated for and as part of a culturally diverse Australia in the present and future:

> As a nation Australia values the central role of education in building a democratic, equitable and just society – a society that is prosperous, cohesive and culturally diverse, and that values Australia's Indigenous cultures as a key part of the nation's history, present and future. (Ministerial Council on Education, 2008)

On several fronts, the highlighting of intercultural understanding as a general capability in the Australian curriculum was not a surprise. Aside from it being a direct reflection of the Melbourne Declaration, the notion had already emerged in various state educational and curriculum policies prior to 2012, especially in educationally influential states such as Victoria and New South Wales. For instance, Victoria's Essential Learning Standards (VELS) curriculum framework, initially introduced in 2005 (Victorian Curriculum and Assessment Authority, 2005), was transformed into its Australian curriculum trappings as the new Victorian Curriculum in 2017, in which the national General Capability of Intercultural Understanding was replaced by the state's Intercultural Capability (Victorian Curriculum and Assessment Authority, 2019b). However, the notion of intercultural education had already been part of Victorian government policy research since before the introduction of the national curriculum (State of Victoria, Department of Education and Early Childhood Education, 2012). This interest was parlayed into another post-national curriculum research project when the Department of Education became a partner in a major research project into how schools were teaching intercultural understanding (State of Victoria, Department of Education and Training, 2015).

What is noticeable is that, by 2015, intercultural education had been established in states such as Victoria and New South Wales, but under the primary principle of multicultural education, of which intercultural understanding was a part. This is the logical obverse of the discussion of terminology canvassed earlier in this monograph. In both states, this emphasis has arisen because governments have framed intercultural education across the political spectrum against the background principle of community harmony and citizenship, founded on knowledge of different cultures or cultural pluralism. In New South Wales, the cultural educational policy is presented as multicultural education, but with a subsection on 'culture and diversity' that is confusingly more intercultural in its expression of intent:

> Multicultural education provides programs promoting anti-racism and community harmony, intercultural understanding and positive relationships between students from all cultural backgrounds ... Understanding contemporary Australian culture helps teachers build culturally inclusive teaching and learning. Students explore difficult questions around power relations, notions of identity, and cultural complexity. Teachers ensure stereotypes are not promoted. (State of New South Wales, 2019)

In Victoria, the notion of multicultural education is based on similar perspectives, but with an apparent better understanding of terminology that provides the policy with greater integrity.

> Intercultural interactions have become a part of everyday life in our increasingly *multicultural* [author emphasis] and globalised world. Developing *intercultural* [author emphasis] knowledge, skills and understandings is an essential part of living with others in the diverse world of the twenty-first century. (Victorian Curriculum and Assessment Authority, 2019a)

The significant aspect of these state policy directives is that, whilst based on the principles of cultural awareness and community understanding, they are not aimed to be *transformative* in the transcultural sense discussed earlier, but merely accommodating. Although they promote strategies such as the importance of language education and anti-racism initiatives, the policies are primarily based on notions that emphasise the importance of cultural *knowledges*, and respect for those knowledges, but not specific engagement with or deep understanding of these ways of knowing: '... central goals of intercultural learning ... [are] cultural awareness, acceptance of cultural differences, and interest in the specific culture of the language being taught, as well as in intercultural topics in general' (Göbel & Helmke, 2010, p. 1572).

The significance of this state-based multicultural interpretation on intercultural education is brought into sharp relief when compared with the conceptualisation of intercultural understanding as a stated general capability within the Australian Curriculum. Whilst the surface focus is very much on the relationships between people, as with the States of Victoria and New South Wales, the documentation is far more explicit in how that knowledge and capability about the components of a particular culture or set of cultures should be used. Intercultural understanding involves students in learning about and engaging with 'diverse cultures in ways that recognise commonalities and differences, create connections with others and cultivate mutual respect' (Australian Curriculum Assessment and Reporting Authority, 2019).

However, the continual tug-of-war between state/territorial governments and the Commonwealth over centralisation of power also meant that the educational agreement regarding the Australian Curriculum gave each state the right to implement the broad curriculum frameworks set up by ACARA in the form that they wished. In practice, this flexibility means that different states, depending upon the political affiliation of the party in power, can devise and emphasise different policies in respect of areas such as intercultural education, just as Victoria demonstrated in its Victorian Curriculum. Indeed, the range of ways in which intercultural understanding is implemented in schools (Halse et al., 2015) only serves to highlight the complexity and diversity of opinion as to its meaning:

> [The] discourses range from intercultural education ... for the recognition of cultural and linguistic difference, to intercultural education as shaped by historically entrenched unequal social relationships between groups marginalised by cultural and linguistic markers. Different conceptions of intercultural education ... different discourses of educational quality ... different strategies for achieving. (Aikman, 2012)

The case of New Zealand provides a singular contrast to both the United Kingdom and Australia, principally because its history has seen a bicultural and bilingual approach to society and education as a result of the 1840 Treaty of Waitangi, which is now considered to mark the founding of the modern State of New Zealand: Aotearoa. In brief, that document set out '... a broad statement of principles on which the British and Māori made a political compact to found a nation state and build a government in New Zealand' (New Zealand Government, 2019). Educationally, the partnership that is seen to be one of the three main principles underpinning modern New Zealand society has been translated into a national curriculum that is infused throughout with elements of cultural education, '... help[ing] schools to give effect to the partnership that is at the core of our nation's founding document, Te Tiriti o Waitangi/the Treaty of Waitangi' (New Zealand Government, 2007, p. 5). Not only is cultural diversity listed as one of the eight guiding principles of the national curriculum, but statements relating to the building of a society that prioritises cultural harmony through education permeate the document. For example, the aim of the national curriculum is to create young people 'who will work to create an Aotearoa New Zealand in which Māori and Pākehā recognise each other as full Treaty partners, and in which all cultures are valued for the contributions they bring; ...' (New Zealand Government, 2007, p. 7). In other words, unlike the United Kingdom and Australian national curriculums, both the concept and actuality of cultural knowledge, understanding and action are infused into the very essence of the New Zealand curriculum framework. By accepting the reality of cultural diversity within the country as the norm, the New Zealand national curriculum is itself transcultural in spirit and the word.

4.2.3 Building education on cultural understandings: the case studies of Asia

The major difference between the Euro-American case studies and the others in this research set is that the latter have developed and built educational systems that are specifically designed to acknowledge and celebrate the culturally diverse nature of their populations, with the ultimate aim of cementing their respective national identities. In India, Malaysia, Singapore and, to a lesser extent, Hong Kong, education is seen as the driver of national unity and progress. The reality in the specific instances of daily life and governing may not be as clear-cut, but as statements of national intent, the respective curriculum frameworks are highly positive in the transcultural mould. They are also dynamic documents, with all the four jurisdictions being unafraid to undertake regular educational reviews since their transition to independence. Such continual self-reflection suggests a determination to make sure that their school educational frameworks are designed to meet the future needs of their own people from a 'home' perspective.

The central place that education for cultural understanding and harmony occupies across the curriculum frameworks of all four case countries/regions in Asia is characterised by the way in which such principles underpin their curriculums as a whole, mirroring the approaches that are evident in New Zealand and the Canadian province of British Columbia. Unlike the situation in Australia, where cultural understanding is predominantly an educational by-product of the national curriculum, a capability that is an outcome of the learning, India, Malaysia, Singapore and Hong Kong see it as a starting point, one of the pillars that guides the curriculum overall. For India and Malaysia, that mainstay takes the form of structuring education around the elements of cultural pluralism, and then using the educational system to meld those different components into one cohesive, national identity.

In the case of India, the principle could not be stated more clearly or forcefully in theory or in practice, with the national curriculum documents being available in twenty-one languages. The intent to mould what are often referred to as the 'multiple realities' of India into a cohesive, unified society is very explicit and reiterated as an obligation for the older generations to pass on the young:

> India is a society made up of numerous regional and local cultures. People's religious beliefs, ways of life and their understanding of social relationships are quite distinct from one another. All the groups have equal rights to co-exist and flourish, and the education system needs to respond to the cultural pluralism inherent in our society. To strengthen our cultural heritage and national identity, they should enable the younger generation to reinterpret and re-evaluate the past with reference to new priorities and emerging outlooks of a changing societal context. Understanding human evolution should make it clear that the existence of distinctness in our country is a tribute to the special spirit of our country, which allowed it to flourish. The cultural diversity of this land should continue to be treasured as our special attribute. (National Council of Educational Research and Training, India, 2005, p. 7)

Such motivations are an example of how former colonies have been able to evolve an educational system that combines liberal elements from the legacy of British colonial education with their own perspectives as underlying concepts. In India's case, as reflected in the quotation above, modern educational practice has its foundations in the multiple heritages of India (Singh, 2013).

A similar focus on national unity through a cohesive school curriculum has been a priority in Malaysia from the time of independence in 1957 (Wong & Ee, 1975; Salih, 1997; Joseph, 2008), albeit framed within an overall government policy of redressing the perceived imbalances of the colonial past by restoring the priority of Malays in society. Consequently, the educational system, whilst catering for the multiethnic population with separate schools (Malay, Chinese, Tamil), sees '… [e]lements of Islam and the Malay culture [being] manifested through various aspects of the Malaysian school curriculum and education system' (Joseph, 2008, p. 185). However, the National

Education Philosophy clearly highlights that, despite the heightened place of Malays in society, acceptance of cultural pluralism is at the core of the ultimate educational goal; that is, social unity within a regional facet on the notion of citizenship:

> Education in Malaysia is an ongoing effort towards further developing the potential of individuals in a holistic and integrated manner, so as to produce individuals who are intellectually, spiritually, emotionally, and physically balanced and harmonious, based on a firm belief in and devotion to God. Such an effort is designed to produce small Asian citizens who are knowledgeable and competent, who possess high moral standards, and who are responsible and capable of achieving high levels of personal well-being as well as being able to contribute to the harmony and the betterment of the family, the society, and the nation at large. (Ministry of Education Malaysia, 2013b, p. E4)

Additionally, the relatively new National Education Blueprint has emphasised this desire for a united, pluralist Malaysian society:

> To foster unity, it is important for students to interact and learn with peers and teachers from various ethnic, religious, cultural, and socioeconomic backgrounds. Accordingly, the Ministry has programmes like the Student Integration Plan for Unity, or Rancangan Integrasi Murid Untuk Perpaduan (RIMUP) to strengthen interaction among student from different school types through co-curricular activities. (Ministry of Education Malaysia, 2013a, p. 12)

In the case of Singapore, a similar emphasis on the role of education as both the creator and maintainer of national unity underpins the curriculum framework. In contrast to Malaysia, however, the Singaporean curriculum documents do not highlight the different ethnic groups that comprise the island state's population. Instead, there is an even more explicit continuous thread throughout that emphasises the need for the educational system to produce citizens who have a strong sense of national, *Singaporean* identity that is founded on a total acceptance of cultural pluralism: 'They also learn values such as respect, responsibility, integrity, care, and harmony; all of which are important for safeguarding our cohesive and harmonious multi-racial and multi-cultural society' (Ministry of Education Singapore, 2015, p. 6). The strength of this commitment is so fundamental throughout the curriculum documents that it is surprising that some comparative school curriculum studies of Singapore and other countries omit any discussion of this cultural pluralist imprimatur (see, for example Australian Curriculum Assessment and Reporting Authority [ACARA], 2018). Of the eight Singaporean Desired Outcomes of Education, the third states that, by the end of their post-secondary education, young people should be 'able to collaborate across cultures and be socially responsible' (Ministry of Education Singapore, 2013). The first seven outcomes culminate in the expectation that all students, by the end of their school education should 'be proud to be Singaporeans and understand a single port in relation to the world' (Ministry of Education Singapore, 2013). Citizenship Education is central to cultural education in the Singaporean context, specifying that it is a national sense of responsibility and obligation to engage 'in appropriate behaviour with other sociocultural groups in both local and international contexts, in a way which would enhance social cohesion' (Ministry of Education Singapore, 2014, p. 4).

Although still very clear in its expectations of cultural learnings, school curriculum in Hong Kong has a quite different context to the previous three case studies discussed. Having been decolonised by the British in 1997, its status as a Special Administrative Region within China means that society, including education, is perpetually in tension with two colonial heritages. Cultural diversity, however, is not as complex as in India, Malaysia and Singapore. Whereas the last three possess multicultural or culturally diverse populations, the vast majority of people in Hong Kong are of Chinese heritage. The difference, however, is between those whom are Hong Kong born and those whom are migrants from China, or the children of migrants. The Hong Kong perspective on cultural pluralism is more influenced by the reality that Hong Kong's economy and structural integrity as a society are very dependent upon its role as a global force.

As a centre of international trade and commerce, cultural compatibility on the international scale and an ability to work and live across many facets of ethnic variation is paramount in Hong Kong. In that context, the educational system is aiming for a regional cohesion that is based on expected outcomes, rather than the reality of existence. It also has to be balanced with the expectations and traditions of China, under which aegis the modern city has been governed for over 20 years. Consequently, it is unsurprising to see both Chinese and English studies as core subjects in Hong Kong schools (Government of the Hong Kong Special Administrative Region, 2019), but neither is it unexpected that 'Moral and Civic Education' is one of the five compulsory general learning experiences as part of the Hong Kong school curriculum (Government of the Hong Kong Special Administrative Region, 2017). In many ways, this particular aspect of Hong Kong education has several characteristics of Confucian philosophy that were discussed in Chapters 1 and 2. As a value-based document, it is significant that the second-ranked value is that of respect for others, within which acceptance of individuality and cultural diversity is a foundational concept, items that are not always viewed as being compatible with the policies and practices of the Republic of China:

> In a diversified society like Hong Kong, it is easy for students to meet people of different backgrounds, abilities, races, religions, beliefs and

lifestyles. When getting along with people having diverse or even conflicting views, students should accept the fact that everyone is unique and try to establish peaceful and friendly relationships with everyone in order to live and work with others in harmony. (Government of the Hong Kong Special Administrative Region, 2017, p. 5)

4.3 And whither the teacher?

One of the most salient shifts in education between the middle of the 20th century and the first quarter of the 21st millennium has been a transition towards the concept and expectation that education of young people now needs to meet and address the reality of an culturally pluralistic global society, one that continues to become more complex and nuanced in its degree and nature. By and large, there is a sign that national curriculum frameworks, or at least those that have a heritage of a British colonial past, are beginning to see such attitudes and aptitudes as being fundamental to existence. Even for those educational jurisdictions where cultural education does not have the priority that can be observed in others, the notion of global citizenship and participation in a cohesive national society holds strong. The question then arises as to what impact this significant, if gradual, shift in educational expectations has on the role of the educator in schools. As was argued in Chapters 1 and 2, the role of teacher as cultural educator has always been a strong component of the role; it is the nature of that role that has begun to shift in dramatic ways.

It is long been evident in learning theories over the last century that the relationship between teacher and student is one of the more fundamental conditions for effective learning. A range of studies have concluded that the influence that a teacher can have on the attitudes and economic progress of a child can be significant. In itself, that would imply that all school educators in educational jurisdictions that have adopted a strong positive approach to cultural education will be required to take on that responsibility. In turn, this would require school educators to have the demonstrated expertise to be involved in such cultural education. It is noticeable, for instance, that both Singapore and Hong Kong have clear statements in their educational policies that indicate that it is the responsibility of all teachers, regardless of level or teaching area, to be involved in the moral and civic education programs that form integral parts of their particular curriculum frameworks. It is therefore not an option that can be avoided by individuals, but one must be accepted and acted upon.

The assessment of teachers' ability to be part of this cultural education process, and the degree to which such considerations should form part of teacher education programs and professional learning activities, is an area that has not received as much research attention as how to teach cultural understanding to students. It is almost as if it is assumed that all teachers will automatically have such expertise, simply because they are trained educators. The diverse nature of contemporary workplaces and classrooms mandates examination of cultures as justifiable components of teacher education. Research does attest to perceptions that teacher preparation programs do not adequately prepare students for these contexts (for example Leh, Grau, & Guiseppe, 2015). In other words, the building of their cultural capacity, or the ability to teach effectively in a culturally diverse environment, is either explicitly deemed to be not taught or has been insufficiently prioritised. What is known is that the travel mobility of pre-service and in-service teachers outside of local institutional and workplace contexts favourably exposes them to diverse environments and appears to improve their readiness for handling cultural complexity (see Halse et al., 2015; Stachowski & Sparks, 2007; Pence & Macgillivray, 2008).

It was this conundrum about the uncertainty of teacher expertise, in a field that has only emerged as a prominent feature of national curriculum frameworks over the last decade or so, that initiated the ongoing research project that is the focus of this particular monograph. The next chapter will explore the nature and reasoning behind the methodology used to explore this area of teacher expertise, as well as exploring some of the contentions behind existing measures of teacher capability and the terminology used to identify that proficiency.

References

Aikman, S. (2012). Interrogating discourses of intercultural education: From indigenous Amazon community to global policy forum. *Compare: A Journal of Comparative and International Education, 42*(2), 235–257. doi: 10.1080/03057925.2012.647465.

Australian Curriculum Assessment and Reporting Authority [ACARA]. (2018). *International Comparative Study: The Australian Curriculum and the Singapore Curriculum*. Sydney, Australia: Australian Curriculum, Assessment and Reporting Authority. Retrieved from https://www.australiancurriculum.edu.au/media/3924/ac-sc-international-comparative-study-final.pdf.

Australian Curriculum Assessment and Reporting Authority [ACARA]. (2019). *The Australian Curriculum*. Sydney, Australia: Australian Curriculum, Assessment and Reporting Authority.

Australian Curriculum Assessment and Reporting Authority. (2019). Intercultural Understanding Learning Continuum. Retrieved from https://australiancurriculum.edu.au/media/1075/general-capabilities-intercultural-understanding-learning-continuum.pdf.

Casinader, N. (2014). *Culture, Transnational Education and Thinking: Case Studies in Global Schooling*. Milton Park, Abingdon: Routledge.

Casinader, N. (2016). Transnationalism in the Australian curriculum: New horizons or destinations of the past? *Discourse: Studies in the Cultural Politics of Education, 37*(3), 327–340. doi: 10.1080/01596306.2015.1023701.

Casinader, N. (2017). *Transnationalism, Education and Empowerment: The Latent Legacies of Empire*. Milton Park, Abingdon: Routledge.

Coulby, D. (2006). Intercultural education: Theory and practice. *Intercultural Education*, 17(3), 245–257. doi: 10.1080/14675980600840274.

Göbel, K., & Helmke, A. (2010). Intercultural learning in English as foreign language instruction: The importance of teachers' intercultural experience and the usefulness of precise instructional directives. *Teaching and Teacher Education*, 26(8), 1571–1582. doi: http://dx.doi.org/10.1016/j.tate.2010.05.008.

Gouvernement du Québec, Ministère de l'Éducation, du Loisir et du Sport. (2019a). *Cultural Geography*. Québec: Ministère de l'Éducation, du Loisir et du Sport. Retrieved from http://www.education.gouv.qc.ca/fileadmin/site_web/documents/education/jeunes/pfeq/PFEQ_geographie-culturelle_2014_EN.pdf.

Gouvernement du Québec, Ministère de l'Éducation, du Loisir et du Sport. (2019b). Culture-Education. Retrieved from http://www.education.gouv.qc.ca/en/contenus-communs/teachers/culture-education/.

Government of Alberta. (2019). Education. Retrieved from https://www.alberta.ca/education.aspx.

Government of British Columbia. (2019a). B.C.'s New Curriculum. Retrieved from https://www2.gov.bc.ca/gov/content/education-training/k-12/teach/curriculum.

Government of British Columbia. (2019b). Positive Personal and Cultural Identity Competency Profiles: Draft. Ministry of Education. Retrieved from https://curriculum.gov.bc.ca/sites/curriculum.gov.bc.ca/files/pdf/PPCICompetencyProfiles.pdf.

Government of New Brunswick. (2019). Education and Early Childhood Development. Retrieved from https://www2.gnb.ca/content/gnb/biling/eecd-edpe.html.

Government of Ontario. (2019). Education in Ontario. Retrieved from https://www.ontario.ca/page/education-ontario.

Government of the United Kingdom. (2019). National Curriculum. Retrieved from https://www.gov.uk/government/collections/national-curriculum.

Government of United Kingdom, Department of Education. (2013). Citizenship Programmes of Study: Key Stages 3 and 4 National Curriculum in England. London. Retrieved from https://www.gov.uk/government/publications/national-curriculum-in-england-framework-for-key-stages-1-to-4/the-national-curriculum-in-england-framework-for-key-stages-1-to-4.

Government of United Kingdom, Department of Education. (2014). Promoting Fundamental British Values as Part of SMSC in Schools: Departmental Advice for Maintained Schools. London. Retrieved from https://assets.publishing.service.gov.uk/government/uploads/system/uploads/attachment_data/file/380595/SMSC_Guidance_Maintained_Schools.pdf.

Government of the Hong Kong Special Administrative Region, Education Bureau. (2017). Secondary Education Curriculum Guide (2017) – Booklet 6A: Moral and Civic Education: Towards Values Education. Hong Kong. Retrieved from https://www.edb.gov.hk/attachment/en/curriculum-development/renewal/Guides/SECG%20booklet%206A_en_20180831.pdf.

Government of the Hong Kong Special Administrative Region, Education Bureau. (2019). Curriculum Documents. Retrieved from https://www.edb.gov.hk/en/curriculum-development/4-key-tasks/moral-civic/curriculum-documents.html.

Grant, C. A., & Chapman, T. K. (Eds.). (2008). *History of Multicultural Education: Teachers and Teacher Education* (Vol. 6). New York, NY: Routledge.

Halse, C., Mansouri, F., Moss, J., Paradies, Y., O'Mara, J., Arber, R., … Wright, L. (2015). *Doing Diversity: Intercultural Understanding in Primary and Secondary Schools*. Melbourne, Australia: Deakin University. Retrieved from https://en.unesco.org/interculturaldialogue/resources/161.

Harris-Hart, C. (2010). National curriculum and federalism: The Australian experience. *Journal of Educational Administration and History, 42*(3), 295–313. doi: 10.1080/00220620.2010.492965.

Joseph, C. (2008). Difference, subjectivities and power: (De) Colonizing practices in internationalizing the curriculum. *Intercultural Education, 19*(1), 29–39.

Kennedy, K. J., Marland, P., Sturman, A., & Forlin, C. (1996). Implementing national curriculum statements and profiles: Corporate federalism in retreat? [online]. *Forum of Education, 51*(2), 33–43. Retrieved from http://search.informit.com.au.ezproxy.lib.monash.edu.au/documentSummary;dn=980404332;res=IELAPA.

Leh, J. M., Grau, M., & Guiseppe, J. A. (2015). Navigating the development of pre-service teachers' intercultural competence and understanding of diversity. *Journal for Multicultural Education, 9*(2), 98–110. doi: 10.1108/JME-12-2014-0042.

Ministerial Council on Education, Employment, Training and Youth Affairs. (2008). *Melbourne Declaration on Educational Goals For Young Australians.* Carlton South: MCEETYA.

Ministry of Education Malaysia. (2013a). *Executive Summary: Malaysia Education Blueprint 2013-25 (Preschool to Post-Secondary Education.* Putrajaya, Malaysia: Kementerian Pendidikan Malaysia. Retrieved from https://planipolis.iiep.unesco.org/sites/planipolis/files/ressources/malaysia_blueprint_summary.pdf.

Ministry of Education Malaysia. (2013b). *Malaysia Education Blueprint 2013-25 (Preschool to Post-Secondary Education).* Putrajaya, Malaysia: Kementerian Pendidikan Malaysia. Retrieved from https://www.ilo.org/dyn/youthpol/en/equest.fileutils.dochandle?p_uploaded_file_id=406.

Ministry of Education Singapore. (2013). Desired Outcomes of Education. Retrieved from http://www.moe.gov.sg/education/desired-outcomes/.

Ministry of Education Singapore. (2014). *Character and Citizenship Education Syllabus - Secondary.* Singapore: Ministry of Education (Student Development Curriculum Division). Retrieved from https://www.moe.gov.sg/docs/default-source/document/education/syllabuses/character-citizenship-education/files/2014-character-and-citizenship-education-(secondary)-syllabus.pdf.

Ministry of Education Singapore. (2015). *Bringing Out the Best in Every Child: Education in Singapore.* Singapore: Ministry of Education. Retrieved from https://www.moe.gov.sg/docs/default-source/document/about/files/moe-corporate-brochure.pdf.

National Council of Educational Research and Training, India. (2005). National Curriculum Framework 2005. New Delhi. Retrieved from http://epathshala.nic.in/wp-content/doc/NCF/Pdf/nf2005.pdf.

New Zealand Government, Ministry of Culture and Heritage. (2007). *The New Zealand Curriculum.* Wellington, New Zealand: Ministry of Culture and Heritage. Retrieved from http://nzcurriculum.tki.org.nz/The-New-Zealand-Curriculum.

New Zealand Government, Ministry of Culture and Heritage. (2019). Treaty of Waitangi: The Treaty in Brief. Retrieved from https://nzhistory.govt.nz/politics/treaty/the-treaty-in-brief.

Office of National Statistics, United Kingdom. (2019). 2011 Census. Retrieved from https://www.ons.gov.uk/census/2011census.

Pence, H. M., & Macgillivray, I. K. (2001). The Impact of a short-term international experience for preservice teachers. *Teaching and Teacher Education, 24,* 14–25.

Salih, D. D. K. (1997). The challenges of Malaysian education in the 21st century. In Z. Marshallsay (Ed.), *Educational Challenges in Malaysia: Advances and Prospects-Proceedings of the Conference Organised by the Centre of Malaysian Studies 11 April 1996* (pp. 1–12). Clayton VIC, Australia: Monash Asia Institute.

Seth, S. (2007). *Subject Lessons: The Western Education of Colonial India*. Durham and London, England: Duke University Press.

Singh, M. (2013). Educational practice in India and its foundations in Indian heritage: A synthesis of the east and west? *Comparative Education*, 49(1), 88–106. doi: 10.1080/03050068.2012.740222.

Stachowski, L. L., & Sparks, T. (2007). Thirty Years and 2,000 Student Teachers Later: An Overseas Student Teaching Project That Is Popular, Successful, and Replicable. *Teacher Education Quarterly*, 34(1), 115–132.

State of New South Wales, Department of Education and Communities. (2019). Multicultural Education (Cultural Diversity). Retrieved from https://education.nsw.gov.au/teaching-and-learning/curriculum/multicultural-education/culture-and-diversity.

State of Victoria, Department of Education and Early Childhood Education. (2012). *Evaluation of the Intercultural Understanding Field Trial*. Melbourne, Australia: Department of Education and Early Childhood Education.

State of Victoria, Department of Education and Training. (2015). Multicultural Education. Retrieved from http://www.education.vic.gov.au/school/teachers/support/Pages/multicultural.aspx.

Victorian Curriculum and Assessment Authority. (2005). *Victorian Essential Learning Standards Overview*. Melbourne, Australia: State Government of Victoria.

Victorian Curriculum and Assessment Authority. (2019a). Intercultural Capability: Rationale and Aims. Retrieved from http://victoriancurriculum.vcaa.vic.edu.au/intercultural-capability/introduction/rationale-and-aims.

Victorian Curriculum and Assessment Authority. (2019b). Victorian Curriculum: F – 10. Retrieved from https://victoriancurriculum.vcaa.vic.edu.au/.

Wong, F. H. K., & Ee, T. H. (1975). *Education in Malaysia* (2nd ed.). Kuala Lumpur, Malaysia: Heinemann Educational Books (Asia).

Chapter 5

Measuring transcultural capacity in teachers

5.1 The notion of professional readiness

One of the most identifiable facets of modernity, wherever and whenever it appears to be taking place, is the notion of accountability, of creating order out of supposed chaos and providing certainty, although it is not always acknowledged as to whom that assuredness applies. Invariably, such validation is sought by those in control or those who have power to guide the direction of society. In the version of modernity that has emerged since the millennium, the prevalence of the neoliberal mindset that has cut across all aspects of society, including education, has seen that notion of accountability being reflected in an accumulation of prescribed criteria and standards in the drive to measure any aspect of human capability, achievement or progress. This is not to say that such standards did not exist previously, but that they have become more visible and, as a result, have generated debates on standardisation and regulation. Before the era of contemporary globalisation, which is generally conflated with the rapid, progressive institution of the Internet since the early 1990s, there were certainly general societal expectations of what certain professions were expected to do. People chose their doctor on the basis of reputation based on everything from ease of manner to rate of recovery; accountants were discussed terms of efficiency or the extent of someone's tax return. And, as discussed in Chapters 1 and 2, throughout British history, teachers have been generally expected to be focused on two primary goals: ensuring the academic achievement of students in the contemporaneous basic skills in literacy and numeracy; and to be a guide in how to be of moral character, which was often defined in terms of being of Christian faith.

But such expectations, often more anecdotal rather than research-based, were only able to function because of the relatively simplified, stratified and slow-changing nature of human society. They were primarily expectations set in terms of the here and now; there was no urgent need to prepare for the future in the long term because the pace of change was steady and relatively slow. Planetary resources were seen to be plentiful, and moral-economic issues such as climate change were not on the general political or social radar; people had the time to adapt to change as they grew older and took on more responsibility for life.

It is often commented upon that one of the features of contemporary globalisation that differentiates itself from previous iterations is the rapidity of the change that it has wrought. In a society that is undergoing such dynamic shifts in organisation, procedure and process, it was inevitable that the pace of change would create a different set of social norms and expectations. Consequently, the age of contemporary globalisation can be also seen to signify a significant phase in the freeing up of individual thought and action. The range of possible occupations has diversified exponentially, even if many specific roles have disappeared, largely as a result of technological advancement. People now have greater opportunity to work in different fields, in different geographical regions and with far more complex employment structures and degrees of flexibility. In spite of the less desirable effects of globalisation that have emerged, such as the growing polarisation between those who have benefited from globalisation and those who have not, and the tensions between local and globalised expressions of culture, there is now greater opportunity for many to have more individual control and management of their lives, whether economically, socially or politically. A corollary of that destabilisation of past patterns and a more secure social existence is that there has been a growing wish to not only find a more universal way to apply the notion of certainty and accountability, but also how best to prepare people for a world that is in such a state of dynamic flux as the norm. Education has had to shift and be more forward-looking, preparing people for a world of difference and change; speedy adaptation is an urgent necessity of now, not a possibility or even probability for some time in the future. The outcome of that wish (or need, depending on the degree of neoliberal conviction) has been the pandemic of regulation that has been applied to a range of employment areas, including education. The extent of such desire for uniformity in expectations and outcomes has been applied to all aspects of educational activity, whether school operations, curriculum, funding and, most of all, the expectations and patterns of teachers as working professionals.

This growth in the desire for universal regulation has not just been intranational, but international as well, with the notion of best practice and benchmarking becoming established as one of the norms in educational thought and research. The nature, outcomes and effectiveness of education across all its various aspects are not just judged on their national relevance, but also on their contribution to comparative considerations at international scale. One result has been, for example, that a number of countries, including Australia, the United Kingdom, Germany, India, Singapore and South Korea, have developed and instituted national curriculum frameworks that have often been based on and influenced by curriculum trends elsewhere. For many years, the Organisation for Economic Co-operation and Development (OECD) has managed a Programme of International Student Assessment (PISA) that has come to both symbolise and enact the ultimate in this desire for certainty and universal standardisation in education. If media debate and political sound bites are any guide for countries such as Australia, the measure of their educational system is not so much the degree to which it meets self-determined national benchmarks, but the country's ranking in what can be seen as an international educational 'egg-and-spoon' race. One of the constants that has emerged out of policy and practice research, however, has been the identification that teacher quality matters, whatever the level of education; it is one of the key factors in determining the degree to which students meet those learning benchmarks, whether internally or comparatively determined.

5.2 Teacher standards and cultural expertise

In Australia, the concern for accountability has been translated into the establishment of several national bodies charged with the regulation of school teaching and teacher preparation, including the Australian Institute for Teaching and School Leadership (AITSL) and the Australian Professional Standards for Teaching (APST), around which graduate teacher education providers now have to be accredited. A similar process has happened in the other regions that form the case study set used in this project, albeit to varying degrees. In itself, the development of such external measures of desired teacher attributes in response to educational patterns cannot be seen to be a negative, and neither is it entirely new. The author, who began his career as an Australian school teacher in the late 1970s, remembers that time as a point when undergraduate Australian teacher education began to transition into degree courses rather remaining at certificate level. Aside from arguments regarding the whole viability and appropriateness of mass student assessments, both nationally and internationally, especially in a multicultural context (for example Crossley, 2014; Waldow, Takayama, & Sung, 2014; Casinader, 2015), the move to create uniformity in both the nature, degree and quality of teacher education can only be viewed as an advancement in providing effective education (however that may be defined) to all children, both nationally and internationally. What can be contested, however, is the degree to which those expectations, now solidified into a regulatory framework, are in alignment with the nature of human society as it exists now, or how it is likely to develop within the next few decades, or within the working lifetimes of the teachers currently being educated. It is on that particular point that concern emerges with the educational jurisdictions represented in this project. In a globalised world where demographic cultural diversity is now the more likely norm and not the rare exception, there is a distinct separation between those educational systems that incorporate elements of cultural understanding as fundamental aspects of teacher education and those who either ignore it, or bury it subliminally beneath more broadly constructed criteria.

Just as was the case with the national curriculum comparative analysis discussed previously (see Chapter 4), there is a separation in this aspect of teacher education between the more established Euro-American industrialised societies and those in the Asia-Pacific, with New Zealand being once more a positive anomaly. Currently, Canada and the United Kingdom are placed where Australia was placed prior to 2010, with teacher education, like school curriculum, being approached differently in each of its provincial educational systems. Nevertheless, these three jurisdictions do have policies that define the general characteristics of a quality teacher in comprehensive, if generalised, terms. However, any specific consideration for the development of teacher expertise in cultural awareness or understanding appears to be subsumed under more generic categories relating to an understanding of student difference. If cultural understanding is specifically mentioned, it tends to be treated in a marginal fashion.

In the case of Australia, the promulgated set of the Australian Professional Standards for Teachers (APST) provides a comprehensive set of expectations across three interrelated domains: professional knowledge, professional practice and professional engagement:

> The Standards describe the elements of high quality, effective teaching in 21st century schools. Seven standards outline what teachers should know and be able to do, providing a nationally consistent description of the role of the teaching professional. Designed by teachers for teachers, the Standards are a public statement of teacher quality. Within each standard, focus areas provide further detail of required skills, knowledge and practice. These are separated into four professional career stages: Graduate, Proficient, Highly Accomplished and Lead. (AITSL, 2019b)

However, in spite of this declaration of a future orientation, the APST effectively confines the ability of a teacher to teach a culturally diverse group to a footnote. Of the 35 focus areas of required expertise across seven standards (see Table 5.1), two are directed specifically at knowledge and understanding in teaching the country's Indigenous peoples, the Aboriginal and Torres Strait Islanders (focus areas 1.4 and 2.4). Aside from that, the APST ignores or, at best, de-emphasises the long-known reality of the increasing cultural complexity of Australia's population. As of the last census in 2016, just over 30% of the country's population were overseas-born, with the top ten countries including England, China, India, New Zealand, Philippines, South Africa and Malaysia; overall, just under half the Australian population has one parent born overseas (Australian Bureau of Statistics, 2019). And yet, the only recognition of this growing trend in teacher expertise in the APST is in Standard 1.3, in which includes teachers having enough knowledge of their students across various facets so that they are able to adjust their teaching accordingly; one of those facets is culture: 'Design and implement teaching

Table 5.1 The Australian Professional Standards for Teachers

Professional knowledge		Professional practice		Professional engagement	
		Know learners and how they learn			
1.1 Physical, social and intellectual development and characteristics of learners	2.1 Content and teaching strategies of the teaching area	3.1 Establish challenging learning goals	4.1 Support participation of learners	5.1 Assess learning	6.1 Identify and plan professional learning needs	7.1 Meet professional ethics and responsibilities
1.2 Understand how learners learn	2.2 Content selection and organisation	3.2 Plan, structure and sequence learning programs	4.2 Manage learning and teaching activities	5.2 Provide feedback to learners about their learning	6.2 Engage in professional learning and improve practice	7.2 Comply with legislative, administrative and organisational requirements
1.3 Learners with diverse linguistic, cultural, religious and socio-economic backgrounds	2.3 Curriculum, assessment and reporting	3.3 Use teaching strategies	4.3 Manage challenging behaviour	5.3 Make consistent and comparable judgements	6.3 Engage with colleagues and improve practice	7.3 Engage with parents/carers
1.4 Strategies for teaching Aboriginal and Torres Strait Islander learners	2.4 Understand and respect Aboriginal and Torres Strait Islander people to promote reconciliation between Indigenous and non-Indigenous Australians	3.4 Select and use resources	4.4 Maintain safety of learners	5.4 Interpret data from learners	6.4 Apply professional learning and improve learning (of learners)	7.4 Engage with professional teaching networks and broader communities

1.5 Differentiate teaching to meet the specific learning needs of learners across the full range of abilities	2.5 Literacy and numeracy strategies	3.5 Use effective classroom communication	4.5 Use ICT safely, responsibly and ethically	5.5 Report on achievement of learners
1.6 Strategies to support full participation of learners with disability	2.6 Information and communication technology (ICT) implement teaching strategies for using ICT to expand curriculum learning opportunities for learners	3.6 Evaluate and improve teaching programs		
		3.7 Engage parents/carers in the educative process		

Source: AITSL (2019a).

strategies that are responsive to the learning strengths and needs of students from diverse linguistic, cultural, religious and socioeconomic backgrounds' (AITSL, 2019a).

Similar imbalances exist in the teacher education expectations in the United Kingdom (England) and Canada, although it could be argued that the terminologies used in their equivalent policies are more directed towards understanding about cultural diversity than the language and concepts used in the Australian case. In Ontario, Canada, which has one of the more developed examples of teacher accreditation, the Standards of Practice for the Teaching Profession lists 16 competencies across 5 domains of learning, including leadership and community. But aside from exhortations to treat all pupils 'equitably and with respect' none of these 16 competencies refer specifically to the notion of cultural diversity (Government of Ontario, 2010). In England, the policy divides teacher quality expectations into two different areas: teaching and personal and professional conduct. Unlike the Australian Standards, teachers are expected to specifically '… uphold public trust in the profession and maintain high standards of ethics and behaviour, within and outside school …'; display '… tolerance of and respect for the rights of others …' and, most explicitly of all, to '… not [undermine] fundamental British values, including democracy, rule of law, individual liberty and only mutual respect, and tolerance of those with different faiths and beliefs' (Government of United Kingdom, Department of Education, 2013, p. 14). In the light of how terrorist acts have impacted upon the United Kingdom in recent years, such statements take on a much heightened significance.

As was the case with national curriculum frameworks, the teacher accreditation frameworks in Malaysia, India, Hong Kong and Singapore are far more explicit in respect of teacher expertise in cultural education. Although their teacher accreditation systems may not be as developed as in, for example, Australia, the emphasis on teachers being able to promote and teach cultural harmony in the name of social cohesion is a foundational aspect of expectations and not just a seeming adjunct. The process of establishing a nationally consistent and regulated teacher education system across the multiple regional complexities of India is controlled by a statutory authority, the National Centre for Teacher Education (NCTE). The NCTE can provide guidelines only, but it is seen as the arbiter of teacher education in the country. Teacher quality and the lack of teacher numbers are constant concerns (Singh, 2013), with only 7% of qualified teachers passing a new eligibility test in 2011. Irregular updates as to the requirements of teacher education courses have taken place since 1993, with the latest occurring in 2014. That particular update saw, for example, the course regulations for a Bachelor of Education degree specifying that the curriculum should include theory and practical '… interactions with the community in multiple socio-cultural environments …' and 'issues of diversity, inequality and marginalization in Indian society …' (Gazette of India, 2014, p. 115). In conjunction with the statements made in the national curriculum framework as to the multiple cultural heritages in India (National Council of Educational Research and Training, 2005), as well as the 2012 Commission that drafted the national vision for teacher education (Government of India, 2012), the importance of cultural diversity expertise for Indian teachers is reiterated on a number of levels.

In Malaysia and Singapore, there are similar expectations of teacher expertise that are aligned with each country's approach to their demographic cultural diversity, but what is also clear is that teachers are expected to have and demonstrate a *personal* commitment to the expected norms of cultural education; it is not just a *professional* requirement. The Malaysian Teacher Standards, devised in 2009, outline three main principles: professional values; knowledge and understanding of education, subject matter, curriculum and co-curriculum and skills of teaching and learning. Professional values are divided into three domains (personal, professional and social) and it is here that the obligations of teachers in cultural education are explicitly set out across several parameters (Swee Choo Goh, 2012). Overall, a teacher is someone who is '… noble in character; has a progressive and scientific outlook; is committed to upholding the aspirations of the nation; cherishes the national cultural heritage; and ensures the development of the individual and the preservation of a united, democratic, progressive, and disciplined society' (SEAMEO INNOTECH Regional Education Program, 2010, p. 55). The set of personal values required includes 'demonstrate[d] respect for cultural diversity and heritage' and 'demonstrate[d] high tolerance and non-discrimination to students in terms of socioeconomic status, cultural values, ethnicity, and religious beliefs' (SEAMEO INNOTECH Regional Education Program, 2010, p. 56).

In Singapore, a focus on developing expertise in building national rather than ethnic identity in a consciously pluralist society is maintained by the National Institute of Education (the only teacher training institution). In its teacher education course, designed to centre on 21st-century skills and thinking, the development of multicultural literacy has high priority (National Institute of Education, 2009, p. 30), and values are now increasingly central to Singaporean expectations. As in Australia, the prime focus of the teacher must be on the needs of the individual child, indicating that they are someone who is '… attuned to the needs of the child as a learner with respect to their individuality, development and diversity' (National Institute of Education, 2009, p. 444)

Once again, of this particular case study set, New Zealand stands out as a form of positive anomaly from the Euro-American sphere. The inherently bi-culturally structured nature of New Zealand society means that teacher graduates are expected to have a similarly oriented cultural empathy and expertise, with the Māori-European dualised heritage being highlighted throughout as a fundamental consideration. The national set of teacher professional standards, which is printed in both English and Māori (Education Council, 2017), reflects and even mirrors the Australian version in many ways; however, it takes the cultural qualities and expertise required for teachers to a new level. Two of the four underpinning values of teacher education are embedded in cultural respect and societal harmony: *manaakitanga* (creating a welcoming, caring and creative learning environment that treats everyone with respect and dignity); and *whanaungatanga* '(engaging in positive and collaborative relationships with our learners, their families and whānau, our colleagues and the wider community)' (Education Council, 2017, pp. 3–4). The third commitment of the code refers to '... respecting the diversity of the heritage, language, identity and culture of families and whānau' (Education Council, 2017, p. 12). The combination of cultural acceptance and facility is, therefore, far more than just a statement of intent; it is an actuality that must be achieved and demonstrated.

The disparity between these two trends – the growing complexity of demographic cultural diversity and the varied emphasis on cultural expertise as a regulated recognition of this trend in teacher standards – creates a question of its own. Aside from exceptions such as New Zealand, why is it that prescriptions of required expertise in the Euro-American sphere tend to ignore or skim over one of the major demographic shifts and educational practice of the last 20 years, especially an aspect that will become more dominant in the decades to come? Is it simply a case of practice yet to catch up with research, or is it more a matter of assumptions being made about the nature of human beings and the professional expertise of teachers? An exploration of this situation will form part of the remainder of this monograph, but whatever the case, the foundational contention of this book is that the characteristics in context of current and future global society not only requires teachers to be more cognisant of the need for this expertise in their professional armoury, but also necessitates that recognition, knowledge and understanding to be incorporated into their professional education and accreditation. This has been supported by recent research studies, including a major Australian research project into how schools teach intercultural understanding (Halse et al., 2015).

It would be quite easy to dismiss a call for teachers to possess some form of accredited cultural education as being a form of excess, with the argument being put forward that cultural matters would be naturally included in any consideration of the needs of any student. One of the more universal pedagogical requirements across all educational systems and approaches is that teachers must focus on the needs of each child. However, such views depend upon the conjecture that all teachers have both an interest and knowledgeable expertise in dealing with matters of culture, and that everyone is sensitive to the needs of people from different cultures. The reality of society as a whole, within any community, and no matter what the socio-political context, is that this will not be the case; there will be a range of views around any particular point. Since teachers are part of society, and in that sense, represent a microcosm of the society in which they live, it is logical to assume that the same range of ideas that exist about cultural difference in a society will be mirrored in the perspectives of the teachers themselves.

This, of course, raises another question of debate: to what degree should we demand or require teachers to be of a certain type of person, one who is seen to hold certain perspectives and expertise in ideas, concepts and values that are deemed to be core to a particular society? Regardless of whichever political forces are in power, such a philosophy leaves society open to the education profession becoming a political football, where careers and expertise are dependent upon the educational philosophy in political vogue. In the area of cultural education, there is evidence that these political nuances have had substantial impact on the direction of educational practice. In Australia, for instance, there was an academic outcry at the way in which conservative governments in the period between 2013 and 2019 intervened with the independent process of Commonwealth academic research grant allocations, with the education ministers rejecting grants – usually sociological and/or in the humanities – that had been initially approved, but did not appear to be compatible with the government's own interpretations of societal priorities. The debate about cultural education is especially fraught because of the political division around the interpretations of, for example, which and whose culture should be prioritised. Such contentions have been, and will continue to be, the source of much educational debate and are often the reason why dealing with issues such as teachers' cultural expertise is sublimated or even ignored completely. The fact remains, though, that cultural understanding is now embedded in many national curriculum frameworks, and yet, to varying degrees, is not part of the explicit expectations placed upon the teaching profession. To that end, it is now even more important to be able to determine a means of determining a teacher's ability to undertake such a responsibility in a way that ensures that teachers can prepare young people for the future world in which they will be adult citizens, a world in which cultural diversity as a basis for societal behaviour will continue to be the norm, not the exception.

5.3 Determining the cultural readiness of teachers

5.3.1 The elements of cultural readiness

In Chapters 3 and 4, I argued that one of the key conceptual identifiers of a transcultural paradigm was that, unlike multiculturalism and interculturalism, it represented an attitude or lens of the world that sees difference as the natural state of society. It was also stressed that the concept was not a total replacement of multiculturalism and interculturalism, but a stage of progression on both, one that was more relevant and appropriate to the modern global societal context. In terms of isolating the elements that comprise a teacher's expertise in cultural education, it is possible to reconfigure the conceptual sequence of multiculturalism through to transculturalism into a format that provides a more concrete base for development.

In one sense, the teaching of cultural understanding can be seen as simply another learning area that has to be taught in schools. Certainly, in the national curriculums of several countries in this research, such as Singapore and New Zealand, the attitudes and content being prioritised are very much built into the curriculum itself. In the case of the Australian curriculum, it is presented more as a capability to be taught across all subject areas. The State of Victoria, in promulgating its variation called Intercultural Capability, also treats it as a curriculum to be taught. The difference is in the components that make up that curriculum, in that to teach cultural understanding in the modern context (that is, in a transcultural fashion) teachers need to acquire a certain attitudinal perspective that enables them to reflect and demonstrate that transcultural outlook.

If the theme of viewing cultural understanding as a learning area is extended, it is possible to argue that, like any discipline, cultural understanding has three forms of knowledge that need to be taught, and which therefore need to be acquired by the teacher in preparation before educating students in this field:

a Propositional knowledge or *multicultural expertise* (the content – facts and information – that needs to be taught): In general terms, this would be the multicultural aspects of cultural understanding; knowledge about different cultures in all aspects of that society.
b Conceptual knowledge, or *intercultural expertise* (the themes that give structure and order to that content knowledge): Intercultural education would play a major part here, as it focuses very much upon communication between different cultural groups in the relevant society and the power relations between them.
c Procedural knowledge or *transcultural expertise* (the skills that help make sense of the propositional and conceptual knowledge, the actions that lead to the ultimate goal): In this instance, the adoption of an attitude that was transcultural in nature would be one of the most important goals of both the teacher's expertise and the children's learning. In essence, this transcultural procedural knowledge incorporates the affective side of social interaction, which can be seen in a proactive '… desire to interact with culturally different others' (Guo, 2010, p. 40).

It is these three broad themes of teacher expertise that form the foundation of the data assessment and analysis throughout the rest of this monograph.

5.3.2 Assessing cultural understanding

The call for a greater urgency for a focus on teacher expertise in cultural understanding should not, and does not, ignore the reality that there has been much work conducted over a number of years in the determination of the level of people's cultural understanding, both within the educational discourse and outside it. It has been a particular focus in the world of business and international relations; indeed, one of the earlier key researchers in the field, Geert Hofstede, was working from within the commercial paradigm. As the degree and complexity of economic and social globalisation have increased, the extent of that interest has become more acute. A wide range of measurements of an individual's cultural understanding have been developed as a result, primarily from the United States.

The diversity of such measurement tools is extensive. For example, in 2006, Fantini and Tirmizi (2006) compiled a list of nearly 100 different 'assessment tools of intercultural communicative competence' that had been developed. Some of the better-known systems on that list included the Intercultural Competence Model (Deardorff, 2006) and the Intercultural Development Inventory (IDI). It is not the intention of this monograph to undertake a detailed comparative analysis of all of these methods. However, in outlining the methodology that was developed for use in this particular project, which is ongoing, there are a number of points that justify expansion and explanation.

a   The overwhelming number of systems on Fantini and Tirmizi's (2006) lists refers to the related notions of cross-cultural or intercultural competence. In the light of the discussion on different forms of cultural education in Chapter 3, there are two concerns with this pattern that will be discussed later.
b   The vast majority of Fantini and Tirmizi's (2006) lists are assessments based on surveys or questionnaires, often referred to as inventories. Many of them are quantitative psychological, behavioural or personality tests, focused on the testing of communication skills and/or cultural sensitivities.
c   Almost without exception, the systems listed have originated from the Euro-American sphere, with the great majority being of US origin and the remainder developed in Europe.

Collectively, these trends suggest that our past approaches to cultural education and the evaluation of cultural expertise need revision and recalibration if we are to develop a form of cultural education – and concomitantly, a form of teacher expertise – that is more attuned to the global and cultural context of 2020 and beyond, rather than the world of the 1970s. First, the notion of *competence*, which dominates perceptions of people's cultural expertise, is very much a *transactional* concept, suggesting the influence of the business world in its development and application. The notion of competence also implies that cultural understanding can be acquired by the mere act of completing a course or the acquisition of a certificate, which aligns with a view that the term was transferred into school education via vocational education, '... where the emphasis on skills and behaviours, rather than content knowledge, was prioritised' (Byram & Gulherme, 2010, p. 5). It treats understanding as purely a learned behaviour and implies that it can be used as needed, rather than necessitating a shift in thinking. As a term, it has been transferred into usage in educational contexts from other fields that are more transactional, such as business and engineering, in which intercultural competence was conceived more in terms of communication across cultural boundaries to enable international projects to be undertaken.

As Deardoff (2011) has highlighted, the plethora of criteria and definitions surrounding the meaning of 'intercultural' has been a major barrier to obtaining any degree of consensus in the field, but the idea of challenging the concept of competence in an educational context has not undergone such scrutiny. In one of the rare occasions of deviation, the Australian State Government of Victoria, in constructing its own version of the Australian curriculum, adopted the term 'intercultural *capability*'. The term is designed to accommodate students being able to '… learn to recognise commonalities and differences, create connections with others, examine the challenges and benefits of cultural diversity and cultivate mutual respect and social cohesion …' (Victorian Curriculum and Assessment Authority, 2019) and appears to differ from the national term of intercultural understanding by being more '… about challenging thinking. It goes far beyond facts about people and cultures to an appreciation of other people's perspectives and a respect for this' (Victorian Curriculum and Assessment Authority, 2019). However, the notion of a 'capability' still infers the notion of a skill that can be learned, a finite qualification. It does not accommodate three key aspects of cultural education that are part of the transcultural paradigm: learning about culture has no endpoint and is continuous; cultural understanding evolves and shifts with life experiences; and cultural difference cannot and should not be isolated as a barrier to be overcome. Instead, the notion of an individual developing cultural *capacity* is far more incorporative of human potential as a quality that is rarely complete and always open to further development. It infers that human expertise can always be improved, especially in relation to an attribute such as cultural understanding that has, and must always, adapt to the changing characteristics of cultural diversity in societies at varied scales: local, national, regional and global.

Second, the conflation between the usage of cross-cultural and intercultural in reference to these assessments highlights the problem of usage that was discussed previously in Chapter 3, as part of the contention that the notion of transculturalism was far more appropriate to and reflective of the modern and future global context. Again, betraying the commercial, transactional historical contexts of much of this work, the persistent use of 'intercultural' suggests an emphasis on the individual gaining enough knowledge to understand how to communicate with different cultures other than our own. Consequently, the context of such assessments continues to assume that cultures are definitive entities that can be easily classified and that the differences between them are barriers to be overcome in the generation of a more homogenous normality.

The overwhelming quantitative approach adopted by these various assessment measures is a philosophical one, part of the ideological neoliberal revolution that has dominated global affairs across all its aspects from the late 1980s. The obsession with the need to provide a simple numerical summary of various aspect of human attitudes or behaviour is, I would argue, part of a search of certainty that arose out the destabilisation of the old norms of global society that came with modern globalisation. Appadurai (2006), in what I consider to be a seminal piece of analysis, *The Fear of Small Numbers*, refers to the fact that the 1990s globalisation created '... an increase in large-scale social uncertainty and ... in the friction of incompleteness' (p. 9). He was writing in the context of the '... large-scale [international] cultural violence' (p. 9) that characterised the 1990s, but I would argue that the contemporaneous rise in the perceived singular 'truth' of quantitative measures, especially in the 'Western' sphere, was part of that attempt to find some means of stabilizing human thought in a world of rapid change.

The innate need to create order out of perceived chaos and simplify reality in order to accommodate a more peaceful existence is part of that linear approach to thinking that has long been identified as part of more Euro-American modes of thought (Nisbett, 2003; Nisbett & Masuda, 2006; Chan & Yan, 2007; Varnum, Grossmann, Kitayama, & Nisbett, 2010; Casinader, 2014). The main difficulty with the linearity of this approach is that it is based on the removal of difference in the search for simplification. In any area of human behaviour, such a fundamental diminution of human complexity is fraught with danger as it encourages blindness towards the very subtle tones of human action that are its very essence, a weakness that is not solved by an equally fervent belief in statistical validation. In the area of cultural expertise in the 21st century, such an ideological approach is even more asynchronous with human reality, for '... the elimination of difference ... is fundamentally impossible in a world of blurred boundaries, mixed marriages, shared languages, and other deep conductivities' (Appadurai, 2006, p. 11). It is those very differences that are acknowledged by the concept of transculturalism as being not just vital, but also part of the *normality* that needs to be accepted. Any assessment of cultural expertise in the modern context therefore needs to place the acknowledgement of those nuances as being to the fore, and not hidden or subsumed within or behind a less contentious agenda.

The observation that Euro-American researchers dominate the field of measurements of cultural understanding is also a reflection of this ideological bias in the preference for the quantitative tools being adopted. They also mirror the particular notion of culture that underpins that approach to cultural understanding. The question of what is meant by 'culture' has been, and continues to be, the subjects of a wide ranging discourse to which I have made my own contributions (for example Casinader, 2016; Casinader &

Kidman, 2018) It is not the purpose of this monograph to repeat or expand that discussion of two basic definitions, but instead, to explore how those understandings might be translated into education on cultural understanding and awareness.

Essentially, conceptions of culture tend to fall into one of two blocks. The first is the more traditional belief that it reflects the values, customs and attitudes of the group of people who have come into agreement regarding a common way of life, even though an individual's interpretation of a culture is very likely to vary in some way from others who ascribe to the same group. To a large extent, this ethnographic class of definitions tends to follow and be followed by the majority of researchers from 'Western', Euro-American contexts that have dominated the discourse. The second formulation of culture is one that emphasises culture as a mindset; a person's culture is more accurately imaged in and by their own perception of identity, which would include acknowledgement of those who might follow a similar interpretation. This line of definition, which has been the focus of several researchers since the 2000s, including the author (for example see Kumar, 2013; Casinader, 2014), and derives from earlier sociological work by researchers such as Geertz (1973), does not necessarily exclude the relevance of ethnographic elements such as language, artefacts and, if relevant, religion. However, it takes the position that a conception of culture is not necessarily *dependent* upon those elements.

A mind-centred conception of culture is far more able to incorporate the notion of the multiple and/or hybrid cultural identities that have become a feature of global demographics, as individuals build identities based on ever increasingly complex worldwide networks. In recognising the fine nuances of cultural identity that have emerged as a major component of the global demography in the modern age, it helps to splinter the crude associations and stereotypes of the past in which culture and cultural identity were all too often seen as going hand in hand with physical characteristics such as skin colour and body shape. A definition of culture that is focused more on the perceptual mindset of those who identify with a particular way of life is able to move beyond such simplistic sequences of logic and recognises the existences of variations within and between cultural identities as a natural, expected occurrence: no culture is fundamentally or consistently homogeneous.

The persistence of the ethnographic 'Western' definition of culture as the unquestioned idea that can be applied to all human existence can be attributed to the dominance of the Euro-American axis in global affairs until the early 2000s, especially in the period since the end of World War II. The post-1945 era can be seen as marking the point in human history when the existence of a multiplicity of cultures and viewpoints, all equally valid (at least to a point), became recognised internationally in the formation of the United Nations. The ideas and outlooks that have long existed across Asia, Africa and

Central/South America are now more visible and have to be included in the general debate as having equal weight. Up until the 2000s, the domination of Western perspectives was assisted in no small manner by the hegemony of the Euro-American media, which have seen themselves as being relevant to not only their local or domestic environment, but also having a rightful and self-evident place in the determination of global opinion. In this context, it is hardly surprising that within the national curriculum frameworks across the Euro-American sphere, the notion of culture, when expressed within an educational context, has tended to follow the established, Euro-American, ethnographic emphasis.

5.4 Project methodology

5.4.1 Overview

The methodology that has been utilised in this ongoing international project has evolved over a decade of research into the notion that the ability of a school educator to teach cultural understanding cannot be taken to be axiomatic as a result of their teacher education, consequent professional experience and professional learning. It has also been constructed to incorporate certain parameters that have not been part of the large majority of the assessment tools designed to date with the general aim of moving beyond the Euro-American-centric parameters with which assessments of cultural understanding have been undertaken. These parameters include:

a   the specific purpose of being more inclusive of multiple interpretations about the nature of culture as a concept and how human beings represent and are represented by it;
b   taking into account that the boundaries between cultures and cultural identities are not as delineated as past and current research seems to suggest, and that an individual's conception of their culture and cultural identity can shift and change throughout their lives as a result of the experiences that they encounter. As a result, an individual's ability to demonstrate cultural understanding can often depend on the context in which they are living; changes to that context throughout life can have dramatic impacts on how an individual perceives their own cultural identity and how they perceive and react to the 'Other';
c   exploring the finer nuances of teachers' understandings about culture, cultural understanding and cultural education, with special attention to the attitudes and reasoning that collectively comprise the components of a transcultural perspective, particularly in relation to cultural difference; and
d   incorporating specific consideration of the globalised nature of current and future world societies.

In particular, the methodology seeks to counter perceived weaknesses in existing tools for teacher assessment of cultural expertise. The preference for quantitative instruments of assessment has been influenced by a number of factors, including ease of administration and analysis, but a major influence has been the belief in numerical and mathematical tools as being self-evidently more valid and reliable than qualitative research, because of '… the rhetorical appeal of numbers – their cultural association with scientific precision and rigor …' (Sandelowski, Voils, & Knafl, 2009, p. 208). The division in intent between the validity of the two basic systems of measurement is no better exemplified by the caution that has to be given to qualitative researchers to avoid converting words into numbers purely for the hope of a more persuasive look (Saldaña, 2016).

The problem of using a quantitative approach to the measurement of teacher attitudes, whether this be about cultural understanding or another aspect of life, is that it does not take into account the importance of context(s) in determining a person's view. It also does not incorporate an understanding that those contexts are not only full of nuances that cannot be de-emphasised in the name of generalisation, but are also ever-changing; no matter how it is named. A reliance on questionnaires and researched statistical expectations is therefore an incomplete and potentially inaccurate approach to assessment of cultural understanding. It is this reference to context and the ever-shifting nature of parameters in a person's life that makes the question-based inventories that are at the base of many assessments of cultural capacity (usually titled as cultural competence) so problematic. Their use may capture a moment in time, but in themselves, they do not help to determine or understand the influences that have led to that particular framing of cultural understanding, nor do they contribute to an understanding of how those ideas might change in the future; no matter how it is named, cultural capacity/competence is '… process that continues throughout one's lifetime' (Matveev & Merz, 2014, p. 123).

By virtue of their very nature, when used in the study of human attitudes, purely quantitative approaches tend to assume that culture and cultural identity are universally consistent concepts and that, no matter where a person originates or lives in the world, their pattern of rationality and thought will be similar. As discussed in Chapters 3 and 4, these associations between cultural background and patterns of thinking were not really questioned in the Euro-American sphere until the early years of the 21st century, and arguably remain a minority perspective. Educationally, some tools have included consideration of the contest between individualist and collective ways of thinking (for example the ICSI – Intercultural Sensitivity Inventory; Bhawuk & Brislin, 1992), but they are relatively few and still reinforce a binary perspective of the culture-thinking link. In a similar vein, tools such as the Intercultural Development Inventory (IDI tend to see cultural capacity as being measured by a linear continuum ranging from denial to adaptation

(Hammer, 2008), when the attribute is a far more complex and nuanced phenomenon. The difference with the methodology applied in this project is that it commences with the acceptance that cultural identity can be fluid over a lifetime and that there are associations between culture and thinking, but that the boundaries between these are neither fixed nor rigid; they do not form a linear transition and are more like zones of transition, often containing features of other culture-thinking associations.

For these reasons, the research project employed in this monograph utilised a mixed methods approach comprising both an online survey and a semi-structured interview. This aligns with the approach adopted by past studies that involved research into cultural understandings of students, such as Deardorff (2006) and Halse et al. (2015). The methodology employed has been developed and validated through its application in four previous research projects into the cultural capacities of teachers, the findings of which have been published in peer-reviewed international outlets (Casinader, 2012, 2014, 2018; Casinader & Clemans, 2018; Walsh & Casinader, 2018)

5.4.2 The components of the methodology

5.4.2.1 Aims

The focus of the research project, which is ongoing, has been to investigate the degree to which teachers in schools demonstrate a transcultural capacity, or the expertise to teach cultural understanding to school students in a manner that is appropriate to the global society in which they will live and work. Aside from looking at the nature and degree of that transcultural capacity, the project seeks to determine the factors that have influenced, encouraged or hindered the development of that capacity by looking closely at the personal and professional contexts surrounding the life of the individual. Through this, the project is aimed at developing guidelines for programs in teacher education and professional learning that would assist prospective and future teachers to either develop or enhance their existing degree of transcultural capacity. A discussion of the learnings to date in terms of recommendations will be the focus of Chapter 7.

5.4.2.2 Participants

As discussed in earlier chapters, the geographical focus of the initial stages of this project has been aimed at educational jurisdictions in regions that were once part of the British Empire and colonial rule. Although the individual circumstances and histories of colonialism are acknowledged and recognised, the fundamental basis of educational systems in each region have the same or similar starting points, regardless of what path or paths have been adopted in the years since the cessation of imperial rule.

Within each region or country used as a case study, the basic unit of investigation was a school or schools, using a sample of ten or more teachers, where possible, from each institution. In order to cover as many variables as possible, it was intended to have a teacher sample from each school that represented the different levels of educational leadership on a ratio of 7:2:1, ranging from classroom teachers through to middle management through to one of the senior staff on the school management team. It was also intended that the sample of ten or more teachers would represent the main learning areas within the school, such English, Mathematics, Science, Geography, History, the creative arts and physical education. The original research design aimed at an initial study of two schools per country/region, one primary and one secondary, which would result in a sample size of 20 teachers in that country/region. Consideration of school sector (government or independent/private) was considered to be less important in this initial phase of research, although attempts were made to ensure that, across the entire project, a range of different school types were investigated.

Over the duration of the research phase from 2017 to 2019, adjustments had to be made according to the individual circumstances found in each country/region. Contact with schools was organised through the author's own research networks rather than educational system administrators in each jurisdiction, as the focus of the project was not, at this stage, on the pattern of teacher expertise in different educational systems, but on that of individual teachers. As a result of unexpected local circumstances, there were occasions when adaptations had to be made to the sample intention of the original research design. For instance, it was possible to only research two primary schools in New Zealand, as no secondary school able to be involved could be found at the time of research. In India, only one school at the research site volunteered their participation, but being a prep-12 school, covering all years of primary and secondary education, it was possible to interview approximately 20 teachers from across the primary and secondary halves of the school. The same occurred in the United Kingdom, where pressures of available research resources resulted in only one school volunteering to be part of the project. Adjustments also had to be made at the time of research as there were a handful of volunteer teacher participants at sime schools who were unable to complete the research process through absence, illness and other factors. A decision was made to exclude any teacher who only completed the online survey, but to include those who had been interviewed, but had not completed the survey. This was because the wide-ranging and conversational nature of the interview enabled a certain degree of question catch-up as the interview was conducted post-survey.

Overall, 135 teachers across 14 schools and 8 countries/regions have participated in the project up until April 2019, with the data research of four schools (three Canadian and one Australian) being funded through a research grant from the International Baccalaureate in 2017. It is intended to extend the project in the future to include a wider range of countries as well as undertaking a more comprehensive coverage of the countries forming part of this particular stage of the research.

5.4.2.3 Data collection

The mixed methods approach adopted for this research consists of two parts: an online survey followed by a personal interview and conducted face to face. The combination of the two data sources was designed to capture information that related to not only the determination of a teacher's transcultural capacity, but also data that would enable a more critical investigation and analysis of the contexts and other factors that might have contributed to the evolution of perspectives of an individual teacher. The questions in both the survey and the semi-structured interview were constructed around the conceptual framework that transculturalism involves essentially an attitudinal shift on the part of the individual; it is not merely a benchmark of behaviour or outlook that can be acquired through the mere act of completing a set of learnings. The survey questions and interview conversations were therefore designed to elicit a teacher's attitude(s) or perspective(s) to the different facets of transculturalism, specifically a positive conception towards change and difference, an affirmative perspective towards globalism and the characteristics of a global society (global mindedness) and acknowledgement that cultures can differ in their approach to thinking, which is a determinant of how effectively a person can work and live within different cultural contexts. These transcultural characteristics were investigated through the study of five themes concerning teacher expertise:

a   Their understanding of thinking and thinking skills.
b   The ways in which they communicate these knowledge and understandings.
c   Their knowledge and utilisation of pedagogical theory and practice.
d   Their experiences of multi-, inter- and transcultural engagement.
e   Their reactions and attitudes to certain scenarios that illustrated the dilemmas surrounding of teaching cultural understanding, such as the boundaries between teaching and indoctrination.

5.4.2.4 Conceptual foundations

The conceptual foundation used to determine a teacher's transcultural capacity was the model of cultural dispositions of thinking (CDT), which was the outcome of the preliminary research that the author conducted into teacher expertise into cultural understanding (Casinader, 2014) and from which the notion of transculturalism originates.

Cultural Dispositions of Thinking

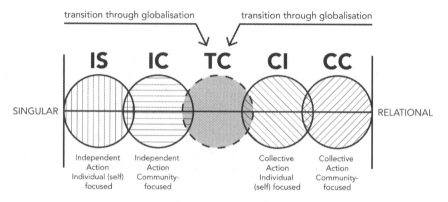

Figure 5.1 Model of Cultural Dispositions of Thinking.
Source: Casinader (2014; reprinted by permission).

The CDT model (see Figure 5.1) was the outcome of the study of 22 school educators from Australia, the United States, Malaysia and Singapore. It is founded on the principles that there is a relationship between culture and approaches to thinking, and that culture is more accurately conceptualised in the context of modern global society as a 'state of mind' than the more traditional ethnographic collection of values, beliefs, artefacts and customary priorities (Casinader, 2014). CDTs are states of mind that reflect a particular cultural approach to specific types of thinking skills. It is important to reiterate that these cultural approaches are not necessarily associated with specific ethnic groups or geographical regions, as is often the case with the more conventional framing of culture. As discussed earlier, culture in this research context is not defined ethnographically, but as a mind-centred entity. Consequently, CDTs are psychological perspectives that reflect a person's collective outlook on people, society and the world, a mind-centred concept that defined more by commonalities in how people perceive their identity (Geertz, 1973; Casinader, 2014).

Within each CDT, people possess a similar cultural outlook and display some consistency in their conception and/or enaction of a thinking skill, classified by differing degrees in the combination of independent (individualistic) and interdependent (collective) elements of thinking. Each CDT therefore reflects different combinations of independent and interdependent traits of thinking; collectively, they embody how people from different cultures conceptualise and communicate the actuality of thinking. Under the model, the different cultural dispositions form a converging, overlapping spectrum (see Figure 5.1), none of which are mutually exclusive. At one end of the spectrum are cultural approaches to thinking that are more aligned with individualistic conceptions of society (IS and IC), matched at the other end by approaches that are culturally more collective in nature (CI and CC) and in the centre of the model, there are those who display a *transcultural* disposition of thinking. These individuals have developed the ability to work within and across cultural contexts that are either individualist or collective, or a shifting integration of the two, depending upon circumstances. Both modes of thinking (individualist or collective) are seen of equal importance, with neither being necessarily superior.

The two CDT groups at either end of the spectrum (IC and CC) are also differentiated by the way in which they approach the thinking skills of individual and community problem-solving. The more individualistic IS and IC thinkers tend to define these as referring to the location of the problem, that is in the individual or the community. However, the more collectively minded CI and CC groups see them as referring to more who is undertaking the problem-solving, there is a much stronger focus on the relationships between people. Transcultural (TC) individuals have the capacity to see the process from both perspectives, integrating as needed, depending upon the situation at the time. It is possible for an individual to shift from one CDT to another throughout their life, depending upon changes in context and circumstance.

The CDT model also incorporates the premise that the move towards a transcultural outlook is influenced greatly by the degree of exposure towards globalising experiences in a person's life; that is, experiences that highlight the features of a global society, including its complexity of cultural diversity. In the initial research from which the model originates, as well as later studies that have employed the CDT model and its related methodology (see, for example, Casinader, 2014, 2018), it was evident that the impact of such experiences generally emerges when teachers are exposed to cultures in different regions of the world, as well as life experiences in regions that offer a great cultural contrast within a person's country of origin. In the 2014 study, for instance, black African educators in South Africa who had a more transcultural sensibility and outlook tended to be those who had progressively moved away from their tribal 'homelands' into other parts of the country during both the apartheid and post-apartheid eras (Casinader, 2014, pp. 107–126). Consequently, those who are involved in more globalised practices in their lives tend to develop a more 'transcultural' cultural disposition, one that is reflected in their attitudes towards change and difference, global mindedness and professional practice. Such findings as to the potential impact of personal and professional travel are not new; a number of studies on the development of cultural capacity amongst teachers have referred to the effectiveness of being exposed to and immersed in life and cultures beyond a person's country of origin, for example Willard-Holt (2001), Pence and Macgillivray (2001), Cushner and Chang (2015), and Halse et al. (2015).

5.4.2.5 The online survey and interview

The structure of the online survey and interview was designed to capture the required depth of data about a teacher's personal and professional background, as well as their attitudes to a range of educational and societal scenarios. The survey itself incorporated the adaptation of an assessment survey instrument developed and used by the Faculty of Education at the University of British Columbia (UBC). The community field experience (CFE) survey was used to assess the impact of a compulsory school placement in a First Nations community within the UBC elementary (primary) pre-service teacher education course (de Oliveira Andreotti, McPherson, & Broom, 2015). The main principle of the CFE tool was that it used a series of affective questions to determine the attitudes and opinions towards certain elements of cultural understanding, using a 5-point Likert scale ranging from strongly disagree to strongly agree. The CFE survey questions were adapted and reconfigured to match the project parameters on teacher transcultural capacity, especially those relating to attitudes towards change, difference and global mindedness. Also included were questions related to professional practice that might shed light on teacher attitudes to specific transcultural elements.

The semi-structured interviews of the teacher participants were held face to face at their school, following their completion of the online survey. The possibility of using virtual conferencing was initially considered, but rejected as the purpose of the interview was not just to gather extra factual information, but to encourage teachers to expand upon the reasons for the attitudes that had been indicated in their surveys. In order for that to occur, a more personal connection had to be established between the researcher(s) and the teachers. Consequently, the interviews were conducted more as conversations than a direct question-and-answer session. A specific set of supplemental questions were asked of each teacher, all relating to their attitudes to more complex situations relating to culture, difference and identity, as well as a comparative discussion as to their personal and professional reactions to these scenarios.

5.4.2.6 Data analysis

The combination of the survey and interview transcript for each teacher was analysed using Dedoose web-based software, which is designed specifically for mixed methods analysis. From the two data sources, a database of the teacher responses was constructed, outlining the nature of their personal and professional experiences. The interviews were transcribed and uploaded into the Dedoose project, along with a descriptor table that summarised the personal and professional characteristics of each individual, including demographics, nature of educational expertise, regions and purpose of travel. This table was populated with data obtained from the relevant interview and the online survey (where this applied). The interview transcripts and survey responses were then coded for expressions of specific individualistic (independent) and collectivistic (interdependent) thinking, using the system employed in the original CDT research project (Casinader, 2014, pp. 147–159). According to the principles of that methodology, which utilises characteristics of independent and interdependent thinking derived from the work of Nisbett (2003), the frequency and proportional balance of the coding of those expressions of independent and interdependent thinking were used to determine the cultural disposition of each teacher (Casinader, 2014, pp. 152–159). The intervals of the relative proportions of each against each CDT are illustrated in Table 5.2.

In order to provide a more nuanced understanding of each teacher's assigned CDT, a quantitative analysis was undertaken of those survey responses relating to the teacher's attitudes towards aspects of a transcultural perspective. These questions could be divided into two subsets: attitudes to change and difference and global perspectives. By focusing on these two divisions, it was possible to conduct a more targeted analysis of the degree to which the identified CDT of a teacher was in line with their personal interpretations of transculturally centred educational situations. There were four parameters or lines of thought tested in terms of attitudes to change and difference, along with three parameters related to global perspectives. Each parameter was investigated through responses to four specific questions.

This second analysis used a system of mean values of agreement and disagreement, similar to the one based on a 5-step Likert scale that was employed by Skamp, Boyes, and Stanisstreet (2004). For each of the statements associated with a particular parameter, a teacher could give one of five answers, selecting the appropriate step on the 5-step Likert scale: strongly agree, agree, neutral, disagree or strongly disagree. There were three stages to the analysis of these responses, which are illustrated in Tables 5.3–5.5. The first was to determine which end of the Likert scale (strongly disagree or strongly agree) was in concordance with a more transcultural view for each of the statements

Table 5.2 Calculation of Cultural Dispositions of Thinking (% Coding)

	IS	IC	TC	CI	CC
Independent	>80	60–79	40–59	20–39	<20
Interdependent	<20	21–39	40–59	60–79	>80
	Independent action Self-focus	Independent action Community focus	Transcultural	Collective action Self-focus	Collective action Community focus

112 Measuring transcultural capacity in teachers

Table 5.3 Direction of Transculturality on Survey Responses (Example)

How do you prepare for new/unfamiliar experiences?	Strongly disagree	Strongly agree
I try to understand as much as I can in advance in order to feel informed.		Positive transcultural
I try not to over plans in order to be open to new experiences.		Positive transcultural
I prepare as much as possible so that nothing surprises me.	Positive transcultural	
In order to avoid unfamiliar experiences, I try to keep things as predictable as possible.	Positive transcultural	
I try to figure out who is right.	Positive transcultural	

connected to a parameter. Table 5.3 shows the determination for one particular parameter concerned with difference.

For instance, Table 5.3 shows the appropriate direction for each of the four statements related to behaviour in an unfamiliar place. It should be noted that not all statements equated strong agreement with a positive transcultural outlook. The responses for each statement were then quantified according to the system outlined in Table 5.5, so, for example, +2 was awarded for a response that was strongly transcultural, whether that was in agreement or in rejection of a statement, a neutral response was coded as zero and so on.

The final stage is shown in Table 5.5. The teacher's scores across all the statements for the parameter in question were averaged out to give a sub-score for that parameter on a range from +2 to −2. A teacher who showed

Table 5.4 Scoring of Degree of Transculturality based on Change and Difference Statements (Example)

How do you prepare for new/unfamiliar experiences?	Strongly disagree	Disagree	Neutral	Agree	Strongly agree	Score
I try to understand as much as I can in advance in order to feel informed.					X	+2
I try not to over plans in order to be open to new experiences.			X			0
I prepare as much as possible so that nothing surprises me.		X				+1
In order to avoid unfamiliar experiences, I try to keep things as predictable as possible.	X					+2
I try to figure out who is right.				X		−1
					AV Score	**+2**

Table 5.5 Calculation of Score on Attitudes to Change and Difference (example)

Parameter	Average transcultural score for each parameter (four statement scores per parameter)
How do you prepare for new/unfamiliar experiences?	+2
How do you approach conflicting perspectives?	+1
How do you behave when you find yourself in a new place?	0
How do you feel about immigration?	−2
During your lunch break after a class, you overhear four people discussing the topics below	
How do you explain economic inequality?	+1
How can the world's problems would be solved?	0
What is the biggest challenge to sustainability?	+1
	AV Score **For attitudes to change and difference** 0.43

a completely comprehensive transcultural perspective would score +2, and one who demonstrated the reverse −2. All the sub-scores for each of the seven parameters relating to, in this case, attitudes to change and difference were then averaged to give a score for that particular transcultural perspective to each teacher. These summary scores were then added to the Dedoose descriptor database so that they could be included in the final data analysis. The Dedoose software enabled analysis of the CDT patterns of the teachers in relation to any one or combination of the descriptor variables, whether by school, country and as a complete set.

In the light of the focus of this monograph, the data analysis that would be the focus of Chapter 6 will be confined to the core interest of this discussion: the degree to which teachers in schools have the expertise to teach cultural understanding appropriate to the nature of a culturally diverse globalised society. It will also reflect upon the ways in which the transcultural capacity of teachers can be developed as part of teacher education programs or enhanced by professional learning programs for in-service teachers.

References

Appadurai, A. (2006). *Fear of Small Numbers: An Essay on the Geography of Anger*. Durham: Duke University Press.
Australian Bureau of Statistics. (2019). 3412.0 - Migration, Australia, 2017-18. Retrieved from https://www.abs.gov.au/ausstats/abs@.nsf/mf/3412.0/.

Australian Institute for Teaching and School Leadership (AITSL). (2019a). Australian Professional Standards for Teachers. Retrieved from http://www.aitsl.edu.au/australian-professional-standards-for-teachers/standards/list.

Australian Institute for Teaching and School Leadership (AITSL). (2019b). Glossary for the Australian Professional Standards for Teachers. Retrieved from https://www.aitsl.edu.au/docs/default-source/default-document-library/glossaryoftheaustralianprofessionalstandardsforteachers.pdf?sfvrsn=8207e93c_0.

Bhawuk, D. P. S., & Brislin, R. W. (1992). "The measurement of intercultural sensitivity using the concepts of individualism and collectivism." *International Journal of Intercultural Relations*, 16(4), 413–436.

Byram, M., & Gulherme, M. (2010). Intercultural education and intercultural communication: Tracing the relationship. In Y. Tsai & S. Houghton (Eds.), *Becoming Intercultural: Inside and Outside the Classroom* (pp. 2–22). Newcastle upon Tyne, England: Cambridge Scholars Publishing.

Casinader, N. (2012). *Cultural Perspectives, Thinking, Educators and Globalisation: A Critical Analysis of the Future Problem Solving Program.* (PhD unpublished doctoral thesis), The University of Melbourne, Melbourne.

Casinader, N. (2014). *Culture, Transnational Education and Thinking: Case Studies in Global Schooling.* Milton Park, Abingdon: Routledge.

Casinader, N. (2015). Culture and thinking in comparative education: The globalism of an empirical mutual identity. In J. Zajda (Ed.), *Second International Handbook on Globalisation, Education and Policy Research* (pp. 337–352). Dordrecht, Netherlands: Springer.

Casinader, N. (2016). A lost conduit for intercultural education: School geography and the potential for transformation in the Australian curriculum. *Intercultural Education*, 27(3), 257–273. doi: 10.1080/14675986.2016.1150650.

Casinader, N. (2018). Transnational learning experiences and teacher transcultural capacity: The impact on professional practice – a comparative study of three Australian schools. *Intercultural Education*, 29(2), 258–280. doi: 10.1080/14675986.2018.1430284.

Casinader, N., & Clemans, A. (2018). The building of the transcultural capacities of preservice teachers to support their employability in a globalised world: A pilot study. *Intercultural Education*, 29(5–6), 589–608. doi: 10.1080/14675986.2018.1500170.

Casinader, N., & Kidman, G. (2018). Geography education, transculturalism and global understanding. In A. Demirci, R. de Miguel, & S. Bednarz (Eds.), *Geography Education for Global Understandings* (pp. 113–128). Cham, Switzerland: Springer/International Geography Union.

Chan, H. M., & Yan, H. K. T. (2007). Is there a geography of thought for east-west differences? Why or why not? *Educational Philosophy and Theory*, 39(4), 383–403. doi: 10.1111/j.1469-5812.2007.00346.x.

Crossley, M. (2014). Global league tables, big data and the international transfer of educational research modalities. *Comparative Education*, 50(1), 15–26. doi: 10.1080/03050068.2013.871438.

Cushner, K., & Chang, S.-C. (2015). Developing intercultural competence through overseas student teaching: Checking our assumptions. *Intercultural Education*, 26(3), 165–178. doi: 10.1080/14675986.2015.1040326.

de Oliveira Andreotti, V., McPherson, K., & Broom, C. (2015). *Crossing Local and Global Borders: Research Project Documentation.* Vancouver, Canada: Department of Educational Studies, Faculty of Education, University of British Columbia.

Deardorff, D. K. (2006). Identification and assessment of intercultural competence as a student outcome of internationalization. *Journal of Studies in International Education*, 10(3), 241–266. doi: 10.1177/1028315306287002.

Deardoff, D. K. (2011). Assessing Intercultural Competence. *New Directions for Institutional Research* (149), 65–79. doi:10.1002/ir.381

Education Council. (2017). *Our Code, Our Standards: Ngā Tikanga Matatika Ngā Paerewa*. Wellington, New Zealand: Author. Retrieved from https://teachingcouncil.nz/sites/default/files/Our%20Code%20Our%20Standards%20web%20booklet%20FINAL.pdf.

Fantini, A. E., & Tirmizi, A. (2006). *Exploring and Assessing Intercultural Competence*. World Learning Publications. Paper 1. Retrieved from http://digitalcollections.sit.edu/worldlearning_publications/.

Gazette of India (2014). Extraordinary: Part III - Section 4. In (Vol. REGD. NO. D.L.-33004/99). New Delhi.

Geertz, C. (1973). *The Interpretation of Cultures*. New York, NY: Basic Books Inc.

Government of India. (2012). *Vision of Teacher Education in India Quality and Regulatory Perspective, Report of the High-Powered Commission on Teacher Education*. New Delhi, India: Ministry of Human Resource Development.

Government of Ontario. (2010). Teacher Performance Appraisal. Retrieved from http://www.edu.gov.on.ca/eng/teacher/pdfs/TPA_Manual_English_september2010l.pdf.

Government of United Kingdom, Department of Education. (2013). *Teachers' Standards: Guidance for School Leaders, School Staff and Governing Bodies*. London. Retrieved from https://assets.publishing.service.gov.uk/government/uploads/system/uploads/attachment_data/file/665520/Teachers__Standards.pdf.

Guo, Y. (2010). The concept and development of intercultural competence. In Y. Tsai & S. Houghton (Eds.), *Becoming Intercultural: Inside and Outside the Classroom* (pp. 23–47). Newcastle upon Tyne, England: Cambridge Scholars Publishing.

Halse, C., Mansouri, F., Moss, J., Paradies, Y., O'Mara, J., Arber, R., …, Wright, L. (2015). *Doing Diversity: Intercultural Understanding in Primary and Secondary Schools*. Melbourne, Australia: Deakin University. Retrieved from https://en.unesco.org/interculturaldialogue/resources/161.

Hammer, M. R. (2008). The intercultural development inventory (IDI): An approach for assessing and building intercultural competence. In M.A. Moodian (Ed.), *Contemporary Leadership and Intercultural Competence: Understanding and Utilizing Cultural Diversity to Build Successful Organizations* (pp. 245–259). Thousand Oaks, CA: Sage.

Kumar, P. (2013). Bridging east and west educational divides in Singapore. *Comparative Education*, 49(1), 72–87. doi: 10.1080/03050068.2012.740221.

Matveev, A.V., & Merz, M.Y. (2014). Intercultural competence assessment: What are its key dimensions across assessment tools? In L. T. B. Jackson, D. Meiring, F. J. R. Van de Vijver, E. S. Idemoudia, & W. K. Gabrenya Jr. (Eds.), *Toward sustainable development through nurturing diversity: Proceedings from the 21st International Congress of the International Association for Cross-Cultural Psychology*, pp. 80–86

National Council of Educational Research and Training, India. (2005). *National Curriculum Framework 2005*, New Delhi. Retrieved from http://epathshala.nic.in/wp-content/doc/NCF/Pdf/nf2005.pdf.

National Institute of Education. (2009). *A Teacher Education Model for the 21st Century, Singapore*. Retrieved from https://www.nie.edu.sg/docs/default-source/nie-files/te21_online_ver.pdf?sfvrsn=2.

Nisbett, R. (2003). *The Geography of Thought: How Asians and Westerners Think Differently…and Why*. New York, NY: The Free Press.

Nisbett, R., & Masuda, T. (2006). Culture and point of view. In R. Viale, D. Andler, & L. Hirschfield (Eds.), *Biological and Cultural Bases of Human Inference* (pp. 49–70). Mahwah, NJ: Lawrence Erlbaum Associates, Inc.

Pence, H. M., & Macgillivray, I. K. (2001). The impact of a short-term international experience for preservice teachers. *Teaching and Teacher Education, 24*, 14–25.

Saldaña, J. (2016). *The Coding Manual for Qualitative Researchers.* Thousand Oaks, CA: Sage Publications Ltd.

Sandelowski, M., Voils, C. I., & Knafl, G. (2009). On quantitizing. *Journal of Mixed Methods Research, 3*(3), 208–222. doi: 10.1177/1558689809334210.

SEAMEO INNOTECH Regional Education Program. (2010). *Teaching Competency Standards in Southeast Asian Countries: Eleven Country Audit.* Philippines: Author. Retrieved from http://www.seameo.org/SEAMEOWeb2/images/stories/Publications/Centers_pub/2012TeachingCompetencyStandards/TeachingCompetencyStd.pdf.

Singh, R. (2013). *India Policy Brief 4: Professional Development of Teachers: The Need of the Hour.* New Delhi, India: Young Lives in India.

Skamp, K., Boyes, E., & Stanisstreet, M. (2004). Students' ideas and attitudes about air quality. *Research in Science Education, 34*(3), 313–342. doi: 10.1023/B:RISE.0000044643.24770.5c.

Swee Choo Goh, P. (2012). The Malaysian teacher standards: A look at the challenges and implications for teacher educators. *Educational Research for Policy and Practice, 11*(2), 73–87. doi: 10.1007/s10671-011-9107-8.

Varnum, M. E. W., Grossmann, I., Kitayama, S., & Nisbett, R. E. (2010). The origin of cultural differences in cognition: The social orientation hypothesis. *Current Directions in Psychological Science, 19*(9), 10–13. doi: 10.1177/0963721409359301.

Victorian Curriculum and Assessment Authority. (2019). *Intercultural Capability: Rationale and Aims.* Retrieved from http://victoriancurriculum.vcaa.vic.edu.au/intercultural-capability/introduction/rationale-and-aims.

Waldow, F., Takayama, K., & Sung, Y.-K. (2014). Rethinking the pattern of external policy referencing: Media discourses over the 'Asian Tigers'' PISA success in Australia, Germany and South Korea. *Comparative Education, 50*(3), 302–321. doi: 10.1080/03050068.2013.860704.

Walsh, L., & Casinader, N. (2018). Investigating the moral territories of international education: A study of the impact of experience, perspectives and dispositions on teachers' engagement with difference in the international Baccalaureate Primary Years Programme. *International Research in Geographical and Environmental Education, 28*(2), 1–15. doi: 10.1080/10382046.2018.1529715.

Willard-Holt, C. (2001). The impact of a short-term international experience for preservice teachers. *Teaching and Teacher Education, 17*, 505–517.

Chapter 6

Transcultural capacity of teachers
A comparative analysis

6.1 Overview

Although the sample case studies were all framed within the general context of being part of the broad-spectrum of British colonial heritage, the contexts of the eight regions studied were all distinctive in one or more ways. As a group, they represented the variety of colonial cultural contexts within which British colonialism operated, regardless of the limitations that have been discussed in earlier chapters. Imperial and legal historians often group Australia, Canada and New Zealand (along with South Africa) as part of the colonial heritage of 'settler societies' that were the major focus of Anglo migrants from Britain throughout the 19th and 20th centuries (Darwin, 2012). However, in the context of the themes of this monograph, such a classification is an overgeneralisation that tends to ignore very important differences in the cultural composition and history of the three regions. In common to all three, of course, is that they represented a colonial space which saw indigenous peoples being dispossessed of their lands and way of life by waves of Anglo-Saxon and European explorers, military forces and migrants. Nevertheless, the way in which the three regions responded and have continued to respond to that colonial history separates them in very distinct ways. For instance, of the three, Australia is the only one to have not negotiated treaties with its First Nations peoples, whereas Canada and New Zealand have built modern societies based upon that very principle. The situation in both countries is not as perfect as that statement might suggest, but notwithstanding any issues that still await resolution, the reality of multiculturalism or cultural diversity is embedded in the governance and structure of society in both countries to a degree that does not exist in modern Australia at this point.

Similar variances and similarities exist amongst the other case studies. Singapore and Malaysia are societies where cultural pluralism revolves around people of Chinese and Malay heritage, but with entirely different emphases that are reflected in their school educational systems (see Chapter 4). Hong Kong is the only one of the case studies that is not a nation-state, having moved from being a colony of Britain to be a special administrative region of China, which has always claimed sovereignty over the islands. India was the

Cultural Dispositions of Thinking

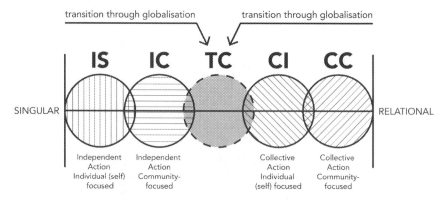

Figure 6.1 Model of Cultural Dispositions of Thinking (Reprise).

Source: Casinader (2014) (reprinted by permission).

primary imperial component of the British Empire, but has a very long heritage of pre-European civilisations that has contributed to its multidimensional cultural, social and economic diversity of the modern day. One aspect of this particular research project was to explore whether these different cultural and sociopolitical heritages and histories have been reflected in teacher attitudes towards teaching about cultural difference. In order to provide a further common point for the research, all schools in which the teacher participants work have self-identified as schools that are looking to educate children in their care for a globalised 21st-century society. If they are to be successful in that objective, it follows that their teaching staff should be equally prepared to take on the challenges of teaching children who had been born into such a society to be prepared to live, work and participate as citizens in the future of that society, however, it might evolve. Under the rationale of the cultural dispositions of thinking (CDT) model (see Figure 6.1), that would mean that the teaching staff in the schools should be as transcultural as possible, or at least, display a CDT (Cultural Disposition of Thinking) as near to it as possible.

6.2 Transculturality as a teacher attitude

6.2.1 General patterns

Under the CDT model, the closer a teacher's determined disposition is to the centre of the converging spectrum, the more globalised is her/his view of the world and the more integrative she/he is of differing cultural perspectives on life, both in philosophy and action. Therefore, if the school wishes to have a teaching workforce that can educate students for the reality of the 21st century, the majority, if not all, of its teachers should have a transcultural disposition, or one very close to it. In terms of the model, that would mean that a teacher would have, at the very least, either an Independent Action-Community Focused (IC) disposition or a Collective Action-Individual Focused (CI) disposition. Both of these perspectives fall on either immediate side of the central disposition, that is transculturalism (TC). It is important to remember that these dispositions have transparent, transitionary boundaries; individuals can morph in and out of two adjoining CDTs over time as the life experiences and learnings change.

Nevertheless, a school that is prioritising the teaching of a 21st-century focused curriculum, with its essential acknowledgements of a culturally diverse society with a strong framework of globalised networks, would need to avoid having a teaching force that was situated mainly on either or both poles of the CDT spectrum: Independent Action-Individual Focused (IS) or Collective Action-Community Focused (CC). Both these distributions are extremes that suggest the teacher involved are too embedded in their own insulated outlook on the world, whether that be on themselves as individuals or on the community as a whole. To be transcultural is to be able to respond to the complexities of the modern cultural world, accepting the reality that any society will contain people from across all five cultural dispositions of thinking. To be transcultural, therefore, is to enable someone to live, work and interact with people from all cultural dispositions of thinking and not to be trapped within the attitudes of any one of them.

On that basis, the results from this research project are very encouraging. As illustrated in Figure 6.2, over 80% of all the teachers were found to exhibit the characteristics of either the TC, IC or Cultural disposition of thinking, with only a small minority (about 12%) being extremely individualistic (IS). The IC and TC categories accounted for nearly 75% participants together on their own. There were no teachers who were seen to exhibit characteristics that would place them in the extreme category of CC.

By and large, then, the majority of teachers in these globally oriented schools can be said to reflect the personal and professional perspectives that align with such an educational philosophy.

This overall pattern was reinforced when the pattern of CDT across teacher participants in each region is observed (see Tables 6.1 and 6.2). For the most part, the overall CDT distribution of teachers – that is, approximately 80% falling within the IC and TC categories, with the IC classification being dominant – was also the pattern in all the case studies (Table 6.1). The very low number of teacher participants in Singapore (Table 6.2) means that no general conclusion can be made about the pattern in that country within this study, although the IC classification for both participants was in line with the general trend.

120 Transcultural capacity of teachers

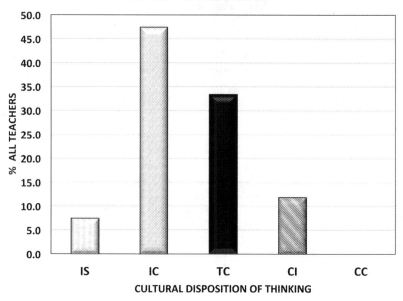

Figure 6.2 CDT of Teachers across All Regions by Percentage of Participants.

Regardless of this overall pattern, there were distinct variations in certain regions that are worth noting. Both Canada and New Zealand are the only case studies to have well over half their teacher participants exhibiting attitudes that reflect a transcultural disposition, even though their combination of IC and TC classifications aligns with the approximate 80% trend overall. They were also the only case studies with over 25% of participants with a more predominant collective-action perspective (CI). Hong Kong, even though 30% of its participants were classified as transcultural, was the only

Table 6.1 CDT of Teachers by Region – by Number of Teachers

	Region								
	Australia	Canada	Hong Kong	India	Malaysia	New Zealand	Sing	UK	CDT Subtotal
IS	1	0	4	0	1	0	2	2	10
IC	16	5	12	11	7	4	0	9	64
TC	8	16	3	4	2	10	0	2	45
CI	2	7	1	1	0	5	0	0	16
CC	0	0	0	0	0	0	0	0	0
Regional total	27	28	20	16	10	19	2	13	135

Table 6.2 CDT of Teachers by Region – by Percentage of Teachers

	\multicolumn{8}{c}{Region}	
	Australia	Canada	Hong Kong	India	Malaysia	New Zealand	Sing	UK	CDT Subtotal
IS	3.7	0.0	20.0	0.0	10.0	0.0	0.0	15.4	7.4
IC	59.3	17.9	60.0	68.8	70.0	21.1	100.0	69.2	47.4
TC	29.6	57.1	15.0	25.0	20.0	52.6	0.0	15.4	33.3
CI	7.4	25.0	5.0	6.3	0.0	26.3	0.0	0.0	11.9
CC	0.0	0.0	0.0	0.0	0.0	0.0	0.0	0.0	0.0
Regional total	100	100	100	100	100	100	100	100	100

case study to have 25% of its participants classified as either IS or highly individual-focused in both outlook and action.

For the purposes of this analysis, these observations will be treated as anomalies that will be discussed separately in Section 6.4, as some of the pertinent aspects of the discussion are also relevant to the findings outlined in Section 6.3.

6.3 The deeper characteristics of transcultural dispositions

As discussed in Chapter 5, two of the key characteristics of the transcultural perspective are a sense of global awareness or mindedness and a positive attitude to change and difference. On one level, a person's sense of globality encompasses the acceptance of globalisation as a process, both in terms of the reality that it has occurred and cannot be wound back, but also in terms of its multifaceted nature. It is not just an economic and social transformation, but one that has cultural, demographic, psychological and individual impacts. At a much deeper level, however, a sense of globality or global mindedness must incorporate an awareness that the impact of global events varies; they have different effects and influences on people and environments in different locations around the world. Not all are positive, and many are negative, or even destructive, on an individual or societal level. In that nuanced frame of understanding, a more comprehensive appreciation of global mindedness accepts and understands the differences that exist around the world as a *natural* state, a core concept within transcultural thinking; it is not just an acceptance of demographic cultural diversity.

In the same way that those with transcultural perspectives are more aware of the nuances in cultural action and cultural identity, being global minded does not mean that people try to perceive societal behaviour and action purely at the general or more holistic level. It does incorporate an understanding of the complexities of variation in world society, that the ways in which people react to global events are often determined by thoughts, actions and

122 Transcultural capacity of teachers

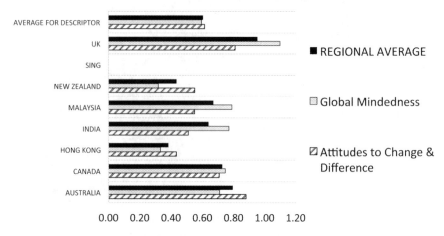

Figure 6.3 Attitudes of Teachers by Region: Global Mindedness and Change and Difference.

influences that are found at the local scale, and not just the global. In short, to be global minded in the transcultural sense is to accept societal difference, cultural and otherwise, as the norm and to not be surprised by its appearance; it sits hand in hand with the ability to adapt to new circumstances.

It was for these reasons that the online survey questions that sought to determine an individual's attitude towards global mindedness focused partly on how that person interpreted the impact of global concerns such as sustainability on human action and behaviour, including professional educational practice in the classroom. Likewise, the situations presented in terms of change and difference asked individuals to determine their attitudes to situations that were unexpected or not in line with that past experiences.

A summary of the attitudes of teachers to these two aspects of transcultural outlooks can be seen in Figure 6.3. As described in Chapter 5, the responses from teachers were processed mathematically to provide an average score for each transcultural outlook on a scale between negative 2 and positive 2. An individual who responded to each scenario and statement in a strongly transcultural fashion would receive an overall score of positive 2; on the other hand, teachers who responded to each scenario and statement in a strongly anti-transcultural fashion would receive a score of negative 2.

Figure 6.3 is based on the average individual score for each region in the measurement of the two transcultural perspectives of global mindedness and attitudes towards change and difference. It also provides an indication of the average score across the two measurements combined for each region. Figures 6.4 and 6.5 show the average scores for each individual perspective

Transcultural capacity of teachers 123

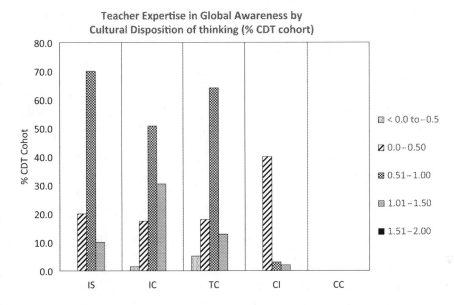

Figure 6.4 Attitudes of Teachers by CDT: Global Mindedness.

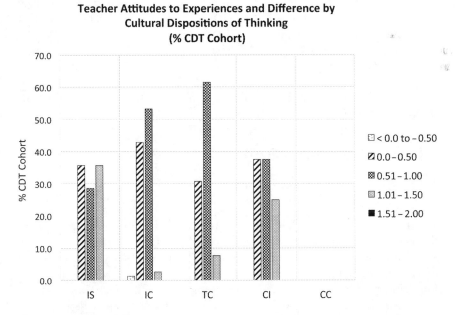

Figure 6.5 Attitudes of Teachers by CDT: Change and Difference.

according to the CDT assessments for the teacher participants. Across these three figures, there are several key patterns to be noted:

a   Scores for teacher attitudes towards change and difference tend to be lower in all regions than scores for global mindedness (Figure 6.3).
b   With one exception, no average score for either criterion was higher than 0.90, out of a possible score of 2.00. The exception was the United Kingdom, which has an average score above 1.00 for global mindedness and just above 0.9 for change and difference (Figures 6.3–6.5). On face value, this would suggest that nearly all teachers sampled had some degree of expertise in these two key aspects of transculturalism, but that relatively few teachers in the sample exhibited the full extent of their potential transcultural expertise; most demonstrated less than half their potential in this area.
c   The region that scored the lowest on each transcultural perspective was Hong Kong. No average score was recorded for Singapore because of the size of the sample and the lack of a survey response.
d   Despite its teacher sample overall having one of the highest proportional rates for transcultural disposition, New Zealand averages low scores on both criteria. Its average score for global mindedness is on a par with Malaysia and India, and its average score for change and difference is as low as Hong Kong.
e   As shown in Figures 6.4 and 6.5, average scores for both global mindedness and attitudes to change and difference are higher in the more transcultural dispositions (TC and IC). In both these CDTs, the great majority of teacher average scores were clustered between 0.50–1.00, out of a possible total score of 2.00. The proportion of teachers with scores higher than 1.00 was higher in the IC (30%) and TC (10%) categories.

Possible reasons for these finer patterns, along with the main overall trends outlined in Section 6.2, will now be discussed in Section 6.4.

6.4   Discussions and analysis

6.4.1   *General considerations*

In many respects, the finding that the vast majority of teachers across all the case study regions were either transcultural, or else one cultural disposition of thinking away from that central disposition, was confirmation of the direction and philosophy taken by the schools that were studied. As outlined earlier, all of the schools had a policy of teaching for 21st-century learning with some following established global education programs such as the International Baccalaureate. In Chapter 4, it was determined that, although the degree of intent varied between regions, all the schools and teachers involved in the study were following international and/or national curriculum frameworks that incorporated the learning of a global framework of citizenship and a broad acceptance of a culturally diverse society. In some cases, the extent of that cultural diversity was expressed in purely national terms, such as was the case in the United Kingdom (England) and India. In others, such as Australia and Canada, that national or provincial sense of cultural diversity was further developed into a global perspective, usually configured into the motion of what it meant to be a global or world citizen. Consequently, it is affirming to determine that the large majority of teachers in those schools, based on the sample, have the general expertise to meet those particular requirements of their school and national/regional educational system.

The variety of cultural dispositions of thinking evident in the teacher participants is also an indication of the reality of any teaching workforce. It would be impracticable and, in many ways, unethical, to assume that all the teachers within any particular jurisdiction would frame their attitudes towards life and education in very much the same way. Just as with any occupation in a society, teachers will represent all the various opinions and life outlooks that exist within that society. This is especially so when teachers across all sectors of school education are considered. It is possible and logical – but not self-evident – to assume that teachers in a particular school sector (that is, government or public, independent, both religious and non-denominational) may have a greater consistency of attitudes that are applicable to working with in that particular factor. For example, it is more probable that teachers working in Catholic schools are either of that faith or supportive of that faith; it is more likely that those who teach in government or public schools have an ethical preference for secular education provided for all, and it is likely that teachers who are working in schools that are international structural or educational philosophy are supportive of that global perspective. However, as an occupational group, teachers will inevitably represent the broad spectrum of opinions in a particular society. It is therefore unlikely and even utopian to expect that all teachers will ascribe to a particular point of view or outlook, whether that be towards cultural diversity or otherwise. Consequently, to find that there was a range of cultural dispositions within this set of sample schools is within the norms of expectation.

What is more significant, however, is that the three CDT groups that dominate the sample are all cultural dispositions that are more inclined to a positive perspective towards global mindedness and difference than not. So, whilst just over one third of the teacher participants were determined to be transcultural (see Figure 6.1), over 40% were thought to be IC (Individual Action-Community focus) and over 10% to CI. Both these dispositions contain a blend of the two opposing cultural perspectives (an individual or collective outlook) and therefore have some understanding, if not totally, of how to work within and across different cultural contexts. The dominance of the IC disposition as opposed to the CI perspective can be seen as a reflection that all the educational systems in the participant regions derived from a Euro-American or 'Western' perspective, or the influence of British philosophy of education, along with input from the North American and European contexts. The notion of individualism is fundamentally a 'Western' concept, and this is certainly a dominating force in the structures of national education, including curriculum, that were discussed in Chapter 4. It is therefore logical that this underlying sense of educated individualism permeated teacher attitudes, even if it is infused with a strong sense of community awareness and action, as embodied in the IC disposition.

Under this assumption, it would be expected that there would be a sign of more collective-oriented CDTs (CI and CC) amongst teachers from the educational systems that are not located geographically within the Euro-American geographical sphere; that is, in regions such as Asia, which has a greater prevalence of community and relationship cultures. However, that was not the case. Table 6.3 shows the breakdown of cultural dispositions by school and region, it is the former Anglo-European settler colonies of Canada and New Zealand that had the greater numbers of teachers who have a CI disposition.

Only 12% of teachers overall possessed a CI assessment (see Table 6.3); of that particular group, nearly half were in Canada and the third were in New Zealand. The teachers in Hong Kong, India, Malaysia and Singapore were together far more concentrated across the TC and IC cultural dispositions of thinking. The reasons for this apparent anomaly lie, I suggest, in the comparative attitudes of these countries towards cultural diversity in both education and, more fundamentally, their structure of society. In the provinces of Canada, as exemplified by Québec and Alberta (see discussion in Chapter 4), the educational systems mirror the emphasis placed by societal governments on teachers being able to teach students about and from the various cultural groups within the province, as well as Canada as a whole. The same emphasis on a program of education in provincial/national identity occurs in New Zealand, where the dual emphasis placed on Māori and European heritages as the bicultural foundation of New Zealand society, including education, means the teachers are required to have a deeper understanding of how New Zealand society sees cultural difference.

As outlined in Chapter 4, those expectations are embedded in the New Zealand national curriculum and its teacher education programs. No better demonstration of that unity of national spirit and acceptance of cultural diversity as the norm was shown by the reaction of the Christchurch community to the mass killing of Muslim New Zealanders in early 2019. One of the most striking images of the media coverage given to the community response to the horrors of that event was seeing New Zealand students from all cultural backgrounds and faiths performing the haka, a Māori dance of respect and unity, to the Muslim community. This embedded acceptance and importance placed on cultural diversity as the norm and

Table 6.3 CDT of Teachers by School and Region

	Australia			Canada			Hong Kong		India	Malaysia	New Zealand		Sing	UK	By number of teachers		By percentage of teachers
	AU-A	AU-B	AU-C	CN-A	CN-B	CN-C	HK-A	HK-B	IND	MAL	NZ-A	NZ-B	SG	UK	CDT Subtotal		CDT Subtotal
IS	0	1	0	0	0	0	2	2	0	1	0	0	2	2	10	IS	7.4
IC	5	7	4	1	2	2	6	6	11	7	3	1	0	9	64	IC	47.4
TC	3	2	3	5	5	6	2	1	4	2	3	7	0	2	45	TC	33.3
CI	0	0	2	3	2	2	0	1	1	0	3	2	0	0	16	CI	11.9
CC	0	0	0	0	0	0	0	0	0	0	0	0	0	0	0	CC	0.0
School total	8	10	9	9	9	10	10	10	16	10	9	10	2	13	135		100

value of a national society in the globalised world is also reflected in the high proportion (50% plus) of transcultural CDT found amongst the teacher participants from New Zealand.

The New Zealand's focus on national unity in acceptance of cultural diversity, and the success of that principle, also suggests a possible reason for why New Zealand scored relatively lower than other regions on assessments of teacher global mindedness and attitudes to change to and difference (Figure 6.3). In their interviews, many of the New Zealand teachers referred to the importance of local community in their school and New Zealand in general, reflecting the significant influence of Māori and Pacific Islander cultures in their sense of identity. Moreover, there was a consistent sense of purpose expressed about the value of communities at different levels, whether this be personal

> Because what (husband) and I often say is that, while I align to Māori values, they're not exclusive to Māori. So, my family is a big, big extended family who are very much part of my life as well. We share food together, and events together, and celebrations together, and they're as part of me … a big part of both of us is the importance of family and extended family … and we all go back, so the whole family …. (Teacher NZ-104)

or within the school:

> So, we have at the beginning of every term, a powhiri … that welcomes new family. It welcomes new students; it welcomes new staff. It's a formal setting, but we do it in our own way, but it's a Māori way of greeting … it's become a really important thing for parents. (Teacher NZ-104)

Culture is seen as a multi-layered concept that is embedded in the daily lives of New Zealanders, with self-determination of identity being fundamental to that principle:

> Their culture is who they are and their surroundings … how they perceive themselves … it's their family, it's their schooling, it's everything, and ethnicity is just a small part of it … it is really hard to think of culture as an ethnic thing. (Teacher NZ-113)

This emphasis on the significance of local community in an embedded multicultural society might therefore provide a national context for teaching about transcultural perspectives, with little need to move into a more comprehensive global context, beyond the close ties that New Zealand has with its Pacific Island nation neighbours. This is not to say that New Zealand teachers are purely nationally focused; however, as will be discussed later, global travel has not played an important part in the personal and professional lives of the

New Zealand teachers surveyed, as it has for participants in other case studies, regardless of the high degree of transcultural capacity evident amongst the New Zealand teacher participants. The findings do suggest that the development of transcultural perspectives in a local context is possible in a highly multicultural milieu where cultural difference is viewed transculturally, as a societal norm and not as a deviation from national homogeneity.

Overall, the highest counts of transcultural or transculturally adjacent dispositions were found in educational jurisdictions of societies that not only accepted the importance of cultural diversity, but have institutionalised that belief into the structure of societal governance and educational provision. Consequently, the great diversity of cultural and ethnic groups within India and the trio of cultural heritages in Malaysian society (even if Malay heritage is emphasised for the stated purposes of equity) are reflected in both educational regions having over 90% of their teachers being classified as being either TC or IC. In contrast, the teachers of Hong Kong show a distribution of CDTs that is skewed towards the individualised pole of the CDT spectrum; both schools have 80% of the teacher participants falling into the IS and IC bands.

In the same vein of argument applied to Canada and New Zealand, this difference in emphasis towards the significance of cultural diversity can be seen as reflecting the greater uniformity of Hong Kong society in terms of culture and ethnic composition. Its population is essentially of Chinese heritage (94%), with the only significant difference being between those who have a long history of Hong Kong connection and those who are from migrant families from mainland China. The remaining 6% are primarily made up of immigrants from India, Pakistan and Nepal, as well as domestic servants from the Philippines, Thailand and Indonesia (Sui-Chu Ho, 2016, p. 74). Such differences are significant enough in Hong Kong society for schools and teachers to reflect upon such factors as teaching and learning design. One principal saw a difference in how parents approached schools about their child's education, with Hong Kong families being '... very protective for them. So, this(sic) kind of children is very timid' (Teacher HK-65). Language is also a barrier: '... some students from mainland China are not as proficient in English ... It's hard to bridge the gap of the diversity so it's one thing to bridge the gap and it's another thing to teach those native speakers something new' (Teacher HK-72). This uniformity of heritage is, however, showing signs of change, placing new demands on teachers who are not used to teaching in a culturally diverse environment:

> multicultural schools are new phenomenon in Hong Kong. In the past, usually local students go to these schools, ex-patriate students go to those schools. People from South Asia go to those schools. We have some government primary schools and secondary schools specially catering for South Africans ... But now things are changing. Why? Because some

schools like ours are having the problem of falling enrolment. We do not have enough local students. (Teacher HK-75)

The more constrained context of the foundation of Hong Kong society also suggests an explanation for why the scores for Hong Kong teachers in the areas of global mindedness and attitudes towards change and difference were distinctively lower than in any other educational jurisdictions (see Figure 6.2). Given the position and role of Hong Kong as an international business hub, the growth and success of which depends upon its global outreach, these more inward-looking perspectives may seem to be somewhat of a paradox. However, the value of English as a life tool and academic success in general is also declining, which suggests a possible future shift in the status of Hong Kong as a globally outward-looking region. Past research has suggested that the children of mainland Chinese migrants have been motivated to educate themselves in Hong Kong because '… they realise that good academic qualifications are necessary for improving their standard of living' (Sui-Chu Ho, 2016, p. 83). However, several Hong Kong teachers mentioned in the course of the interviews that they were seeing a shift:

Nowadays they have more opportunities to do other things ... they don't see education as the most important thing in life. People usually consider a good education as the only way to change their lives, so to speak. But nowadays they think that there are other ways ... They can go to insurance. They can become an estate agent and so on. And all these people in Hong Kong make a lot of money .... (Teacher HK-75)

These new points of separation in a formerly homogenous Hong Kong-style Chinese-heritage society are also having other educational impacts because, along with the generational changes since the re-absorption of Hong Kong into China in 1997, they have created multiple groups of students with different needs. The children of Hong Kong immigrants now include those with at least one parent living in mainland China, those who have arrived in Hong Kong in the last few years, and the children of all the non-Chinese residents (Yuet-Mui Yuen, 2016, p. 201). The divisions are accentuated by the advantages held by those who can speak English, who:

... normally belong to the upper class .... Their parents probably speak English as well. So, these people have a better command of English normally ... and choose to study overseas. Those who don't ... cannot go into a local university, (and) tend to go to China and Taiwan nowadays. More and more people are doing this. Our students like to go to China and Taiwan very much, because often they are not that bad in science subjects, or in history, geography, and so on. But they almost always fail English. So, they cannot get into a local university. They cannot go to an overseas university. But in China and Taiwan, English doesn't count. At least not as heavily. (Teacher HK-75)

6.4.2 *The significance of exposure to cultural diversity*

As discussed in Chapter 5, previous studies have shown the value and importance of serving and pre-service teachers experiencing different cultural environments as a means of developing the cultural capacity (see Section 5.3.1). These conclusions are strengthened by the findings of this research project into two particular ways: firstly, that there is a correlation between degree of transcultural outlook in a person and the professional travel experience of the teacher participants; and secondly, that the value of new cultural experiences is reflected in their attitudes in respect of their pedagogical strategies for enabling students to learn about and accept cultural diversity as a societal norm.

6.4.2.1 *Personal and professional travel experience*

One of the strongest patterns revealed by the project was confirmation that teachers' openness to cultural difference is greatly influenced by the degree of their personal and travel experience outside the location of their cultural or birth origins. In the course of the survey and interview, teacher participants were asked to nominate regions and countries to which they had travelled in specific detail. Consequently, it was possible to identify precisely the degree and extent of an individual's travel experience. As illustrated in Figure 6.6, teachers who were either transcultural or very close to that cultural disposition (TC, IC or CI) had all undertaken personal or professional travel.

Further, whereas a large proportion of the teachers in each of the four cultural dispositions identified had travelled within up to four regions (Figure 6.5), the teachers who were transcultural or IC in disposition with the only groups to have travelled up to eight different regions (Figure 6.7). It was these teachers who were far more varied in their travel and therefore cultural experiences; for instance, it was these teachers who had travelled to more than one continent rather than, as an example, focusing the geographical extent of their travel experiences on Europe, no matter how comprehensive their coverage of that continent might have been.

The impact of these travel experiences was reflected in the comments made by participants about how their views about culture, cultural difference and their own cultural identity had been influenced by travel, with several themes prominent. One of these was the impact of travel on their notion of global society by opening their eyes to cultural diversity:

> ... it gave me a very acute understanding of what it is to be a world citizen, but also an acute understanding of the importance of roots. (Teacher UK-123)

132　Transcultural capacity of teachers

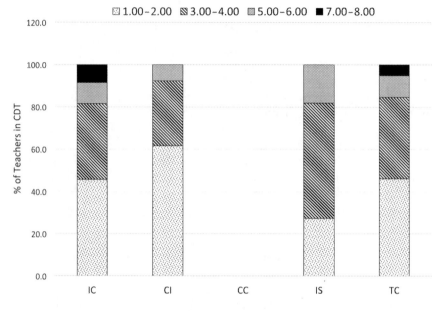

Figure 6.6 Number of Regions Visited by Cultural Disposition of Thinking (Percentage of Teachers in CDT).

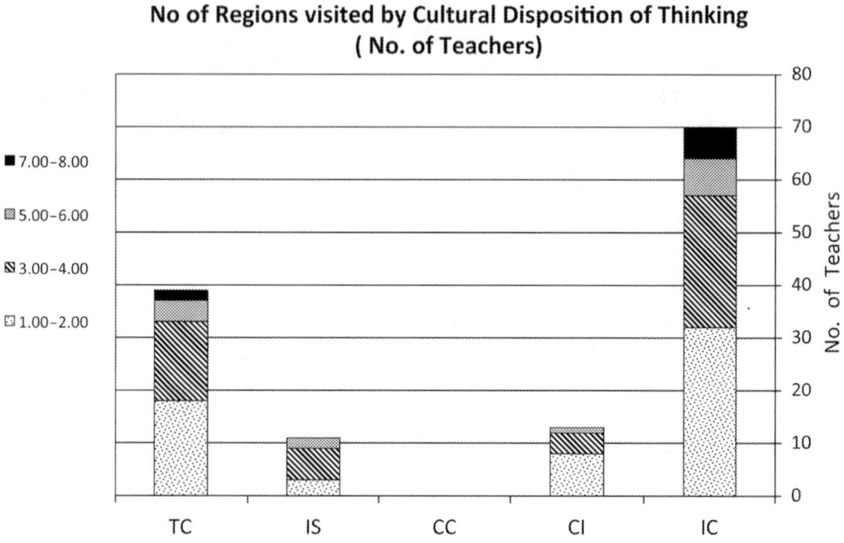

Figure 6.7 Number of Regions Visited by Cultural Disposition of Thinking (Number of Teachers in CDT).

it changed my view of the world ... my ability to communicate with people from different backgrounds and enjoy the diversity of the people on this planet. (Teacher UK-131)

... going to these countries opened my mind, opened my mind to possibilities in the field of education .... (Teacher SG-121)

... what I've brought back to school and teaching from that is an appreciation of differences. So just it's always sort of in my mind and on my radar that people live differently. (Teacher AU-05)

Knowing that the world is a much larger place then Singapore. (Teacher SG-122)

A second theme was the influence of travel on their notion of culture and identity, inevitably freeing it up by emphasising the varied nature and fluidity of the term around the world:

Travel is very enriching. It breaks down lots of barriers in people's thinking, I think. You can't really understand a culture until you've lived in it and been part of it. (Teacher NZ-121)

... we have these sort of characteristics and it's easy to define ourselves around these characteristics. It's easy to define the 'Other' as not belonging. So ... culture (was) created to make people feel they belong. (Teacher AU-14)

... cultures .... obviously there's language, there's religion, there's geographic background and you throw them into a melting pot. Even politics and other things can create a series of circumstances that define a people. The further you travel, the more you realise probably there's not one whole definition. (Teacher AU-10)

In opening up teachers' perspectives on culture and the world, though, the impacts on some participants were far more profound, opening up new confidences in their own identity, cultural and otherwise:

In my faculty I was the only Malay Malaysian, and I mixed around with the British and the national, international students. And that really ... boost(ed) my confidence level ... I could become like a new me. (Teacher MZL-92)

It makes you look at the larger purpose for education, look at how there is a constant change in the global landscape, and also look at how our children should be prepped for that kind of experience. To look at things from a broader perspective. (Teacher IND-79)

... normally in Hong Kong, the pace is fast, and we expect everything to be done efficiently ... when I was in Sweden, I needed to queue up like for two hours just to get the key for my hostel room. At that time,

I it was quite uneasy for me because I didn't expect that to take a long time. (Teacher HK-58)

The cultural experience alone, working alongside so many different nationalities; people I'm best friends with, people from around the world... (Teacher CN-46)

However, further analysis of these travel patterns also indicates that there are hidden nuances to the possible influence of travel on transcultural capacity. Earlier, it was established that case studies such as Canada and New Zealand had the highest proportions of teachers with transcultural or near transcultural capacities, with the United Kingdom also well represented (Tables 6.1 and 6.2). Nevertheless, it was then determined that, in terms of global mindedness, along with attitudes towards change and difference, teachers in regions such as Canada and New Zealand did not score as high as teachers in the United Kingdom, Malaysia and India. An explanation for this apparent paradox can be seen in Figures 6.8 and 6.9, which show the travel experience of teacher participants in each case study, illustrated in both numbers and proportions of teachers.

The patterns in Figures 6.8 and 6.9 show that the pattern of teacher travel experience by CDT hides the fact that most teachers in the research sample had not been to more than four different regions, a figure that includes their location of work and (if different) their origin of birth. There was great consistency on this point across Australia, Canada, Hong Kong and Singapore. New Zealand and India are strikingly different with 80% or more of teacher participants not having travelled to more than one country. In contrast, teachers in both United Kingdom and Malaysia all had extensive travel experience and were the only case studies to have teachers who had travelled to eight regions. This depth of variation in travel experience offers an explanation for why, as identified earlier, teachers from these two countries scored high on global mindedness and attitudes to change and difference. The extent of their outlook had been influenced by the greater range of cultural differences that they had experienced.

The limitations of the sample size in each case study notwithstanding, these seeming contradictions suggest two important conclusions about the role of travel in building transcultural capacity:

a Extensive travel into places outside one's place of cultural origin has a clear impact on the development of global mindedness and positive attitudes towards change and difference. The degree of impact is dependent upon the variety of culturally different places that comprises that pattern of trouble; the more diverse the range of cultural experiences, the greater the development of transcultural perspectives.
b The development of transcultural perspectives within teachers is possible without the benefit of extensive international travel, if certain conditions are present.

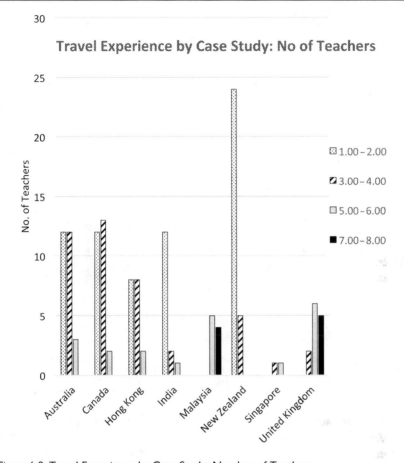

Figure 6.8 Travel Experience by Case Study: Number of Teachers.

The nature of such conditions and the wider implications of these conclusions for the development of transcultural capacity in teachers will be discussed in Chapter 7.

6.4.2.2 *Living and meeting cultural difference*

A corollary of the travel experiences that were a feature of the nearly all teacher participants in the project was their influence on teachers' pedagogical conceptions of how best to teach people about the nature and value of cultural diversity as a natural feature of a society. One of the key interview questions asked teacher participants to reflect on whether knowledge, understanding and *acceptance* of cultural difference was best achieved by people just meeting cultural difference or whether it was far more

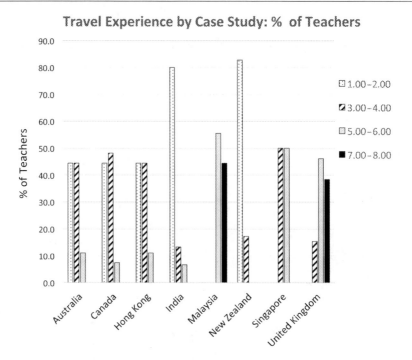

Figure 6.9 Travel Experience by Case Study: Percentage of Teachers.

important for them to live cultural difference. The concept of meeting or living difference was left to the individual to interpret as they saw fit; however, if explanations were requested, the notion of meeting difference was defined as simply introducing and illustrating different ways in which people lived to students, whether that be by conducting classroom activities or by more cursory visits to different areas. Living difference was defined as experiences that embedded an individual in the life of another culture, even for a short time.

As Figures 6.10 and 6.11 show, the vast majority and proportion of teacher participants, especially those identified as being TC or IC in their cultural dispositions, saw *living* difference as being the more effective avenue to cultural knowledge and understanding than just meeting with cultural difference; it was the only way in which people could learn and understand the significance of what it was to be in a culturally different place. In particular, they highlighted the value of living difference in eradicating stereotypical assumptions that there is only one 'right' way to live: 'There's a big wide world out there, and people look different, speak differently, behave differently, have different morals, values, et cetera. And our way isn't necessarily

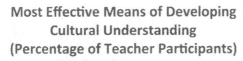

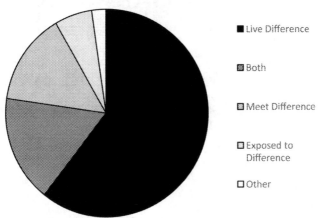

Figure 6.10 Living or Meeting Difference: Most Effective Means of Developing Cultural Understanding by Percentage of All Teacher Participants.

the right way' (Teacher AU-8). In gaining an appreciation of how others live and see the world, '... it (gives) them the tools to understand other people's cultures too, so they can relate better to them as people ... helps them grow as learners' (Teacher NZ-107). Living cultural difference is more effective than simply meeting it at face value because it is learning by doing, and is not a mere presentation of facts:

> I'm a strong believer of exponential learning ... exponential learning requires you to have a chance to link ... using the external environment, linking the external environment through your senses, the five senses, ... the filter through which you link the external environment to your internal environment. When that clicks, you're able to empathise with the situation and empathy is achieved ... you have a better understanding of the issues, you'll be able to differentiate, talk about the differences and link with it. (Teacher SG-01)

> I think they have to live it because I don't – I'm Māori. I don't live like a Samoan or a Tongan person but my kids in my class help me and you have to use what they know. So, yes, I research things for Samoan language week, but I go to my kids who can fluently speak – their parents to help me out, bring in their parents to help teach things because that's their culture, not mine. Even though I'm facilitating that learning,

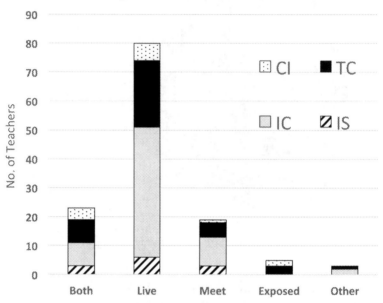

Figure 6.11 Living or Meeting Difference: Most Effective Means of Developing Cultural Understanding by Number of Teachers and CDT.

> I don't live it and I'm not a part of it but the kids in my class are. So, what I try to do is work on their strengths and some of my kids are fluent in Samoan, so they'll help me with the words. They'll help me understand what I'm trying to say or what I'm trying to teach and how to teach it properly. (Teacher NZ-108)

What Figures 6.10 and 6.11 also show, though, is that many teachers with these same CDTs saw learning about cultural understanding to be a multi-part process that was usually ongoing. A school may enable a child (or teacher) to meet cultural difference and thereby develop a basic appreciation and understanding about cultural difference, but it was usually later in life that people might act upon that beginning and improve their cultural capacity:

> … experiencing it as an adult, I think you get it so much more if you're actually in it. Because it creates that empathy as well, you actually – you're

not just seeing theories of how different people live, but you're actually experiencing it yourself. (Teacher AU-4)

Others extended the idea of merely 'living' cultural difference to one step further: the significant benefits of *immersion* in cultural difference. Nevertheless, such a goal could only be achieved through a dual approach of meeting and living difference within the school:

> There's nothing like experiencing it. It's nothing like being immersed in something. But I think it has to be a combination of both. But with technology, they can do so much, even in a primary school. You try and have that combination of drawing on what's happening in your school, the people in your school, or in your community. (Teacher AU-8)

Despite the overwhelming support for *living* cultural difference, it is not the case that teacher participants were unaware of the difficulties involved in creating such educational experiences within the school environment:

> There's a kind of gap there, meeting and living ... clearly learning by doing is something, which is helpful, but there are certain things culturally that it can sometimes be difficult for students to actually 'live'. The closer you get to the living, the better, I think. (UK-123)

Many pointed out the cost of activities such as overseas trips for students and staff, but others also suggested that such circumstances were not barriers to creating culturally different experiences for students and schools and it is up to schools to do what they can. It was more a matter of taking children out of their zone of cultural comfort with them a safe space and giving them the opportunity to 'live' the feeling of cultural uneasiness:

> At primary school we can introduce the kids to it, so they can meet it and they can see the differences. And if they want to then go and extend their learning, then they can. They could go onto to then living it. (NZ-116)

In the garden of cultural education, teachers can 'just put these seeds into their heads so that they can start looking, and that's what I mean by education' (Teacher MAL-96). Schools are unable to do everything because of the inevitable time and other resource restraints, but they can set the foundation for future lifelong learning: 'Having gone and lived difference in Africa, I can say living it has definitely more of an impact, so you do what you can do, but in this environment the best we can do is have them meet (cultural difference)'. (Teacher CN-34)

Within this broad pattern, there were a handful of teacher participants who argued that the act of teachers organising opportunities for school students to meet or live cultural difference should not be, and was not necessarily, the key point in developing cultural capacity. They argued that it was the teacher as a role model of behaviour and a person with demonstrated cultural capacity, that was more important and far more influential. In other words, it was not necessarily the pedagogical or professional expertise of the teacher that was the crucial factor, but their transcultural capacity- as illustrated by their personal behaviour - that was more fundamental in encouraging students to develop their own transcultural ability:

> If you are a good teacher and have good pedagogy, then it's just a part of what you do in your classroom, and it is tipped into that cultural identity/cultural capital that your students have. You create that understanding with the children that you have in class because you're giving them an opportunity to share about them, to talk about their culture. (Teacher AU-102)

With three Indian teachers, that translated into ensuring that older, discriminatory cultural practices such as the caste system were not evident in their classrooms:

> In my classroom, irrespective of your caste, creed or …. or where you stand in the community in terms of your economy, it's secondary for me. All of you are equal. There are certain rules which are to be followed when you are – you are all in uniform … you're wearing a uniform that means we are all in the same level … If you speak in a very mean way, I think that shows your culture. So, I think we (teachers) have to be, as a human being, more open. (Teacher IND-82)
>
> It is more important for us is to respect different cultures here. It's about the way we do things here … we are more focusing on how we need to be managing ourselves or, if you so call it, developing (students') emotional intelligence in terms of respecting and accepting cultures. (Teacher IND-83)
>
> The way we put across should be to see every religion and every culture (as equal). You should be good; you should do good deeds. At the end of the day, that is what it should be. How we are going to put across to the kids, that's very important. (Teacher IND-77)

For a teacher in New Zealand, it was important to make those transcultural values visible to the student:

> … it's not just about talking about it – it is living it and it's making it, in your classroom – and I'm speaking from a teachers' perspective. It needs

to be seen, it needs to be heard, it needs to be part of your everyday. (Teacher NZ-102)

Others expressed the view that making general statements about the choice between meeting and living cultural difference was not the main concern, because the classroom practices of teachers needed to be based on the context and needs of the students in their own school, which were not necessarily the same that were present in another school. For a New Zealand teacher, the multicultural nature of her school might have reflected the diversity of New Zealand society, but it did not reflect the complexity of the world elsewhere:

> They're not fully exposed to that ... they meet kids in class who are from a certain place or from somewhere else and have a different religion, but ... not ... the mass numbers of it. In London, I could sit on a bus ...and there could be 50 different people speaking 50 different languages. (Teacher NZ-105)

6.5 Conclusion

The extent of the information gathered from the extensive mixed methods research underpinning this project is such that it will provide data for future consideration and publication for some time to come. As stated earlier, the focus of this particular monograph and its context is the ability of school educators to undertake the teaching of cultural understanding and to isolate some of the qualities that comprise that expertise. To date, the findings indicate that there is variation amongst schoolteachers in their capacity to teach cultural knowledge, understanding and acceptance in an transcultural manner that is both relevant and appropriate to world society in the middle part of the 21st century, a world in which cultural diversity must be accepted as the norm and not treated as a problem of exception. This variation exists even in schools that operate under educational philosophies and programs that acknowledge the particular conditions of this time in history and the influence that it is having on the demands for education. The project has also reinforced past research that there are certain parameters that seem to encourage and promote the development of transcultural capacities in teachers, especially those relating to personal and professional travel to areas and cultural environments outside that place of origin. The question remains, however, is how to translate these patterns into practical and practicable educational systems and practices that will better enable school educators to be prepared to teach in the world of the 21st century, with particular attention to the demand for that expertise in teaching within, about and for the acceptance and reality of cultural diversity. That debate will be the subject of the final chapter of this monograph.

References

Casinader, N. (2014). *Culture, Transnational Education and Thinking: Case Studies in Global Schooling*. Milton Park, Abingdon: Routledge. (Reprinted by permission.)

Darwin, J. (2012). *Unfinished Empire: The Global Expansion of Britain*. London, England: Penguin.

Sui-Chu Ho, E. (2016). In search of equal and excellent basic education in Hong Kong. In M. Kwan-Choi Tse & M. H. Lee (Eds.), *Making Sense of Education in Post-Handover Hong Kong* (pp. 73–94). London, England: Routledge.

Yuet-Mui Yuen, C. (2016). Changing student diversity, changing cultures and changing education policies. In M. Kwan-Choi Tse & M. H. Lee (Eds.), *Making Sense of Education in Post-Handover Hong Kong* (pp. 200–214). London, England: Routledge.

Chapter 7

Building transcultural capacity in teachers

Implications for teacher education and professional learning

7.1 Overview

The primary drive for the research on which this monograph is based was twofold: first, a belief that school education in cultural understanding has become increasingly essential as a result of the impact of globalisation on the cultural demography of local and world society; and second, a concern that teachers in the modern age were lacking the professional expertise to take on that responsibility. As has been argued in Chapters 1 and 2, the teaching of cultural understanding is not a new addition to the expectations and obligations of a teacher. Within the context of this research, which is positioned on the legacy of education in the British idiom, there has always been an element in the role of a teacher that is focused on the teaching of cultural expectations in knowledge, skills and behaviour. What has been transformed, however, is the focus of that cultural understanding. Up until the mid-20th century, within the British historical sphere, the notion of cultural understanding in the educational context was primarily centred around the transmission of culture, one that reflected the supposed British imaginary or way of thinking, or the communication and reinforcement of a specific way of life. It was not until the globalised context of the World War II and its post-conflict tensions, which, for the first time, saw the world teetering on the brink of possible human extinction, that the central goal of education and cultural understanding began to evolve into a wider context. It transitioned into one that was designed to create an understanding and acceptance of others, with the intention of reducing and hopefully removing the ignorance and national insularities that had led to armed global conflict.

By the middle of the first decade of the 21st century, the expectations about cultural understanding had become widespread enough to be incorporated into the national educational frameworks of a number of countries. The case studies in this particular research project span four continents, the societies and educational systems of which had their origins in British society more specifically, and Euro-American (Western) attitudes more generally. Despite this, the multitudinous threads of debate, argument and conflict surrounding the nature of what cultural education in schools have meant that, in the views of this researcher and others, the field has become mired in outdated and irrelevant conceptions of culture that are not appropriate for the world of the 21st century. That same confusion has also led to an expectation that teachers will somehow naturally have the expertise to deal with a demographic phenomenon that was unprecedented in world history, an expectation that is based on certain assumptions about the nature of culture and the impact of contemporary globalisation on cultural identity. It is that particular expectation that has been the core challenge addressed by this monograph, commencing with the proposition that school teachers need to possess a new form of cultural expertise, that of transculturalism, in order to have the capacity to deal with the circumstances surrounding the need for cultural education in the middle of the 21st century.

In the context of what has been conceived as the first phase of an ongoing research project, the primary foundations of this research were essentially optimistic. It hypothesised that schools that were actively involved in the teaching of a curriculum and educational philosophy that emphasised the characteristics of a contemporary and globalised world society would be more likely to have teachers that had the expertise to implement such an educational mission. Nonetheless, as discussed in Chapter 6, the findings of the research project have highlighted three central aspects about the comparative state of teacher transcultural capacity:

1 Whilst teachers within these contemporarily focused schools had some degree of transcultural expertise, a sizeable proportion had gaps in their knowledge, skills and attitudes that meant that their proficiency had only been developed to approximately 50% of their potential. Given the range of contexts in which these teachers were working (see Chapters 5 and 6), it suggested that the reasons for this gap could not just be put down to either length of career or lack of educational experience. As illustrated in Figure 7.1, all of the cultural dispositions comprised teachers who represented a wide range of teaching experience, from less than 5 years to over 21 years. Educational ability based on length of experience was therefore of little significance in determining degree of transcultural capacity. Instead, the reasons must lie in the nature of teacher education programs and/or professional learning and development opportunities that are provided to and undertaken by teachers in the course of their career.
2 Transcultural expertise was more developed in teachers who had undertaken experienced high degrees of personal and professional international travel. Such involvements also gave teachers a more advanced knowledge and understanding of global mindedness as well as a greater appreciation of the nature and value of change in difference in human societies.
3 Nonetheless, there were a number of teachers, especially in Canada and New Zealand, who had developed a high degree of transcultural

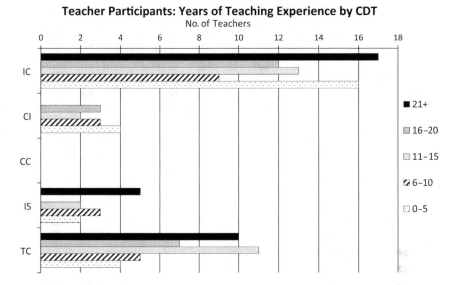

Figure 7.1 Teacher Participants: Years of Teaching Experience by CDT.

capacity and yet had not undertaken a great deal of international travel. This suggests that there are other factors, aside from international travel, that can also create the conditions and contacts for the development of transcultural expertise.

7.2 Cultural displacement: the basis of developing expertise in cultural diversity as the norm

7.2.1 The existing evidence

The principle that cultural understanding can be developed within school educators through programs that facilitate international travel experiences is one that has been investigated and discussed previously. The conclusions have been consistently positive, with travel experience leading to increased cultural literacy (Halse et al., 2015). The pattern of improvement appears to be uniform, whether the programs are designed for pre-service teachers during their teacher education courses, or as professional development for teachers working in schools. The research also seems to indicate that this development of expertise is observable in all teachers, regardless of the cultural context of the educational systems in which they are being educated or in which they teach, and regardless of whether they are from within the Euro-American paradigm. Research in the Republic of Korea has found, for instance, that the more they interact and live with foreign nationals, the greater is the South Korean tolerance for being part of a multicultural environment, an attitude that was not a feature of Korean traditional society and culture (Kim & Jeon, 2017)

One of the major points on which researchers agree is that any measure taken to develop a teacher's cultural understanding must lead to a renovation of attitude and outlook within the individual. It is not just about gaining more content knowledge about cultural understanding, which can be equated with multicultural knowledge, but is more '... a transformation of the external formal knowledge into something much more meaningful ... personal intellectual growth ... it is about reconstruction and reconceptualisation within the teacher' (Adeleman Reyes, Capellla-Santana, & Khisty, 1998, p. 112). This is one reason why the notion of attaining 'cultural competence' by doing a single certification or course is unrealistic and an oversimplification of what cultural understanding actually means. A transformation in attitude is not instantaneous and occurs gradually over time, not as a consequence of a single act. Whatever initiatives are put into place must 'jolt' the teacher out of existing assumptions and habits, as '... being entrenched in one's own culture can be a barrier to responding to cultural difference' (Tambyah, 2019, p. 120); they need to develop an heightened awareness of the existence and implications of issues relating to cultural identity, which can become far more acute with increasing cultural diversity within a place (Halse, 1999). The value and impact of living and working in international environments are effective measures because they highlight '... the diversity of human experiences, [the] demands of personal examination of one's own values and [the] recognition of sociopolitical realities and power relationships within our society' (Guillaume, Zuniga, & Yee, 1998, p. 156). Through such experiences, teachers – regardless of the length of their teaching careers – have their '... eyes ... opened to others' beliefs and educational practices – others' way of thinking, doing, and being. They [step] outside of their comfort zones and [stretch] their personal and professional limits in ways conventional student teaching could never achieve' (Stachowski & Sparks, 2007, p. 131).

In order to achieve the maximum impact of using international travel as a developer of cultural understanding, whether that be multicultural, intercultural or transcultural, the general agreement has long been that such programs cannot be left to chance or casual osmosis:

> Despite the cost and organisational complexity of setting up these programmes, a tightly structured international practicum in a 'similar but different' setting alerts pre-service teachers to the complexities of teaching for cultural and socio-economic diversity as part of teachers' knowledge. (Tambyah, 2019 p. 120)

The results of a targeted approach are substantial, with teachers being affected on a range of personal and professional levels: '... increased confidence, a better appreciation and respect for differences of others and other cultures, and an awareness of the importance that feedback and reflection play in professional and personal growth' (Pence & Macgillivray, 2001, p. 23).

For teachers in schools, the success of any professional development is determined by the expertise and guidance of the school leadership:

> … principals and teachers with extensive experience with ethnic diversity and intercultural situations inside and outside of school were more aware and proactively engaged in building the intercultural capabilities. This was vividly illustrated in two schools where the principals had experienced the intercultural benefits of overseas study and supported their less experienced teachers to also do an overseas study tour, all of whom returned to take up intercultural leadership roles in their schools. (Halse et al., 2015, p. 43)

Nevertheless, in spite of this general approval of the usefulness of international life experiences in building cultural capacity, research has also indicated a number of potential flaws in the strategy, all of which are interdependent to some degree. In the first place, whether undertaken in teacher education or as professional learning for career teachers, the process is inherently self-selective. International travel, especially if designed to incorporate a period of residence in a specific place and interaction with locals, is resource intensive, both in terms of time and money. This means that, unless the cost of travel is covered by a third party, a teacher's ability to undertake such professional learning is limited by the extent of their financial resources. Furthermore, unless the international program is compulsory, it is more likely that those who volunteer for such opportunities are those who possess some degree of cultural expertise and wish to employ or extend it (Casinader & Clemans, 2018). The teachers who might accompany students on school-organised, study-based overseas trips are themselves selected on the basis of a range of other factors, including reliability, organizational ability and rapport with students; possessing any assessed degree of cultural capacity may not be one of the significant criteria, even if the experience proved to be invaluable in developing their own transcultural expertise (Casinader, 2018). A study of pre-service teachers who applied for an international school placement as part of their undergraduate course showed that those '… who are inclined to apply for optional international placement experiences tend to already possess a prior degree of transcultural thinking and attitudes as a result of their prior personal and/or professional, life experience' and that '… recruitment strategies should consider intentional targeting of students for whom international travel is less familiar …' (Casinader & Clemans, 2018, p. 605), along with an evaluation of the students' previous cross-cultural activities.

Length of time spent abroad and the background and perspective of those who were constructing the learning program internationally have also been noted as concerns. Researchers such as Fabregas Janeiro, Lopez Fabre, and Nuño de la Parra (2014) have argued that stays that are of less than 3 months' duration are not effective. Although short-term stays do have a '... positive effect on emotional and intellectual growth of preservice teachers ...,' they do not facilitate deep cultural understandings or interactions (Malewski & Phillon, 2009, p. 58). They may '... increase knowledge but do not necessarily promote respect for cultural diversity, positive attitudes or behaviour, or develop the skills to work with diverse students' (Ohi et al., 2019, p. 242). This superficiality of short overseas tours was highlighted by one of the Australian teacher participants. Although he was speaking initially in the context of developing the cultural understandings of students, his point was made with a wider context in mind:

> I'm dead set against taking kids on tours. I just think, do that with your family ... I would much rather them go and have a lived experience in a homestay overseas, for however long, and get to know people at a deeper level and form bonds with people. I'd rather these kids go to France for longer, meet up with some former colleagues of mine that I've been working with and have that really fantastic experience and a reciprocal experience. I think that is probably what I consider to be lived experience and exposure to culture. And hopefully, some understandings will come. [Teacher AU-14]

The research outlined in this book reveals that study abroad does not invariably lead to shared cultural understandings or interpretations. Additionally, the planning of a program that does not involve the input and knowledge of people from the cultural milieu being visited (Melnick & Zeichner, 1997) is being framed purely on an outsider's perception of difference in the area and culture(s) being visited, with opportunities for genuine learning and understanding about difference being lost.

7.2.2 The notion of cultural displacement

Whether undertaken personally or professionally, as part of a course or a professional learning opportunity, the success of international travel experiences in developing some degree of cultural capacity means that the basic principle of that experience needs to be somehow employed in any cultural education program. As this monograph has outlined, though, there are other ways of developing transcultural attitudes within teachers than a pure focus on international travel, for the teachers in Canada and New Zealand had one of the lowest levels of international travel experience and yet they contained the highest proportions of school educators with a transcultural disposition of thinking. In order to develop a more contemporary and relevant transcultural perspective, such initiatives must go beyond the superficial and obvious. The transformation in attitude that is embedded in transculturalism – the outlook that cultural difference is not only a societal norm, but should not be seen as a problem or barrier – does not evolve naturally from just gaining knowledge about other cultural environments (multiculturalism) or the way in which different cultures can connect and interact (interculturalism). It comes from a realisation about the nuances of cultural difference, the impact that these can have on people's lives and how this matter is reflected educationally, ideas that are often identified as the ultimate aim of any international experience; teachers are learning about '… borderland pedagogies that integrate processes of dialoguing, reflecting, posing questions, position-taking, and building bridges to connect the intellectual with the experiential and to connect the work of the classroom to local communities' (Hardee, Thompson, Jennings, Aragon, & Brantmeier, 2012, p. 218).

The essence of the catalyst that drives that transformation is *cultural displacement* or cultural dislocation, the learnings that derive from physically and psychologically being embedded in a culturally unfamiliar environment for a period of time. By participating in such experiences – for it has to occur on multiple occasions – an individual deliberately challenges their own knowledge, expectations and assumptions as to what is the norm, what is different and what is likely to happen. It is through navigating through such uncertainties that the nuances of a modern interpretation of cultural understanding become understood and absorbed, laying the pathway for the evolution of a transcultural perspective. The greater and wider the range of cultural environments to which a teacher is exposed at a deeper level, the more profound the development of their transcultural capacity.

7.2.3 Implementing cultural displacement: teacher education and professional learning

If *cultural displacement* is to be one of the key foundations for any program that aims to develop transcultural capacity within teachers, it needs to be comprehensive in scope; in short, it needs to be undertaken by all educators within a particular educational organisation, whether that be pre-service teachers who are undergoing teacher education as part of an undergraduate or postgraduate course, or the teaching staff within a particular school. The initiative cannot be selective or optional, but has to be enabled as a mandatory component in a teacher education course or as part of a serving teacher's professional development. The teaching of cultural understanding is not discipline or subject specific, even if some of the content might seem to be easier to incorporate into some areas such as English, Geography and History. As a professional attribute, transcultural capacity is represented by an openness to difference and change that can be applied to any learning area, regardless of context.

Within teacher training institutions, in practical terms, this condition means that all undergraduate or postgraduate students undergoing teacher education need to participate in a more targeted program of school placements throughout the duration of a course. If, for example, a student has 4 years of teacher education with eight periods of school placement overall, it should be compulsory that at least 50% of those placements take place in cultural environments that are outside the student's own life experience. Such a condition should not be an option within a teacher education program, but a compulsory parameter that students need to be aware of prior to applying for and being accepted into a teacher education course. Possessing a transcultural capacity is not expertise that is only applicable to certain teachers; as has been argued throughout this monograph, teaching in the modern societal context means that all teachers need to be, and should be, teachers of and about cultural understanding in the modern idiom.

Given that it is highly unlikely that funds could be provided, either by the institution, the student or an external sponsor, for all students in a course to participate in a program based purely on international school placements, the onus devolves to the institution to find ways in which the experience of cultural displacement can be provided at a much lower cost to both the student and the institution. One possible avenue is illustrated by the examples of the personal and professional histories of several teachers in Canada and New Zealand who were assessed to have a transcultural capacity, but who had not undertaken extensive international travel, if any. Invariably, these teachers had been born and grown up in the more regional parts of their country, away from the large urban centres, and had progressively moved from place to place as they developed their professional and personal careers. In other words, their experience of cultural difference was gained through being immersed in local communities from different parts of their province and/or country. Quite apart from any tourist-like travel, they had life experience of melding themselves into a variety of community ways of life that required them to adapt and respond to new circumstances. As one Canadian teacher expressed it,

> When I think about my identity, it's not the place of where I am right now. It's a nationalist kind of approach to being Canadian. I've had opportunities to experience culture, but they are limited because they have a North American draw to them. But the concept of the feeling [cultural awareness] is inside, and experiential for me is the lived experience for me. I take what I have lived. (Teacher CN-54)

Evidence of a similar progression in transcultural understanding was found in cross-cultural research conducted by the author in South Africa, Malaysia, Australia and the United States. One of the most transcultural South African teachers, a black African principal, had gradually moved away from his designated homeland area under the apartheid regime throughout his career, experiencing life in so many different parts of the country that he had become a language expert in all of the designated 11 national languages (Casinader, 2014).

Within a teacher education course, this can translate into the relevant institutions putting in place a system of professional practice school placements that requires all students to be involved in different school locations around their state, country or even city. Within any urban area of reasonable size, socio-economic conditions and cultural characteristics can vary greatly, and schools in those different regions reflect those same differences. Consequently, a pre-service teacher can experience similar feelings of *cultural displacement* as part of their teacher education if they are required to be involved in a school whose socio-economic and cultural environment is in contrast with, for example, the area in which they live and/or the schools they attended as a young person. For an institution to promise all pre-service teachers that they will provide school placements that are within easy reach of their existing place of residence is to remove one of the major components of teacher education over which the institution has some control. A program of eight school placements over a teacher education course that incorporates one international placement in a country and culture with which the student is unfamiliar, a regional placement in a rural area, one school in a different state or province and a fourth in an unfamiliar location within a student's own residential urban area will provide a comprehensive and varied set of experiences in cultural displacement that will prepare that individual for teaching in a range of school environments, both local and global. Such a detailed, targeted program requires substantial time and expertise to organise and implement, but it is addressing one of the key aspects of professional expertise that graduate teachers in the 21st century need to acquire; the benefits are substantial and considerable:

> teacher education needs to take into account the more cosmopolitan, transcultural contexts for teachers' work. This can be achieved through teacher education programs that are less parochially framed and more focused on transportable, transferable professional skills and adaptable knowledge that is widely recognised throughout Australia and elsewhere. (Widegren & Doherty, 2010, p. 20)

Such adaptable principles are not new ideas in teacher education. For instance, when the author was undertaking teacher training in Australia during the mid-1970s, the conditions of teacher placement across three school experiences over 1 year included a condition that one placement should be in an inner city school and that another should be in an outer suburban school, with strong encouragement to do at least one placement in the rural areas of the state. Twenty years ago, Merrell Ligons, Rosado, and Houston (1998) argued that pre-service teachers should be placed in different school settings so that they obtained an understanding of different cultural environments.

Any sense of a school feeling that students were just being parachuted into local communities without support could be resolved by building up a deeper relationship between the school community as a whole and the teacher education institution.

Similar principles in cultural displacement can be applied to professional learning programs designed to build transcultural capacity in serving teachers. Professional development programs that focus on the building of knowledge and pedagogies tend to be prevalent, but if they are one-off events that are not connected to a long-term, deliberate program of capacity building, then long-term impact is unlikely. A recent, major Australian research study (Halse et al., 2015) demonstrated that building professional capacity in teachers through '… scaffolded professional learning activities … throughout the project, [along with] high-level, external, expert support to self-directed, peer support' (p. 12), was one of the three key components in '… equipping teachers and schools with the skills to develop the intercultural capabilities specific to their students, staff and communities' (p. 12).

However, the focus of this particular project was the notion of intercultural capability, not transcultural capacity. If teachers are to develop this more enhanced form of cultural capacity, one that is more relevant and appropriate to the cultural environment of schools and societies in the 21st century, then their professional learning programs need to contain the same elements of cultural displacement that have been discussed in relation to teacher education. Once again, resource issues and financial constraints are inevitably factors that come into play, not only between educational sectors (for example, publicly funded government schools versus independent or private schools), but also between schools from the same sector, but which are located in contrasting socio-economic and cultural environments Not all schools have the resources to follow the policy of one school in the research project, which offered built-in support for teachers to undertake international educational study visits during term breaks as long as there was an educational question to be investigated. However, there are a number of cost-effective measures that could be implemented to build transcultural capacity across a school's teaching workforce.

Teacher exchanges are now a common feature of schools that have international links through their membership of globally centred educational organisations, some of which are philosophically based, such as the Round Square and the Council for International Schools, and others such as the International Baccalaureate, which are curriculum based. Other, better-resourced schools in the Euro-American sphere have campuses in a range of countries outside that context, such as some Australian schools, which have campuses in China and Thailand. Nonetheless, there is no barrier to educational administrative regions organising teacher exchanges for a reasonable length of time (for example, one term) between schools that fall within their own jurisdiction. A planned program that saw all the teachers within a school being involved in the building of a long-term reciprocal relationship with another school that was located in a completely different socio-economic and cultural context, but within the same city or state/province, is well within the scope of achievable strategies in the present day. In the same vein, schools from all sectors have often developed ongoing relationships with other schools in different countries through unexpected means, and more often than not through the meetings of principals at various kinds of educational conferences. The impetus for such school-based and long-term teacher development programs aimed at building transcultural capacity must inevitably come from the leaders involved, whether that be of individual schools and/or of the authorities in charge of certain educational sectors and jurisdictions.

7.3 A personal epilogue: the cultural elephant – premonitions for the future

My own career as an educator has spanned almost 40 years and two distinct phases: first, over 30 years in Australian school education, combined with a variety of international collaborations and activities; and second, the current phase as an educational researcher within a major university faculty of education. Consequently, although the context of the school research contained within this monograph has been deliberately comparative and international, the reality remains that the base of my comparisons will inevitably be the Australian context.

One of the inescapable conclusions that derives from my own professional experience and the research with which I have engaged has been the realisation that Australian school education has one major deficiency when it comes to developing expertise in cultural education amongst its teaching workforce. In a country that has become increasingly multicultural over the last 60,000 years, especially over the last two centuries, the Australian teaching workforce remains solidly Anglo-European and does not reflect the variety of cultural backgrounds that are now part of the Australian community at large (Santoro & Allard, 2005). This is not a concern that is confined to education (Wilkinson & Bristol, 2017); the voices that point to the doggedly unrepresentative nature of politicians in Australian state and national parliaments have become increasingly louder. Following the Federal Government elections in May 2019, public commentary was very open in praising the appointment of the first Indigenous parliamentarian in the lower house of the Australian parliament as the first Indigenous Minister for Indigenous Affairs. As notable as that appointment was, it is more a travesty and reflection of the current state of Australian society and education that it had to be noted at all.

One of the best means of developing cultural capacity within any professional community, or any community at all, for that matter, is to see the leadership of that community in all its areas as reflecting the nature of that community. Throughout my school teaching career, I can count on one hand the number of times that I was not the only person of colour at an educational conference, apart from any educational professionals who were attending from Asia or the Pacific. In all the schools in which I taught, which covered all three school sectors in Australia (government, independent and Catholic), I was the only non-Anglo-European within the management structure, even at the faculty head level. The irony is that, in contrast to my visible presence as a person of Sri Lankan heritage, I was born in England and have spent all of my life living in places that were very much part of the British Empire; I am Anglo-European in much deeper ways than the obvious.

Such cultural monotony still dominates the Australian school education workforce today. The result is that it is rare for school children from non-Anglo-European cultural backgrounds to see a teacher with whom they might feel a cultural connection. Those who suffer from racism often refer to this lack of role modelling in their teachers as one of the factors that impacts upon their sense of well-being (Walton et al., 2014; Priest et al., 2019). Perhaps even more concerning than the lack of cultural diversity within the Australian school teaching profession is the dearth of apparent interest in redressing that particular point. It is noticeable that all the surveys of Australian teachers over a number of years (McKenzie, Kos, Walker, & Hong, 2008; McKenzie, Rowley, Weldon, & Murphy, 2011; McKenzie, Weldon, Rowley, Murphy, & McMillan, 2014), including the major OECD TALIS reports (OECD, 2014a, 2014b), do not request any information about the cultural background of the participants. The major focus is on whether you are overseas-born and if you are of Indigenous heritage, but there is no interest at all in the ethnic or cultural background of the individual, especially for those who were Australian-born. Under the assumptions being made by these surveys, the importance to me of my Sri Lankan heritage and the fact of my ethnic difference are totally ignored as irrelevant.

The persistence of this Anglo-European domination has been reinforced by other aspects of the research project that is the basis of this monograph. One of the elements that was investigated was the cultural and ethnic identities expressed by the teachers in each school. Of the 27 teachers in Australian schools that participated, only one was not Anglo-European, a person who had come to Australia for his tertiary education from East Asia and had only chosen to move into teaching after his initial degree. The same pattern of cultural uniformity was evidenced in the characteristics of the teachers from the UK school, but comments from those participants and the school leadership illustrated that they were more aware of the implications and potential concerns arising from such a situation. In one sense, the teachers themselves were determined to counterbalance the reality of that fact by being extensive travellers, people who made a point of placing themselves in cultural environments that were outside their normal experience. As discussed earlier, this was one of the major factors in developing the strong degree of transcultural expertise that was evident in the teachers who participated in the research. What was dominant in the other case studies, however, was that any cultural diversity in the country at large was mirrored in the same way by the range of backgrounds of participating teachers. This was particularly true in a country such as New Zealand. Across the two schools that participated in the research, there were a number of individuals who were of Māori heritage, Pacific Island background or from multiple heritages. Many were married to people who were also from a different cultural heritage, seeing their life experiences as being part of their cultural learning, the lessons from which they were able to bring into classroom practice.

The situation in Australia is further complicated when the notion of leadership is brought into the equation. Recent research has confirmed that the same pattern of Anglo-European monoculturalism exists with Australian school leadership (Wilkinson & Bristol, 2017); the '… continuing homogeneity of school executive staff who lead increasingly diverse communities in Australia is a major ethical and moral issue which contemporary school systems need to seriously engage with and address' (Wilkinson & Bristol, 2017, p. 21). In terms of developing the transcultural capacity of teachers, this disjuncture between the reality of the Australian community in the 21st century and the cultural composition of Australian teachers and their leadership remains highly problematic. For educators to see cultural difference as being a norm in society, which is one of the most fundamental aspects of the transcultural perspective, they need to see that norm being made visible, expressed and encouraged, not only within the school workforce itself, but also amongst its leadership. To be transcultural as a school educator is not a form of expertise that is, or should be, the domain of any particular cultural or ethnic group. It is, however, a necessary disposition in current world society that can/will only ever be fully realised when the cultural diversity within a teaching workforce is in alignment with that of the community that it serves, wherever that may be in the world.

References

Adeleman Reyes, S., Capelila-Santana, N., & Khisty, L. L. (1998). Prospective teachers constructing of their own knowledge in multicultural education. In M. E. Dilworth (Ed.), *Being Responsive to Cultural Differences: How Teachers Learn* (pp. 110–125). Thousand Oaks, CA: Corwin Press.

Casinader, N. (2014). *Culture, Transnational Education and Thinking: Case Studies in Global Schooling*. Milton Park, Abingdon: Routledge.

Casinader, N. (2018). Transnational learning experiences and teacher transcultural capacity: The impact on professional practice – a comparative study of three Australian schools. *Intercultural Education, 29*(2), 258–280. doi: 10.1080/14675986.2018.1430284.

Casinader, N., & Clemans, A. (2018). The building of the transcultural capacities of preservice teachers to support their employability in a globalised world: A pilot study. *Intercultural Education, 29*(5–6), 589–608. doi: 10.1080/14675986.2018.1500170.

Fabregas Janeiro, M. G., Lopez Fabre, R., & Nuño de la Parra, J. P. (2014). Building intercultural competence through intercultural competency certification of undergraduate students. *Journal of International Education Research, 10*(1), 15–22.

Guillaume, A., Zuniga, C., & Yee, I. (1998). What difference does preparation make? Educating preservice teachers for learner diversity. In M. E. Dilworth (Ed.), *Being Responsive to Cultural Differences: How Teachers Learn* (pp. 143–159). Thousand Oaks, CA: Corwin Press.

Halse, C. (1999). *Encountering Cultures: The Impact of Study Tours to Asia on Australian Teachers and Teaching Practice.* Melbourne, Australia: Asia Education Foundation.

Halse, C., Mansouri, F., Moss, J., Paradies, Y., O'Mara, J., Arber, R., ... Wright, L. (2015). *Doing Diversity: Intercultural Understanding in Primary and Secondary Schools.* Melbourne, Australia: Deakin University. Retrieved from https://en.unesco.org/interculturaldialogue/resources/161.

Hardee, S. C., Thompson, C. M., Jennings, L. B., Aragon, A., & Brantmeier, E. J. (2012). Teaching in the borderland: Critical practices in foundations courses. *Teaching Education, 23*(2), 215–234.

Kim, J., & Jeon, H. (2017). Anti-multiculturalism and the future direction of multicultural education in South Korea. *Curriculum Perspectives, 37*(2), 181–189. doi: 10.1007/s41297-017-0025-7.

Malewski, E., & Phillon, J. (2009). International field experiences: The impact of class, gender and race on the perceptions and experiences of preservice teachers. *Teaching and Teacher Education, 25,* 52–60.

McKenzie, P., Kos, J., Walker, M., & Hong, J. (2008). *Staff in Australia's Schools 2007, Canberra.* Retrieved from http://docs.education.gov.au/system/files/doc/other/sias2010_main_report_final_nov11_2.pdf.

McKenzie, P., Rowley, G., Weldon, P., & Murphy, M. (2011). *Staff in Australia's Schools 2010: Main Report on the Survey, Melbourne.* Retrieved from http://docs.education.gov.au/system/files/doc/other/sias2010_main_report_final_nov11_2.pdf.

McKenzie, P., Weldon, P., Rowley, G., Murphy, M., & McMillan, J. (2014). *Staff in Australia's Schools 2013: Main Report on the Survey.* Melbourne, Australia: Australian Council for Educational Research. Retrieved from http://docs.education.gov.au/system/files/doc/other/sias2010_main_report_final_nov11_2.pdf.

Melnick, S. L., & Zeichner, K. M. (1997). Enhancing the capacity of teacher education institutions to address diversity issues. In J. King, J. E. King, E. R. Hollins, & W. C. Hayman (Eds.), *Preparing Teachers for Cultural Diversity* (pp. 23–39). Columbia University, New York, NY: Teachers College Press.

Merrell Ligons, C., Rosado, L. A., & Houston, W. R. (1998). Culturally literate teachers: Preparation for 21st century schools. In M. E. Dilworth (Ed.), *Being Responsive to Cultural Differences: How Teachers Learn* (pp. 129–142). Thousand Oaks, CA: Corwin Press.

OECD. (2014a). *New Insights from TALIS 2013: Teaching and Learning in Primary and Upper Secondary Education.* Paris, France: Author.

OECD. (2014b). *TALIS 2013 Results: An International Perspective on Teaching and Learning.* Paris, France: Author.

Ohi, S., O'Mara, J., Arber, R., Hartung, C., Shaw, G., & Halse, C. (2019). Interrogating the promise of a whole-school approach to intercultural education: An Australian investigation. *European Educational Research Journal, 18*(2), 234–247. doi: 10.1177/1474904118796908.

Pence, H. M., & Macgillivray, I. K. (2001). The Impact of a short-term international experience for preservice teachers. *Teaching and Teacher Education, 24,* 14–25.

Priest, N., Chong, S., Truong, M., Sharif, M., Dunn, K., Paradies, Y., ... Kavanagh, A. (2019). *Findings from the 2017 Speak Out Against Racism (SOAR) student and staff surveys.* Retrieved from Canberra: http://csrm.cass.anu.edu.au/research/publications.

Santoro, N., & Allard, A. (2005). (Re)Examining identities: Working with diversity in the pre-service teaching experience. *Teaching and Teacher Education*, *21*(7), 863–873.

Stachowski, L. L., & Sparks, T. (2007). Thirty years and 2,000 student teachers later: An overseas student teaching project that is popular, successful, and replicable. *Teacher Education Quarterly*, *34*(1), 115–132.

Tambyah, M. (2018). Intercultural understanding through a 'similar but different' international teaching practicum. *Teaching Education*, 30 (1), —105–122. doi: 10.1080/10476210.2018.1453795.

Walton, J., Priest, N., Kowal, E., White, F., Brickwood, K., Fox, B., & Paradies, Y. (2014). Talking culture? Egalitarianism, color-blindness and racism in Australian elementary schools. *Teaching and Teacher Education*, *39*(0), 112–122. doi: http://dx.doi.org/10.1016/j.tate.2014.01.003.

Widegren, P., & Doherty, C. (2010). Is the world their oyster? The global imagination of pre-service teachers. *Asia-Pacific Journal of Teacher Education*, *38*(1), 5–22. doi: 10.1080/13598660903474155.

Wilkinson, J., & Bristol, L. (2017). The unexamined constructions of educational leadership. In J. Wilkinson & L. Bristol (Eds.), *Educational Leadership as a Culturally-Constructed Practice: New Directions and Possibilities* (pp. 7–22). Milton Park, Abingdon: Routledge.

Index

Note: Page numbers in **bold** indicate tables; those in *italics* indicate figures and those followed by "n" indicate note.

ability 38
acceptance, principle of 47
African communities 31
Age of Colonialism 40
Age of Enlightenment 37, 39
Age of European colonisation 3
Age of Industrialisation 30, 34, 40
agricultural revolution (18th century) 34
Anglo-European legacy, cultural education 73–79
Anglo-European monoculturalism 155
Anglo-Indians 4
Anglo-Saxon Britain 32
APST *see* Australian Professional Standards for Teaching (APST)
Arnold, Matthew 22
Asia (case studies): cultural education 79–83; *see also specific countries*
asynchronicity, problems of 61–62
Australia 90; Anglo-European monoculturalism 155; British colonial heritage 117; CDT of teachers by school and region 126, **127**; cultural demographics **11**; curriculum 72; education, culture and faith 16; education system 153–155; OECD TALIS reports 154; teacher standards and cultural expertise 90–91, **92–93**
Australian Curriculum 78
Australian Curriculum Assessment and Reporting Authority (ACARA) 61, 76, 78
Australian Institute for Teaching and School Leadership (AITSL) 90
Australian Professional Standards for Teaching (APST) 90, 91, **92–93**

British colonial heritage 117; *see also specific countries*
British colonisation 12, 22; imperial period of 71–72; multicultural nature 12; teacher's role 18–19
British educational morality: global professional, teacher as (phase 3) 43–48; layperson as teacher, rise of (phase 2) 34–42; overview 30–31; religious as educator (phase 1) 31–33
British Empire 10, 29, 36, 105, 118, 154; Decolonisation and political independence from 50; evolution of education within 71; of 19th and 20th centuries 41; *see also* British colonisation
Buddhism 16, 17, 18, 19, 20

Canada: British colonial heritage 117; cultural demographics **11**; cultural displacement 148–149; cultural dispositions by school and region 126, **127**; curriculum **72**; teacher standards and cultural expertise 91, 94; transcultural capacity of teachers, assessing 150
Canadian Royal Commission of Bilingualism and Biculturalism 57
case studies 10–13, **11**
Catholicism 17
Ceylon (Sri Lanka) Burghers 6, early education 40–41
Cheng-Tek Tai 50
China, 'Middle Kingdom' 8, rebirth of 56
Chinese Empire 3
Christianity 16, 18, 19, 23
civilisational symbols 3

Index 159

Collective Action-Community Focused (CC) disposition 119
Collective Action-Individual Focused (CI) disposition 119, 126, **127**
colonisation 2–3; impacts of 5; migration and 6; trade and 6; *see also* British colonisation; European colonisation
communication technology(ies) 1, 43, 65
community field experience (CFE) survey 110
community(ies): contemporary globalisation and 30–31; religious as educator 31–33
Confucian Heritage Culture (CHC) 18
Confucianism 16, 18, 20; British colonial rule and 22; compassion 50; Confucian/Chinese positions on learning *vs.* 'Western' democratic conceptions 49–50; moral educational focus 21; Other principle and 23
contemporary globalisation 1–2, 3, 4, 7; age of 30–31, 89; outcome of 50–51; singularity of 8; *see also* globalisation
cosmopolitanism: contemporary 7–10, 49; modern 7–10; older forms 5–7; philosophical views 7–8
Council for International Schools, the 152
cultural competence 146
cultural demographics, case study summary **11**
cultural difference: acceptance of 135–136; case studies 10–13, **11**; concept 13–14, 38; cosmopolitanism, of past and the modern 5–10; cultural understanding 1–2; culture, faith and morality 14–25; discussion parameters 10–14; global acknowledgement of existence 55–56; globalisation, nuances of 2–5; living and meeting 135–141, *136–138*; teaching for 1–25
cultural displacement: existing evidence 145–148; implementation 149–153; notion of 148–149
cultural dispositions of thinking (CDT) model 107–110, *108,* **111, 118**; collective action-community focused 119; collective action-individual focused 119; independent action-community focused 119; independent action-individual focused 119; teacher participants (years of teaching experience) 144, *145*; of teachers across all regions 119, *120*; of teachers by region 119–120, **120–121**; of teachers by school and region 126, **127**; transculturality, as a teacher attitude 118–124, *120,* **120–121**
cultural diversity: living and meeting cultural difference 135–141, *136–138*; personal and professional travel experience 131–135, *132, 135*; significance of exposure 131–141
cultural education: asynchronicity, problems of 61–62; changing notions and contexts of 57–62; global imperative 55–57; interculturality 60–61; multiculturalism 57–59; new construction criteria 63; overview 55–57; paradigm of 66, *66*; transcultural approach 65–67, *66*; transculturalism 63–67; UNESCO, formation of 55–56; *see also* education
cultural education, policy and practice: Anglo-European legacy 73–79; case studies of Asia 79–83; contradictions and expectations 73–79; international comparisons, disjunctures 70–72; overview **72**, 72–73; teacher's role 83–84
cultural identity 13–14, 56–57, 65; mind-centred construction 65; new perspective *64*, 64–65; *see also* transculturalism
cultural readiness, of teachers: cultural understanding assessment 98–103; elements 97–98; procedural knowledge (transcultural expertise) 98; propositional knowledge (multicultural expertise) 98; substantive knowledge (intercultural expertise) 98
cultural self-determination 45
cultural understanding 1–2; education for 79–83; Euro-American-centric parameters 103; faith *vs.* 19–25; older forms of cosmopolitanism 5, 6; procedural knowledge (transcultural expertise) 98; propositional knowledge (multicultural expertise) 98; substantive knowledge (intercultural expertise) 98; and teaching expertise 28–53; *see also* cultural education
culture-faith associations 17
culture(s): concept of 13–14, 102; defined 5; Euro-American-centric parameters 103; faith and morality 14–25; and global imperative 55–57; hybrid 6; mind-centred conception 102;

mind-centred construction 65; as a mindset 102; traditional belief 102

data analysis 110–113, **111–113**
data collection 107
decolonisation, post-1945 56–57
de la Parra, Nuno 148
democratisation: of education 39, 46–47, 46n1; principle of social justice 47
demographic movement: cultural impact 3–4; *see also* migration
Dewey, John 29, 46, 46n1

East India Company 40
education: attributes 13; concept of 28–29; culture and faith 16–19; democratic conceptions of 46–47, 46n1; democratisation of 39; and faith, relationship between 44–45; globalisation, impacts 7; as moral citizenship 28–29; spiritual beliefs and 16; of teacher 151; 'Western' democratic conceptions *vs.* Confucian/Chinese positions on learning 49–50; *see also* British educational morality; cultural education; education system(s); intercultural education; multicultural/pluricultural education; teacher(s)
Education Act of 1870 36, 40
education system(s) 9; Education Act of 1870 36, 40; European Middle Ages 32–33; European philosophers, influence of 37–38, 39; Factory Act (1833) and 36; former British colonial territories 50; Hong Kong 82–83; India 80; Malaysia 80–81; mass education 35–36; post-1945 revolution 43–48; Reform Act of 1832 36; Roman Empire 32; Singapore 81–82; *see also* education; teacher(s)
educators *see* teacher(s)
empathy 61
enculturation 29
Erasmus 47
Euro-American axis 3, 4
Euro-American-centric parameters 103
Euro-American sphere 46; multicultural education 57; multiculturalism, adoption 58; teacher standards and cultural expertise 91, 95–96
Euro-American/'Western' civilisation 19, 56
Euro-American/'Western' cultures 21, 51
European colonisation 2–3; multiculturalism and 12
European empires 3
European Middle Ages: education system 32–33; layperson as teacher, rise of 34
European Union 10
expansive globalisation 4
extremism 52

Fabre, Lopez 148
Factory Act (1833) 36
faith: *vs.* cultural understandings 19–25; culture and 16–19; education and, relationship between 16–19, 44–45; indigenous religions 19; moral citizenship and 21; New Religious Movements 19; World Religions 19
The Fear of Small Numbers 101
First Nations: identification of 8; moral citizenship 24; religions in 19

Georgian calendar 4
'global imaginary' 64
globalisation 1; commercial and trade centrality to 8–9; contemporary 1–2, 3, 4, 89; education, impacts 7; expansive 4; 19th century 2; nuances of 2–5; singularity of 8; 21st century 2
global professional, teacher as 43–48
Good Samaritan parable 24
Great War 39–40, 48
guidance 37
Gundara, Jagdish 60

Hinduism 16, 20
Hofstede, Geert 9, 99
Holocaust 56
Hong Kong 117; case study 82; CDT of teachers by school and region 126, **127**, 129–130; cultural demographics **11**; cultural pluralism 82; curriculum **72**; curriculum frameworks 79; educational system 82–83; teacher standards and cultural expertise 94
Hong Kong Special Administrative Region 12
humanism, concept 49
hybrid culture(s) 6

ICE (Intercultural Education) 9
Inca Empire 3

Independent Action-Community Focused (IC) disposition 119
Independent Action-Individual Focused (IS) disposition 119
India: British colonial heritage 117–118; case study 80; CDT of teachers by school and region 126, **127**; cultural demographics **11**; curriculum **72**; curriculum frameworks 79; early education 40–41; education system 80; multidimensional cultural diversity 118; 'multiple realities' 80; pre-European history 12; teacher standards and cultural expertise 94–95
indigenous religions 16, 19; moral educational focus 21; religious as educator 31–33
Industrial Revolution 34
intercultural capability 100
Intercultural Competence Model 99
Intercultural Development Inventory (IDI) 99, 104
intercultural education: concept 100; *vs.* multicultural education 60–61; principles 45; *vs.* transcultural education 66, *66*, 67; *see also* education
Intercultural Education 60
intercultural expertise (substantive knowledge) 98
intercultural interactions 77–78; state-based multicultural interpretation 78
interculturality/interculturalism: concept 60; global context 60–61; *vs.* multiculturalism 61–62; 21st century 61–62; *see also* multiculturalism; transculturalism
Intercultural Sensitivity Inventory (ICSI) 104
International Association for Intercultural Education (IAIE) 60
International Baccalaureate, the 152
internationalism 30; *see also* globalisation
Internet 1, 43, 88; development 4
interpersonal skills, teacher 28
Islam 10, 16, 17, 19, 20, 24

Janeiro, Fabregas 148
Judaism 16, 17
Judeo-Christian faith 16, 17, 19, 20

Kant, Immanuel 7, 8; on education system 37, 38, 39
Khan, Genghis 3, 4

layperson, as teacher 34–42; European Middle Ages 34; mid-19th century 35–37; socio-economic transformation and 35; 20th century 40; *see also* education system(s)
living cultural difference 135–141, *136–138*; *see also* cultural difference
Locke, John 37–38, 39

Malaysia: case study 80–81; CDT of teachers by school and region 126, **127**; cultural demographics **11**; cultural pluralism 117; curriculum **72**; curriculum frameworks 79; education system 80–81; National Education Blueprint 81; National Education Philosophy 80–81; teacher standards and cultural expertise 94, 95
Malaysian Teacher Standards 95
mass education, system of 35–36; *see also* education system(s)
Melanesians 4
migration 1, 4, 64; colonisation and 6; cultural identity and 65; historical, impacts 5; post-1945 era 58; rural-urban migrants 34; *see also* demographic movement
Mill, John Stuart 22
mind-centred conception, culture 102
mindset, culture as 13, 102
Mongolian Empire 3
Moon landing (1969) 43
moral citizenship 20, 21, 24; education as 28–29; emergence of concept 44; teacher's role and 28, 29; *see also* British educational morality
morality 14; development, in child 37–38; *see also* moral citizenship
Moyn, Samuel 44
Mughal Empires 12
multicultural expertise (propositional knowledge) 98
'multicultural-intercultural' debate 62
multiculturalism 12; adoption, factors 58; criticisms 58–59; initial context 57–59; *vs.* interculturalism 61–62; socio-economic contexts 58; state-based interpretation 78; 21st century 61–62; use of 58–59; *see also* interculturality/interculturalism; transculturalism
multicultural/pluricultural education: concept 57; *vs.* intercultural education 60–61; New South Wales 77; objectives

58; origins 57; *vs.* transcultural education 66, *66*; Victoria 77; *see also* education

National Centre for Teacher Education (NCTE) 94
National Education Blueprint (Malaysia) 81
National Education Philosophy (Malaysia) 80–81
National Institute of Education (Singapore) 95
natural human rights, doctrine of 4
Nature's law 39
Nazism 56, 57
NCTE (National Centre for Teacher Education) 94
neocolonialism 12
neoliberalism 2
New Religious Movements 19
New South Wales, multicultural education 77
New Zealand 155; British colonial heritage 117; cultural demographics **11**; cultural displacement 148–149; cultural dispositions by school and region 126–129, **127**; curriculum **72**; teacher standards and cultural expertise 91, 95–96; transcultural capacity of teachers, assessing 150
19th century, globalisation 2; *see also* post-1945 revolution

OECD (Organisation for Economic Co-operation and Development) 89–90
OECD 2013 TALIS Report on International Perspectives on Teaching and Learning 9
OECD TALIS reports 154
online survey 110
Organisation for Economic Co-operation and Development (OECD) 89–90
Orthodox Christianity 17
Other 41; Confucianism and 23
'Other,' teaching for: contemporary globalisation and 31; education, culture and faith 16–19; faith *vs.* cultural understandings 19–25; overview 14–16; teacher as moral guides 48–53

Peel, Robert 36
'The People' 8
Persian Empire 3

PISA (Programme of International Student Assessment) 90
planetary resources 88–89
Plato 29
policy and practice, cultural education in: Anglo-European legacy 73–79; case studies of Asia 79–83; contradictions and expectations 73–79; international comparisons, disjunctures 70–72; overview **72,** 72–73; teacher's role 83–84
political 'ostrichism' 5
polysemics 61
Portera, Agostino 60
post-colonialism 2, 3
post-1945 revolution: decolonisation 56–57; education system 43–48; international conflict, minimising 57; migration patterns 58; multiculturalism 57–59
post-war cultural education 9
procedural knowledge (transcultural expertise) 98
Programme of International Student Assessment (PISA) 90
propositional knowledge (multicultural expertise) 98
Protestantism 17

Reform Act of 1832 36
religious as educator 31–33
Republic of Korea 145
Rizvi, Fazal 7
Roman Catholicism 17, 32
Roman Empire (BC 27–476AD) 3; education system 32
Round Square, the 152
Rousseau, Jean-Jacques 29
rural-urban migrants 34

Scott, John 35
SEAMEO INNOTECH Regional Education Program 95
self-determination 13
self-reflection 21
Silk Road 6
Singapore: case study 81–82; CDT of teachers by school and region 126, **127**; cultural demographics **11**; cultural pluralism 117; curriculum **72**; curriculum frameworks 79; education system 81–82; teacher standards and cultural expertise 94, 95

Index

Singaporean Desired Outcomes of Education 81–82
social justice, principle of 47
Society for Promoting Christian Knowledge 35
spiritualism 16
standards and cultural expertise, teachers 90–97; Australia 90–91, **92–93**; Hong Kong 94; India 94–95; Malaysia 94, 95; Singapore 94, 95
Stoics 7
student and teacher, relationship between 83
subcultures 17; *see also* culture(s)
substantive knowledge (intercultural expertise) 98
Symons, Jellinger 35

TALIS report (2008) 9
teacher(s): ability, assessment 83–84; building transcultural capacity in 143–155; cultural education (current policy and practice) 83–84; duality in role of 52; education 151; evolution of 39–40; as global professional 43–48; intercultural capability 100; interpersonal skills 28; layperson as, rise of 34–42; as moral guides towards 'Other' 48–53; religious as educator 31–33; role of 28, 29; and student, relationship between 83; transcultural capacity, comparative analysis 117–141; transcultural capacity measurement 88–113; transculturality as teacher attitude 118–124, *120*, **120–121**; *see also* education; education system(s)
teacher(s), British educational morality and 30–48
technology, globalisation and 4; *see also* communication technology(ies)
trade: colonisation and 6; cultural contacts and 5; globalisation and 8–9
traditional belief, culture as 102
transcultural capacity in teachers, building: cultural displacement 145–153; cultural elephant –premonitions for future 153–155; existing evidence 145–148; implementation 149–153; notion of cultural displacement 148–149; overview 143–145, *145*
transcultural capacity in teachers, measurement of: aims 105; conceptual foundations 107–110; cultural dispositions of thinking (CDT) model 107–110, *108*, **111**; cultural readiness, elements of 97–98; cultural understanding, assessment 98–103; data analysis 110–113, **111–113**; data collection 107; online survey and interview 110; participants 105–107; professional readiness 88–90; project methodology 103–113; standards and cultural expertise 90–97, **92–93**
transcultural capacity of teachers, comparative analysis: aspects 144–145, *145*; CDT model 118–121, *120*, **120–121**; cultural diversity, significance of exposure 131–141; living and meeting cultural difference 135–141, *136–138*; personal and professional travel experience 131–135, *132*, *135*; deeper characteristics 121–124; discussions and analysis 124–131; overview 117–118; transculturality as teacher attitude 118–121, *120*, **120–121**
transcultural education 65; *vs.* intercultural education 66, *66*, 67; *vs.* multicultural/pluricultural education 66, *66*; paradigms 66, *66*
transcultural expertise (procedural knowledge) 98
transculturalism 63–67; conditions for approach *64*, 64–67, *66*; factors 64; goals 63; as new construction criteria 63; transpatiality *64*; *see also* interculturality/interculturalism; multiculturalism
transculturality, as teacher attitude 118–124, *120*, **120–121**
transpatiality *64*
travel experience, personal and professional 131–135, *132*, *135*
Treaty of Waitangi (1840) 78–79
21st century: asynchronicity, problems of 61–62; globalisation 2; interculturalism 61–62; multiculturalism 61–62; transcultural capacity in teachers, building 143–144; transculturalism 63–67

UNESCO 5, 44; formation of 55–56; work of 45
UNESCO Guidelines on Intercultural Education **45**
Union of Soviet Socialist Republics (USSR) 56

Index

United Kingdom: CDT of teachers by school and region 126, **127**; colonialism 19; cultural demographics **11**; curriculum **72**; teacher standards and cultural expertise 91, 94

United Nations 4, 5, 43; establishment of 43, 44, 55–56; General Assembly 56; international harmony goal 55; Security Council 56; sociocultural generosity 56; Universal Declaration of Human Rights 45–46

United States 58

Universal Declaration of Human Rights 45–46

Victoria, multicultural education 77

Victorian Curriculum in 2017 77, 78

Victorian Multicultural Commission 62

Victoria's Essential Learning Standards (VELS) 76–77

Wesleyan Training Institution 35

'Western' culture 10; *see also* Euro-American/'Western' cultures

'Western' democratic conceptions *vs.* Confucian/Chinese positions on learning 49–50

Whitlam, Gough 57

World Religions 19

World War I 48

World War II 39–40, 44, 55, 71, 102, 143; causes and realities 56; evolution of global society after 43

Zhong Guo 8

Printed in the United States
By Bookmasters